Journey to Awareness
and Beyond

the warrior of peace is the path
that the Highest Masters walked
for changing paradigms :

2009

Journey to Awareness and Beyond

with Modern Technology and Ancient Wisdom

Paving your Path to Empowerment and Transformation with Brainwave Biofeedback and your Inner Keys

&

Keys to the physiology of happiness,

The joy of well-being of body and mind,

Responsible Open Self-Expression.

Dr. Liana Mattulich
&
Dr. David Paperny

Cover Design

Yang is the sky. In the sky is a human brain map in a high state of Awareness from inner work that generates freedom, seen as the three flying birds. Yin is the color of Mother Earth with the light of wisdom pulsing from her heart. The drop of water is the element that joins the sky to the earth in rain, as nutrition—and like the human body made of liquid crystalline fluid containing memories and information. The center black dot is a Singularity cradled in a Quantum Field web. The rocking and singing of the cosmic cycles are illuminated by the kiss of rainbow light as the Singularity's infinite life potentials wake up.

Image concept by Liana Mattulich; art by Michael Huebner.

This book was printed in the United States of America.

To order additional copies of this book, contact:
Xlibris Corporation
1-888-795-4274
www.Xlibris.com
Orders@Xlibris.com
50229

Contents

*To all the masters, teachers, students, friends,
team, biological family and soul family
for your contributions to this work
and living these concepts as tangible reality.*

About the Authors

Dr. Liana Mattulich became a physician in 1963, providing medical and preventive care in Argentina. She was a pioneer in biofeedback from 1973, Founder and Director of Biofeedback Center of Buenos Aires in 1980, and Founder of LABA (a Chapter of the Association for Applied Psychophysiology and Biofeedback) in 1995. A Fellow of BCIAC and certified in EEG, she was President of CAAPB, 1998-2001. For over 25 years, she has practiced and taught Zen and Tibetan meditations and exercises from native South American cultures and the Sufis, all incorporated in her professional work. After years of retreat in a Buddhist monastery, she realized the need to become a bridge between the scientific approach and ancient wisdom, which she made possible with the foundation of the Inner Key Center. She has had a private practice in the United States since 1991, with both national and international clients. In Denver, Colorado since 1995, she is currently Director of Inner Key Programs. www.InnerKey.com

Dr. David Paperny graduated from the UCLA School of Medicine in 1977, is a Board Certified Pediatrician, and Associate Clinical Professor of Pediatrics at the University of Hawaii School of Medicine. An Adolescent Medicine specialist at Kaiser Permanente in Hawaii for over 25 years, he is a Fellow of both the American Academy of Pediatrics and the Society for Adolescent Medicine. He is Certified and an Approved Consultant in Clinical Hypnosis by the American Society for Clinical Hypnosis, and also Certified in Brainwave Biofeedback by the Biofeedback Certification Institute of America. He is a member of the Association for Applied Psychophysiology and Biofeedback as well as the International Society for Neurofeedback & Research. www.TheMindSpa.info

Forward

Why read this book? To explore your mind and your reality. Why explore your mind? Because *you want more* than you commonly experience. You are the result of over 40,000 years of human evolution, yet you are unaware of most of the automatic functions and workings of your body and your mind. Moreover, there are abilities which we all have, which have withered over the eons, but can be rejuvenated.

There are many traditions around the world which approach reality, consciousness and health in different ways. Our Western experimental scientific approach has limitations because it ignores valuable assets in these traditions. Jesus spent some 12 years of his early life (recently accounted for) in the East, before returning to the Middle East to share some of those keys to reality. Moses, Buddha, Mohammed, and Jesus all learned some of these inner keys, and the amazed masses worshipped them and their views of reality.

Knowledge is power. Empowerment is knowing the inner workings of your body and mind, allowing you to go Beyond. There exist suppressed aspects of the mind (keys) which you can discover. Eastern philosophy and practices understand that we are inextricably linked to our Earth, both physically and energetically. Subtle energies studied in the East provide millennia of empirical experience that offer Westerners the opportunity for new knowledge and growth. Western science is just beginning to address this broad experience as scientific technology is more able to measure and affect them.

Brainwave biofeedback (also called Neurofeedback), described below, is one of the best currently available methods for expeditious empowerment.

It is a technology that can be applied for personal growth and change that can help correct personal problems as diverse as Attention Deficit Disorder in children and drug addiction in adults. This *non-invasive technique* is well documented to help people with chronic pain, migraine headaches, anxiety disorders, PMS, seizure disorders, and a number of other conditions. Brainwave biofeedback practitioners worldwide are now also using it for both adults and children who have learning problems, depression, sleep difficulties, and many other health and psychological conditions. This approach is as cutting edge as current brain chemical research, but also grounded in the most ancient understandings of human health.

Most people know about biofeedback, but brainwave biofeedback is far beyond traditional biofeedback, like the space shuttle is beyond the first airplane. The brainwave biofeedback process uses computerized biofeedback to help the individual learn *self-regulation of the mind-body*. The mind and body are not separate, but rather an integrated whole with self-regulating mechanisms which are quite taxed in our modern society. Brainwave biofeedback enlists the person's own self-regulatory mechanisms to create a state of optimal functioning, which leads to lasting changes after sufficient training sessions. *Brainwave feedback allows people to develop skills which would otherwise take years to learn through traditional approaches such as meditation.* After many years of meditative work, monks in monasteries are able to generate high gamma brainwaves (a state of open consciousness—enlightenment); then the mandalas of Tara and Shiva (sacred images for these practices) on which they gaze begin to take on new meaning and form in their higher awareness states. It is likely that neuromodulators and neurotransmitters (chemicals naturally created in the brain) facilitated by sacred sounds, when used together with body movements (from different spiritual practices), allow *Intention* to be reinforced by High Will. These practices actually create new patterns in the function and physiology of cellular networks.

How does someone learn to regulate his or her brainwaves? An audio-visual display responds when one is producing desired brainwave patterns. This information helps the person learn to *make easy transitions between different brainwave states*, rather than being *habitually stuck in one state*. For example, the depressed person is often stuck in a low arousal state. The anxious person's brain may be producing too much high frequency brainwave activity; that person can learn to make the transition to a more relaxed, lower arousal state. The child or adult with an attention problem may have trouble making the shift to an alert and focused brainwave state. The person with a substance abuse problem may produce high arousal brainwaves and not enough of the "feel good" brainwaves. Brainwave biofeedback teaches *a natural, permanent tool*. Before training, the brain is habitually locked in limited patterns, and after training, *the brain becomes more flexible and under conscious control.* Specific brain-based training techniques can identify and address neuro-physiological processes and issues with *precision and speed* unmatched by traditional approaches. These interventions are specific enough to abort a migraine headache in progress without drugs, and general enough to promote the development of *empowerment* and *creativity* in most individuals.

What can such **transformational technology** do for healthy people? It is believed that we use far less than 30% of our brainpower. Optimal Performance Training with brainwave biofeedback facilitates mental adaptability and *higher level brain functions.* It is commonly used to develop optimum performance in professional athletes by training brain operations to *peak performance.* The ***evolution of higher consciousness*** is both a group and individual process. Each individual who expands his or her consciousness or *awareness* will have an effect on many others. Many trainees report considerable personal spiritual growth. High tech brain training offers an effective, verifiable way to accomplish progress—a doorway to reach higher abilities and levels of awareness. Many people find themselves uncomfortable with approaches such as yoga, meditation and spiritual empowerment practices, but some find it easier to accept the benefits of transformative experiences when they come in the form of a technology. Brainwave biofeedback is *the* most holistic use of such technology.

People all over the world devote a great deal of time and energy learning to regulate their brainwaves. They just call it different things: transformation work, meditation, or personal healing. Zen monks, yogis, Sufis, Chi Gong masters and others spend 20 years or more learning to reach specific states of consciousness, thought to be healing states. They are trying to reach a state of freedom, creativity, flexibility, effectiveness, and a more calm and centered way to live. Many eventually become empowered leaders and make a real difference on this planet.

Biofeedback is non-medical, time-tested and proven performance technology, currently used by such people and groups as: many top universities, Price-Waterhouse Resilience Institute for Performance Improvement, Fortune 500 Companies, US Military Academy's Center for Enhanced Performance, US Olympic Training Center, professional athletes in the NFL and PGA, US Army Marksmanship Team, Public Sector Management Development Centers, corporate executives, and—most important—individuals who want to strengthen their brainpower to accomplish their goals. Decades of research on human brainwaves, how the brain works, and how we can enhance its functionality have produced highly effective methods for strengthening brain power. Dr. Mattulich and Inner Key have decades of experience in using this advanced Western technology, but uniquely—also incorporate the most effective Eastern mind-body techniques for personal growth.

Brain training approaches are just that, enhancement training. There is, however, no magic or instant transformation. They require the same kinds of work as do traditional mental approaches as well as ongoing personal practice of new skills and paradigms. This breakthrough technological approach does allow a **more precise, targeted training process that produces results relatively quickly.** With the techniques discussed in this book, the speed and intensity of technological training is enhanced by the use of acupressure, meridians and other Eastern techniques. This approach uses a variety of standard biofeedback technologies along with a comprehensive brainwave biofeedback neuro-integration training system. It is an innovative, high-speed awareness leadership empowerment program, representing the most evolved methods beyond usual transformational programs and philosophies.

David Paperny MD, FAAP, FSAM, cASCH, BCIA-EEG

Chapter 1

THE FOUR GREAT QUESTIONS

"To be, to feel, to think, to imagine, to know. Behold the order of the main stages in the circuit of human life."—Mikhail Naimy

Who am I? Where do I come from? What should I do? Where am I going?

The good news is: Now you can *wake up* from all the limitations in which our social, educational, physical, mental and emotional conditions hold us—a narrow "comfort zone"—and find the answers. Dreams only become true reality when we move on from the past and make the effort to learn. New understandings, some from scientific fields, and others from opening your perceptions in different dimensions, will bring back your inner power of *Being*. When the path of inner wisdom is traversed, you will know *who you are*! You have already taken the first step in this journey.

Who am I ?

The usual answer to the question "Who am I ?" is obvious: You are a man/woman, You are a worker/student, You are (your name). This, however, limits us. It is not the whole truth. More than the sum of our titles, roles, and tangible forms, we are a composite of bodily aspects:

- **The physical body**—the molecular center operated by Mind and the biochemistry of emotion. When harmonized, it is the vehicle for manifestation of the energetic and electromagnetic bodies.
- **The energetic body**—the center or source of chi or prana—life energy. When developed, it allows a person to access universal wisdom, as well as lessons from his/her most poignant individual experiences through the ages.
- **The electromagnetic body**—the center and axis of metabolic change, influenced by gravitational and other forces. When this subtle field is intensified, it acts as a bridge for physical, emotional, mental and spiritual functions.

Matter and energy are our *physical realms*. However, we *are "alive,"* and that subtle component is *Life Force*. We know scientifically that dead bodies have matter, but the many kinds of detectable energies are gone. Ancient wisdom described Life Force as a *bridge of transformation* that it is centred deep in the bottom of the spine (Kundalini sleeping serpent) as fire of red colour—that of the blood. Translate it to modern language as an *infrared spectrum emission*. And, that we are. The *physical body* and the *infrared emission body* is: Life Force—intelligent, dynamic and aware. Our infrared emission body is listening to our *Soul*, a library of past experiences.

This wonderful physical body and the second part of the Life Force in us is completed and enhanced by a third component, *the Spirit*. This is the realm of the consciousness of the Mind. The mind is a vehicle that can *express the light of the spirit* as creator and discoverer with all our inner power (called by society, paranormal functions). Mind can do these because we have a wonderful matter realm: *the brain and nervous system*. Being alive is a precious *opportunity* to go beyond the frontier of that narrow undisciplined mind to regain inner power of *human awareness* and open the door to freedom. This physical body is a most amazing machine, a living system that contains all the elements we need for being **who we really are!** *Life Force* is the warm dynamic infrared frequency that permeates all of the realms of our being. Your essence is light. Light is photons, and photons move at the speed of light.

Where Do I Come From?

We as human beings are more than we appear. Take a moment with *your real nature*. Many times in poems as well science it is expressed: "Humans are dust of stars . . ." Our matter has the same molecules as our planet and other universal bodies. Shamanic journeys teach about different dimensions and realms. Science now reveals that "the *Observer* of an experiment can alter what happens in the experiment because of the Observer's influence on the Quantum field" of physics. We have a Soul that goes beyond matter and travels into time (backward and forward). Soul is our personal "recollection" of experiences, which can be retrieved by special techniques. That information can help to gain wisdom from the past (or the future) from where you came and move you from entrapment in old paradigms to a new freedom.

Soul is metaphorically centered in our physical heart (or just to its right). In Eastern tradition, the soul is recognized in a special "meridian" of the chest, capable of expressing real Love, beyond the duality of: good/bad; sex/gratification; possession/slavery, etc. It is a fountain of the Highest Compassion as it transcends the root of all problems and can change reality. The knowledge that the open soul gives us (from the power of recognition of our higher purpose and mission) is the knowledge of the *Meaning of Our Lives*. These qualities of life we consider to be "paranormal functions" are actually "normal functions." The realm of higher frequencies beyond the energy band of the soul is where it can "see" with clarity and is free of linear sequential time. There we find no duality, have no attachments, and even become free of the usual forces of physics, including gravity (ref 1). This energy band or "*presence energy*" emanates from the body, creating *new* possible realities. We are **all** these *qualities of energies, frequencies, and matter* in one reality that can transform and change. Where do we come from? From our Highest Being that is a mirror reflecting ourselves. Shown recently in physics: "**One** particle can be in two different places at the same time." This is paradoxical thinking, or maybe a new concept explaining from where we came.

What should I be doing?

Your level of purpose, the meaning of your existence, and the commitment that you want to invest in your daily path is your choice. There is no good or bad, heaven or hell; only *you with you*, dream or reality, in creation or destruction. Any "movement" that you do makes space-time present here-now. Dream dreams, and life happens. Create reality, and you can *choose*. No judgments, no pressures, and no maps with the designation "you are here." Life is a mystery which can be conquered, discovered and enjoyed.

Beyond your parents and their mistakes and what the environment, doctrine, dogma, and culture did to you, you have inside you the inner key to unlock the chains and run free. The best word for that Key is *gratitude*. Be grateful to those human beings that brought you here—even if you are the product of a rape. Don't miss this lifetime opportunity by using blame, excuses, justification, rationalization, and self-pity. We are more than physical body, but without this wonderful vehicle, *evolving* is an aspiration gone unfulfilled.

Comfort with the known, and fear of the unknown is common and often protective of our bodies. But fear of the unknown is weak in *warriors* and *explorers*. Just as caution is part of our genetic makeup, it is also engrained in our physical genes to go where nobody has gone before, to explore new frontiers, spaces, and dimensions. To explore new lands, to face new situations, to *make known the unknown* is our heritage. With that comes a need to give less importance to *attachments*. Warriors let go of the past, take the happy memories, and move on. It has never been easy, and it will not be easy, however, *the unknown is our path and future*.

Where am I going?

The journey "home" can be a difficult task. This planet is a small piece of matter in the Milky Way galaxy, and all of us are but a grain of sand in the infinite possibilities of many realities. Regaining inner power is knowing *our spaceship, our psychophysiology*, which needs to be understood as a personal fingerprint, different from the every day complex interactions with other people. From that knowing, you are the Observer in space-time beyond apparent human frontiers. Is this idea too subtle or too unclear? Then start with one desire—to know *more*. And to go beyond limited awareness . . . you need *freedom*. One can be a black hole being, coming back again and again in incarnations, only consuming. The other option is to be a free bridge of joyful, infinite possibilities.

We are held by our contracts and warranties of pledges and ideas, and this creates a matrix, a field of our individual space-time, in which we have a "life," and to lose it is to pay a high price. We need to *keep our promises* during the incarnation in which we create those commitments, or we will come back into another physical body which will allow us to accomplish that pledge. One must *erase* the personal story, *move on* only with the happy memories, and *let go* of the past. To do so means to: *clean our present life of the chains of broken promises*. With this *new clarity* we are ready to know there are bridges (also called doors) to transcend when we want to evolve. The bridge between the *gamma state* (high awareness that can be measured in brainwave maps) and our "*original smile*" (a Buddhist concept of high enlightenment, a state reached by few Masters) is beyond rational explanations in words. It is because in that bridge/door, the Quantum Observer, and we, are **ONE**. It is an a-dimensional, a-temporal state, where we, as Absolute Totality with internal divinity, know the Unknown. Our *last face* in this evolving path of transformation is the distillation our *essence*, also called our *"original smile."* The body is then beyond matter-form in a realm of infinite possibilities. We may go to the starting point of universal life, without science or the usual concepts that our human mind can grasp. It is in these fields of infinite possibilities where our identity as human merges with the supreme uncreated being. In some schools of ancient wisdom, this is called the: *Unknown Pristine Field.*

Where you are on the path

The truth is: There is no store in this universe where you can buy "awareness" or "ascension" or "enlightenment" at any price. The path to take is one of constant self-discipline to build that quality of energy which is called High Will. This chemistry of our energetic skin happens to us *from us*; it is neither something that we can buy in a shopping mall, nor is it a miracle from some god or a blessing from a guru. To make yourself *different* is a commitment to inner work and only can be done *from you to you.* Let the past and its habits go, and focus long on self-discipline. It is self-discipline that creates the healthy proportion of High Will (energy that increases inner power) in our Dantien (the primal force energy center). Then our life **changes.** The chaos inside is transformed into clarity of a new reality of open perceptions. The "big, deep, transparent lake" (a metaphor about calmness and clarity, often used in inner work) becomes an open book—a space without time—where we read our inner joyful peace. When people are fragmented by many desires, attachments, and dualistic views, they are not capable of sustaining a commitment.

An open attitude and new internal power over the physiology and personality can unlock doors of *unlimited potentials.* Nobody walks for us, nobody can digest our food, and nobody can breathe for us! Only we can do that for ourselves. It is so simple, such common sense, but there exists a most difficult moment in the inner path. When that new reality or dimension in which we are ready to immerse ourselves beyond the past is near, then the ego personality—the wild mind—rears its head. The older neuron circuits are resisting. This stems from two problems: the *feeling of abandonment* and the *fear of the unknown.* Since separation at birth from the mother's body, the limits imposed by societal educational rules and the essential knowledge in the genetic code that *we are evolving-adapting,* all facilitate the creation of specific neurochemistry—habits. Habits give the personality a soil where wild grass and weeds grow, and not delicious herbs to season our life. Victim attitudes, tyrannical relationships, tragedies, and sexual compulsions are the roots of feelings of "neediness and needing attention." Suffering is chosen over being alone because the "beliefs" can't imagine being healthy and happy by one's self.

Absurdity is found in modern society which sells you insurance for everything, at every moment in your life, and for your death too. It denies *impermanence,* pretending that tomorrow will be the same day as it is today. What a boring life! Walking, breathing, and dreaming are never the same; your body is a regenerative organism where cells die and are reborn every minute. In real life, all is "change," but we are taught in human relations to be the same; it is safe that way; you are protected. If you agree to be contained in a box of lullabies and pleasure, then don't think, don't get out, just obey. Perhaps it is time to take on our roles as *warrior beings,* and we can fulfil our destiny in this society, and look for the next question with courage and determination. To be the creator of the journey is a daily commitment. Beings with unlimited inner power have internalized the universal *respect for all forms of life.* Inner work is unlocking and opening doors of wisdom, using *inner keys.*

According to scientific research, different areas of the human brain have specific functions. Therefore, inner work includes changing the following parts of the nervous system:

- The oldest, deeper brain which controls the body's reflexes, reactions to emergencies, and breathing.
- The hypothalamic/limbic brain that modulates the emotions and neurochemistry.
- The prefrontal cortex which elaborates and integrates emotional and cognitive responses.
- The autonomic network as a functional web composed of interconnected areas of the brain and spinal cord. It receives and provides information which modulates behavioral states and unconscious bodily functions, and also dialogues with the immune system.

We can call the *interaction* of these parts of the brain "the monkey mind." There are two ways in which this monkey mind expresses itself: as the wild animal and as the domesticated pet. The wild monkey mind engages in impulsive, undisciplined mental responses. Compulsive and addictive behaviors originate here. It is the aspect of human intellectual capacity that only skims the surface of a situation, rather than delving into the depths of an issue. When uncontrolled, it contributes to the deterioration of the person's quality of life, and limits his/her optimal development.

The monkey mind, however, can be domesticated so as to nurture our personal growth, rather than suppress it. With training, awareness, and discipline, we can employ our wiser mind to help realize our goals. Normally, without special development, the monkey mind deceives us about who we are. We need a broad perception to reveal all of the aspects of our being; the analogy is that a prism can allow us to see the rainbow colors that a ray of light contains.

One must learn to develop the acuity of the senses and employ exterior mirrors (biofeedback) until learning the ability to recognize and react positively to the inner signals provided by the body and its internal systems. State of the art technology allows the individual to more rapidly learn self-regulation in daily events. Optimal training is a combination of new western science with older eastern teachings of visualizations, analogies and metaphors, breathing techniques, exercises and movements. The objective is to broaden attitudes with maturation of inner power and intention.

There is the opportunity to expand perceptions of *what life is,* including:

— A dynamic system of transformative power.
— Awareness capable of creating a higher quality of joyful personal evolution.

As for ancient wisdom, we see that shaping the life of a learner of any discipline starts with changing the person's inner attitude. Examining values and *purifying thoughts and feelings* are basic to the initiation of any transformation. For example, in yoga instruction, before students start with the Hatha (posture), or the Prana (breathing techniques), the teacher gives them Yamas and Niyamas: rules for living a purified life. These parameters shape one's mind, calling for deep pathways of compassion, clarity, respect, cleansed feelings and self-healing. Empowerment comes after many hours of practice and strong commitment to inner work. (Note that the approaches presented in this book are not intended as a substitute for medical advice or psychotherapy.)

Change is essential

The nature of society (and the person) is to resist change and transformation. Currently, the acquisition of material goods and the attainment of personal power overly influence our world. Humanity, as a whole, needs an attitude of increased respect and appreciation for all life forms. This will not happen overnight, since the evolution of society is slower than the transformational process of individuals.

Many people feel a deep need to use their innate capacities to the maximum, yet are hesitant to do so because their communities or social situation do not permit it. As a result, they may feel isolated and can become fearful. In spite of this, however, some people have the courage to search for a deeper meaning of life and existence.

True leaders model qualities such as resilience, self-regulation, efficiency, effectiveness and wisdom. They are an inspiration for others and plant seeds of creativity and responsibility in the community. Their unbiased, clear vision encourages groups to use consensus building in the harmonious unfolding of life on earth, where every life form is respected in its process of co-evolution in the universe for establishing peace and well-being.

When and how change is possible

Inability to change is likened to "blinders" that limit perceptions of the world. Pleasure, fear, attachment, grief, anger and pain are all driving feelings that push our emotional buttons in daily life. We are often slaves to our ignorance, our emotions, and the structured windows of space-time in which we are immersed. By removing these blinders—limiting forces—we can change our internal response to external events, freeing ourselves from an "attitude of suffering." We can live fully, and in the now.

Everything has a point of origin. But life is an unfolding process of continuous beginnings. To initiate changes and move most efficiently, we need to be aware of the shifts and cycles in our personal physiology, and in nature. Observation of universal patterns demonstrates that *change is a constant force* with its own rhythmic cycles. Individuals who desire to modify their lives in a conscious manner have to prepare themselves through self-discipline and awareness. **Correct timing** is crucial for transformation; we must take advantage of propitious times and specific windows of opportunity in order to speed up and intensify our development of wisdom. This process involves exhibiting *flexibility* in more aspects of our life so that we can cultivate and store higher qualities of energy.

Real intention and strong courage are necessary to accomplish higher purposes. One must get past ideas of self-importance and preconceptions. In the case of brainwave biofeedback, there are those who would doubt that technology has much to offer, and beleive that they must struggle without help. Others may feel that meditative-mindfulness states from biofeedback training could not possibly have "spiritual value." Some actually feel that there must be dedication and "long suffering" (unconscious religious mandates), or that technology-assisted self-regulation learning could not be a path to enlightenment.

Here, we present carefully selected precision tools of modern science and technology, and combine them with the knowledge from the greatest truths of ancient wisdom, in a unique blend of interactive and transformative power. You can experience learning in all of your dimensions: mind and body, feeling and energy. *Your inner freedom flourishes when you own your physiology, thoughts and acts.* At this moment, what you are reading may cause old fears and doubts to mix with your deep desires to be a successful individual and to maximize your optimal potential. You are not an "ugly duckling." You are a "swan," and with discipline, a bit of effort, and a lot of fun, you will fly beyond frontiers.

Within a few weeks of exercises and inner work, your different intelligences will discover new layers of meaning in metaphors, motion, and in joyful inner work. Wisdom from the depths of your heart will bring clarity and light into your life. You can develop successful ways of being physically healthy, preventing premature aging, making your behavior efficient in daily life with energy and accomplishment. You can feel totally joyful in all the aspects and dimensions that you are . . . and fly free of past limitations, like the beautiful swan.

> *"The human brain is an enchanted loom where millions of flashing shuttles weave a dissolving pattern, though never an abiding one, a shifting harmony of sub-patterns.*
> *It is as if the Milky Way entered upon some cosmic dance."*
> —*Sir Charles Sherrington*

Five Aspects of You

Your *Physical body* is the most obvious aspect of the self since you see yourself as a body distinct in time and space. Your biology at the cellular level is in balance, automatically senses external influences, and adapts to change. Each cell contributes to a greater whole. The physical aspect has the least amount of true consciousness.

Your *Mind* organizes reality through thought. It is made of individual thoughts, emotions, sensations, and current memories and beliefs which both operate you and guard you consciously and unconsciously. *The Mind can be anywhere and imagine anything.* It is free to perceive the world, but it will never be able to fully comprehend all of itself. You are consciously aware of yourself as the sum of your thoughts, desires, wishes, dreams, and emotions. Most of our thoughts are collective and are literally programmed inside us by society.

Your *Spirit* is your vital "light force." Your body is made 80% of water and 20% of a collection of lifeless chemicals, assembled by an incredible design that knits together every cell in your body and energizes it with this Chi, Qi, Prana, spark of life, or Universal Light of Creation, at a very high frequency.

Your *Soul* is the recollection of all the experiences of this and so many past lives that you have been. The identity of your Soul itself is from the basic vibration, or hum, of the universe. This vibratory connection allows pure consciousness—the love, joy, ecstasy and bliss of being light of pure consciousness. You are truly multidimensional. You are soul-aware when you can experience everything through high love and compassion, or when you have the perception of ecstasy or bliss.

Your *Essence* is purest connection that transcends space-time, and is "One with the absolute"—a-dimensional and a-temporal. It is a paradox of reality that you can have that presence and interconnectedness—the same paradox as a particle existing at two different places at the same time (University of Colorado, Quantum physics research).

What am I ?

This question can be answered in many ways. Let's use information from the sciences. You are non-linear dynamic system in a state of anisotropy. The human body is the most dynamic system in the scale of life forms in this planet. At every level, organs, tissues, cells interact constantly as non-linear oscillating waves of electric energy (brain, heart, etc.). It is the unpredictable, impermanent, and random fractal geometry and dissimilar paths in the body-space which are characteristic of being healthy and alive. From physics we know the velocity of propagation of electromagnetic energy is not equal in all directions (it is anisotropic). In the physical body, an acupuncture meridian is a preferred path where a certain quality of energy moves. Non-coherent areas of brainwave activity sometimes represent a healthy but chaotic condition, since chaos may be the seed of creativity.

For the immune system, the non-linear dynamic anisotropy is characteristic of those activities where intelligence, information, energy and matter evolve in a continuous equilibrium of variability, dissolution-creation, and neurotransmitters—all changing our emotions and giving "sense" to our life reality. The *body is a physical electro-chemical structure* and the *immune system is chemical-emotional realm*. Both are coupled, and they interact in a non-linear way. The *mind is our "identity"* in the electromagnetic field, and involves both of these realms.

Matter is the miracle of atoms, particles, and possibilities in dynamic movement. Science can measure energy emissions from cells, and has shown that certain energy frequency wavelengths can either enhance or diminish the multiple functions of our highest mental potentials. Nature created intelligent doors for these three systems to interface. It seems to an outside observer that the process of creation and dissolution is chaotic.

However, we find that chaos naturally creates *fractal* geometric states, by generating attractor points where self-organization can start, creating a new level or state that evolves. These *points* are the doors where the immune system listens for normal, healthy physiology.

When actions allow us to distill the energy called Chi, (ancient wisdom teaches many ways such as martial arts, pranayama, meditation, etc.), our realms are capable of listening and intertwining in non-linear interface with subtle energies. *Awareness and self-regulation of our physiology* in the context of our entire energy spectrum transforms and evolves us, making us the owners of our subtle bodies, the soul and the spirit. Focusing Chi can bring finer perception to the chaos of our wild mind, then re-wire our brain-body with *creative plasticity* inherent in our nature, and create structures beyond our apparent limitations.

The *soul* realm has the *information of who we are* in our time and space. Soul is in the basic form of a band of energy of the spectrum (called Qi in eastern teaching). This space (electromagnetic field) is dissimilar in the cardinal directions because of the speed of propagation relative to our chaotic environment where most of us exist. What does this have to do with an internal spiritual path? It is the creation of *awareness of Qi energy* by different psychobiological techniques that decodes the language, information, and the inner power of our spirit-selves.

When the mind is disciplined, the structure of the extra-meridians, normally in chaotic movement, begins to display self-organized points of communication. They are called the *attractor points*, and in oriental medicine, the *spiritual points*. These new attractor centers in our five aspects (body, immune system, mind, spirit and soul) intertwine and bring awareness of the quality of our essential nature: *our spirit*. The physiology of spirit was intensely studied for 3,000 years. Now, science has the technological capability to measure and prove the existence of these realms of subtle reality. With special psychobiological exercises over years of trial and error, many can discover and practice non-linear and dynamic learning of the inner power of altered states. They know about subtle energy formation (Chakras) and a periodicity of some energies in the spirit realm (Shushuna, Ida, Pingala, Kundalini).

Correct timing is crucial in this quest for the highest potentials in our time and space while alive. The entire universe is connected in a non-linear, dynamic system of anisotropy . . ."As above is below." We are immersed in the many realms of our planet, as part of the solar system, and the galaxy—together—only a grain of sand in this universe. So, how do we evolve, and in what direction? How do I reach the speed of the fractal geometry of inner power? If I am more than matter, energies and information, who am I? Science can measure our electrical, chemical, and magnetic aspects, but subtle energies are two other parts of the spectrum. They are: *Qi = Soul* and *Kundalini = Spirit*.

Awareness is the individual-state of inner power with pristine wisdom. However, *Beyond Awareness* is a non-linear dynamic system in a state of anisotropy, which you are. We call that: Knowing the *Unknown Pristine Field*.

Nourishment of The Physical Body

Human beings need various types of sustenance at different times and places. Location and lifestyle impose distinct limitations on our quality of food, water and air. Proteins, carbohydrates, fats, vitamins and minerals are basic nutrients for the body, but we can survive deprived of these for many weeks. We cannot, however, thrive without water for more than a few days, and breath is the most essential of all. A few minutes without oxygen and our physical lives will terminate.

Maintaining the body's stability and efficient balance is a complex metabolic process involving the immune system, hormones, enzymes, electrical currents, blood circulation, and many other factors. The nervous system, via nerve impulses, releases neurotransmitters and neuromodulators (chemical cocktails) that allow for inter—and intracellular communication.

The physical body represents the integration of the physical, energetic and electromagnetic dimensions. It needs to be cherished and cared for as a "one of a kind" treasure. Balanced food intake, an environment without pollution, exercise in a rhythm appropriate to age and physical capacity, and honoring the body's need for sleep are basic necessities for well-being. Gentle discipline and loving attention can maintain healthy physiology.

> *"All the substances necessary for the maintenance of the life of the*
> *organism, for psychic work, for the higher functions of consciousness*
> *and for growth of the higher bodies, are produced by the organism from*
> *the food which enters from outside:*
> *The food we eat, The air we breathe, Our impressions.*
> *All functions are interconnected and counterbalance one another."—*
> *Gurdjieff*

Nourishment of The Energetic and Electromagnetic Bodies

The Asian concept of subtle energy is expressed by the words Ki, Qi, or Chi. The symbol for this word combines the radicals for "vapor" and "rice." We know that raw rice, before it is transformed (cooked) by the vapor, gives very little nourishment to the body. This oriental analogy can be compared with the development of *High Will*. Chi is the distilled product of food after the heat of metabolism is applied. Similarly, *High Will* arises from the synthesis of breath and special exercises with the warmth of *attention*. Chi travels through (the acupuncture) meridians, and the *High Will* energy supports immune functions. This unique form of energy is capable of integrating and providing vital nourishment, leading us into another dimension of Awareness.

The scientific world recognizes that our bodies have an electromagnetic field as well as other forms of electrochemical energy. Photons, gamma rays and the light from beyond our solar system all reach us. These spectrums of energy interact with ourselves and our planet. They are necessary for our healthy development, growth and for life on earth. They are as essential to our sustenance and survival as are air and water. In photosynthesis, plants use light to create oxygen which is released into the atmosphere. Sunlight enables a metabolic balance of Calcium in our bones; gamma rays act on genetic materials of our cells providing mutant forms—change.

Science and Common Sense

Recent advances in science in this millennium have revealed new information in many fields; most are related to fundamental and technical increases in knowledge of chemistry, medicine, quantum physics, mathematics and astronomy. These advances provide us with a better overall comprehension of life and reality as a sequence of events with strong rules of cause and effect. However, there are some paradoxical concepts that make us aware of the necessity to maintain an open mind in understanding the essence of reality. For instance, at one time it was thought that the world was flat and now we know it is a pear-shaped sphere; last century the speed of light was the limit of velocity, but not today; and recently science has proven that one particle can be detected in two places at the same time. Many phenomena once considered paranormal (or miracles) are explainable. We need to maintain mental flexibility and be willing to reevaluate precepts once considered infallible.

The latest information is readily available to us through books, videos, magazines, schools, newspapers, television, radio, and the Internet. These resources generate ideas that nourish the mind and personality, and change beliefs, values, and perspectives. One must take responsibility for seeking out the truth, while employing healthy skepticism when navigating on the information highways.

As a compliment to our intellectual understanding, we must utilize *empirical common sense*. If we engage only in a narrow, linear, academic approach to life, we simply categorize the data we receive. Inflexible belief systems limit personal growth! Ancient wisdom includes common sense based on experience: and an awareness of the interconnectedness of all things. Common sense with empirical science is not better or worse than experimental science; it is a complementary tool, allowing old and new approaches to have an integrative win-win relationship. Once modern science can *measure* empirical experiences, these then become aspects of "modern" science.

> *"In self-observation we must differentiate between the four basic*
> *functions of the body-machine:*
> *the thinking, the emotional, the moving, and the instinctive."—*
> *Gurdjieff*

Truths at this moment

Dear Reader,

I am sure that with new developments in technology, hitherto unknown concepts will become easier to discover, adopt, practice, learn, and apply. Today's professionals, proficient in their skills, will create better interfaces between technology and humans, improving learning speed and accuracy. Therefore, we can assume today's truths will be changed in the future. The same will likely happen to some of the ideas expressed here. Evolution is part of the process of life. To remain attached to a group of concepts or techniques, without respect for what can be learned from progress, is to try to dam the flow of life. When I was 15 years old, I read a book written by Gandhi. In his prologue he admitted that some of the ideas in his current book contradicted what he had written fifteen years before. With those very humble words, he explained that probably in another fifteen years, his truth would evolve and change again. This is my exact position today. I hope that the next generation will combine these ideas with good judgment and new discoveries to produce continuous growth and improvement in human life.

What is written in these pages offers you a journey, not linearly expressed, but with common knowedge and scientific information linked. Included are ways to nurture your smile along with academic understanding. However, here is what will happen: This is not a drama, a novel, or scientific report, but it is a bit of all that, and beyond. You are invited to take this journey, unique and infinite as snow crystals singing, and as memorable as the wonderful storytellers that you have known in your life. The intent is to help you see the grain of sand as well as the big picture of the universe. We hope to facilitate your inner way of walking a path of self-development in a similar context to those of the sages, but at your own speed. The best way for these pages to benefit you is to think with an open mind, looking at each paradox as a pathway in non-linear time, or as a map in the chaos to a new order that is attainable here and now. Taste some wisdom techniques and smell new movements. They will bring you the opportunity to discover, express and sustain your inner freedom, and perhaps flow beyond!

Begin by taking time to do the exercises; practice discipline; jump into the deeper meaning of words that you use in daily life, and flourish in more accurate language. Let go of older paradigms that restrict your emotions, and flow in the joyful reality of your body where you will discover: we are flying together as swans . . . not ugly ducklings.

Liana Mattulich

Chapter 2

CONSCIOUSNESS AND REALITY

"Nothing in current science can account for consciousness, yet consciousness is the one thing we cannot deny. The exploration of this final frontier has now become imperative. Now, more than ever, we need to understand our own minds, and our sentience, so that we can achieve our true inner potential."
—Peter Russell

"Our scientific power has outrun our spiritual power. We have guided missiles and misguided men."
—Martin Luther King, Jr.

At some point in history, a split occurred and we ended up with Science and Religion. Science limited its study to the material world and the Church took charge of the metaphysical realms. Now, with science studying consciousness, we are beginning to reintegrate Spirituality and Science. People are now having experiences that are not explained by old scientific paradigms, and we are now reconsidering our cultural and religious views of reality.

Unconscious Mind

Our everyday thoughts are on three levels: conscious, subconscious, and unconscious. The unconscious mind is a vast unseen. It holds all our past experiences, everything we have ever thought, felt, experienced, or sensed in the past. It is possible to access the functioning unconscious mind, motor programs and immune system through use of symbols, archetypical ideas, personal affirmations, specific sounds, rhythms, music, and vibrations with special qualities. By using and integrating these modalities we are able to *recall* universal messages of wisdom deep within. However, fear is responsible for most of the obstacles to progress and change in one's life. Fear usually originates with *imagery* residing in the unconscious. Each image has an affective or emotional component attached to the memory. Procedures such as Eye Movement Desensitization and Reprocessing (EMDR) and Thought Field Therapy (TFT) can disconnect the emotional bridge to the image, rendering the unconscious image neutral.

EMDR is an information processing therapy where the patient focuses on memories in sequential doses while simultaneously moving the eyes side to side. Possible targets for EMDR processing are distressing memories, situations that elicit emotional disturbance, traumatic incidents, or any other emotional obstacle preventing development of specific skills and behaviors. The patient identifies the most vivid visual image related to the memory and its related emotions and body sensations, then focuses on the image or negative thought and body sensations while simultaneously moving the eyes back and forth (bilateral optical-cortical stimulation). It often produces profound relief in a short time. After EMDR processing, patients generally report that emotional distress related to the memory has been eliminated, or greatly decreased. Importantly, these emotional and cognitive changes usually result in spontaneous behavioral and personal change.

TFT is another method which can help eliminate emotional blocks to progress. It is a self-administered treatment that uses tapping on *energy meridian points* along with EMDR-like bilateral optical-cortical stimulation while focusing on the targeted negative emotion or problem. TFT has been developed since 1980 by psychologist Roger Callahan who treated 97% of 68 phobic patients successfully in an average treatment time of 4.3 minutes (Callahan, 1985). A study by Sakai and Paperny reported impressive changes in self-reported subjective units of distress (SUD) in 1594 applications of TFT, treating 714 patients. For Post Traumatic Stress Disorder, TFT is reported to be the most rapid treatment compared to other new therapies. For Traumatic Incident Reduction (TIR), the standard treatment mean duration was 254 minutes; for EMDR, it was 172 minutes, for Visual Kinesthetic Dissociation, it was 113 minutes, but for TFT, 63 minutes.

Subconscious Mind

The subconscious controls all the involuntary processes of the body, i.e., the regulation of respiration, digestion, circulation, etc. It works 24 hours a day. *Habits* and *beliefs* come from the subconscious. To be in control of your life, you must be in charge of how and what you think, both consciously and subconsciously.

In the more subconscious layers of the mind, the central structures of the brain regulate feelings, and to some degree, sensory perceptions and emotions. Here, analogies and metaphorical stories have a profound effect on helping the mind recognize previous thought patterns and redirect them, enabling the individual to take new actions. Learning self-hypnosis as well as vivid, graphic and precise imagery of physiological processes can assist in transforming the inner attitude.

Conscious Mind

In the mystery that comprises our brain and mind lives what we call neurons (nerve cells). They "speak" in complex and dynamic interchanges of chemical/electrical language patterns. All three layers of the mind, unconscious, subconscious and conscious, understand this language. These neurons provide feedback into every cell and molecule of our bodies. They serve as the anatomical and energetic bridges across the different realms of our beings.

The conscious mind is the one we use for everyday volitional activities. In the cognitive realm, *words* are the primary instrument of the intellect or conscious mind. When somebody speaks to us, our "monkey-mind" often interjects itself prematurely, thus robbing us of the opportunity to reflect and touch our inner silence. This wild animal aspect pushes us to answer impulsively, without diving into the deeper processes of thought. Thus, the mind often engages in unproductive activities in daily life; some very common ones include:

1) Self-incrimination: recurring thoughts that destroy self-esteem and are not easily driven away.
2) Self-pity: embodiment of the role of victim, where one is unable to take responsibility for his/her actions.
3) Anger: everything elicits a response of blame or anger. The person is not capable of forgiving or seeing love inside or outside.
4) Dependency: one cannot take personal responsibility and lives attached to others, lacks courage and/or cannot handle the fear of solitude and loneliness.

5) Selfish immaturity: living willfully for the moment with focus on undue self-gratification, avoiding seeking meaningful purpose of support for others.

6) Fear and worry: living in the past or future; having an obsessive approach to life. Fear disallows deep Joy. Joy is the absence of Fear.

These various patterns are repeated by the mind, producing an incessant internal dialog, often sabotaging our opportunities for a satisfying life. *Inner silence* will become more accessible with training. It is only in the space of silence that clear, true thoughts come through and expand our awareness. Outside conditions often seem to regulate our emotions, moods and actions. In reality, daily life is a miracle in process: fertile in opportunities with the potential for great productivity.

"Those who dispute, do not see."—Chuang Tsu.

Making the Decision to Take Responsibility and Let Go

There may be a need to spend time in a healing environment with competent professionals who assist in the process of releasing a suffering attitude, in reducing the pressure from emotionally charged memories, and in creating a new life of freedom. Recovery is a decision and commitment to *live in the present,* and a willingness to become self-reliant. To remain living in yesterday's pain, depending on help from others, is to ask for a solution from the outside that can only come from the inside. The average human being, in order to maintain the charade of showing only positive attributes, spends excessive time and energy in keeping the door shut on unpleasant memories and feelings. The following analogy illustrates this.

Imagine yourself in a big room; this room represents your life. It is where you store all the memories of your life experience. Some are accepted and displayed readily. You are proud to maintain these memories, such as: the card sent to you by your former sweet heart (it represents an attachment that is sustained past its time), a stuffed toy that reminds you of a friend, the colorful picture of your family, or the diploma for which you studied so hard and is now an old piece of paper on the wall. These things give us comfort, credibility, or even a sense of security. Or they can be souvenirs, markers on the road of our life's past, which can be used to help us better understand the present and to help guide us into the future. There are some memories, however, that you do not want anybody to know about: failures, deceptions, emotional pain, culpability, worries, etc. All these charged feelings are stored as big air filled balloons in a closet totally out of view. You may be the only one who knows they exist. As these balloons accumulate, you suffer and become weak by having to use energy to keep them inflated and hidden. You cannot give them up; you are forced to keep that door closed, and your energy is increasingly drained in the effort. You are never free to feel joy from the full depth of your being.

We can accept and process memories of events that were once very painful. But first, the effort is to change our perspective about the event, using a two-step process. We go back into the situation with compassionate understanding as to how it may have come about. Then we need to recognize that the memory is no longer a useful reality, and that we waste energy devoted to keeping it repressed.

One can only be in the freedom of the current moment by *letting go* of the suffering attached to the past. By *releasing* the pain of our previous experiences, the balloons may continue to exist, but are greatly deflated as they rise up in the sky, and occupy less space and energy in our memory. We have grieving in our nature, but should not consume today's life in an endless state of grieving and suffering over what happened in the past.

Intelligence Quotients

We develop different intellectual capacities and talents in life; science now has accepted the existence of many types of intelligence such as:

- linguistic (part of IQ tests)
- spatial (part of IQ tests)
- logical/mathematical (part of IQ tests)
- emotional ("EQ")
- musical/rhythmic
- body-kinesthetic
- interpersonal
- *intra*personal

We are complex and sacred beings. Often simplistic labels are employed to describe us, yet life is abundant with opportunities allowing us to flourish in the world in different ways. The more we open the inner spaces of intelligent communication among the parts of our being, the more our potential blooms into a song of joy. ("Being" refers to the whole reality of a person, the physical aspect with energetic realms and electromagnetic fields superimposed.) Transformation is a process of developing this basic form or seed that we are, and supporting our growth and maturation into Joyful Beings.

On the other hand, when we *believe self-limiting concepts* that may have originated through labels or belief systems generated by others, we are putting up barriers beyond which we are unable to grow. When a child is diagnosed with attention deficit disorder (ADD) in regard to their behavior without a complete evaluation, she/he may be unjustly given a label that can destroy the will and motivation for personal growth. It could very well be that this child has one of the new generation brains with immense *creative* potential, new areas of functioning and many more wonderful possibilities (not fitting well in our standard educational system)—all of which could be lost because of the misapplication of a diagnosis and/or inappropriate use of medication.

When one overvalues IQ, this restricts the ability to be receptive to new perspectives without judgment, while often possessing a low emotionally functioning "EQ." Then there are those who constrain their intellectual pursuits in a circumscribed fashion, whether by imposition of dogmas, belief systems, family rules, cast, ethnic limitations, social stratification or educational elitism. These limited views trap them in restricted frames of reference.

Forty thousand years of human evolution has provided an innate intelligence hidden in the subconscious mind and in the human nervous system capable of feats of which we are hardly aware. Humankind is on the verge of experiencing revolutionary changes in mental capacities. With the opening of the many information highways and current technology requiring multi-tasking, now the younger generations receive much more external input in the first three years of life than an adult would process in a lifetime just one hundred years ago. Whenever an organ like the brain is more utilized, it must grow and develop connections among new cells. That is the current situation in the brains of children at this time. Only with a "new Key" from all the dimensions of our being, can our deeper abilities manifest and our *evolution make a quantum leap* in this present millennium.

> *"Socrates said that if people know what they should do, they will do; but he underestimated people's ability to fail themselves. Everyone knows what they should do, but how many people actually do it?"*
> —Tsai Chih Chung

With ancient wisdom techniques, discipline and practice, our bodies can develop and self-regulate the flow of different qualities of energies. Now modern science can help us using new technology to become successful in precisely and efficiently managing this energy spectrum. Stephen Hawking,

PhD, of the University of Cambridge, is further expanding our knowledge of the universe by providing a crucial link between the radiation of black holes and the laws of thermal equilibrium with the environment. When we study his findings, we can conceive of the death of our physical body as our energy body passing through a wormhole to another dimension. Our essence (energy body) is conserved even as our material form changes completely. Recent controlled scientific studies of mediumship by Dr Gary Schwartz certainly confirm this premise of the survival of consciousness after death of the physical body. Matter, consciousness and energy are never destroyed, but are interchangeable.

In a few more years, technology and science should allow us to understand the complex role that human *energetic physiology* can play in daily life. If one chooses to ignore the research and recent scientific discoveries regarding energy and quantum physics, it will be easy to remain locked into old ideas with narrow frames of reference. Self-actualization is a multifaceted path. To understand and accomplish this takes effort, but we can sparkle as diamonds in the light when the Keys open us.

Science and Multidimensional Reality

In order to understand the complexity of the human body, we must see the universe as a multi-dimensional reality. Each person is a microcosm, reflecting all the realities of the macrocosm which science is presently analyzing and beginning to verify.

Recently, at the National Institute of Standards and Technology in Boulder, Colorado, Dave Wineland, PhD and Chris Monroe, PhD demonstrated the paradoxical concept that one particle can be in two different places at the *same time* (ref 2). This experiment gives credence and support to an ancient concept that *the essence of a human being can co-exist in (or be comprised of) more than one space-energy-dimension.* Scientists are applying this concept to the development of a new prototype high-speed computer: a quantum computer.

Western science is also beginning to seek understanding of the differences between "energies" and "forces." At Oxford University, experiments have been manipulating *light* subjected to the influence of greater and lesser gravitational forces. Laser beams passing through nonlinear optical materials enhance and suppress vacuum fluctuations, leaving regions of positive and negative energy. Gravitational fields can act as convergent lenses which focus positive energy, while acting as divergent lenses for negative energy. (Note that the word "negative" used in conjunction with "energy" has no unfavorable connotation.)

Universal Mind aka Quantum Mind

The Mind (particularly the unconscious) probably actually exists beyond our computer-like brain organ. It is linked with Universal Intelligence of all things. Brain is a conduit, but Mind has no limitations or boundaries. Our brainstorms and breakthroughs are actually vibrations from the Universal Mind. Although neurons in our brains help form the *awareness* of a thought, actual thought itself does not originate in the brain at all. The brain is like the TV receiver in your home, not the TV station. Thought is a result of the Mind, and the perception of a thought comes *through the brain*.

Other names for Universal Mind are Quantum Mind, Quantum Field, Akashic Record, Mind of God, and the Zero Point Field; they all represent the singular root of all consciousness, extending *back* for eons, but also years *ahead* into the future. This model of timelessness explains the universe best, and provides physicists the bridge between Mind and matter that best fits current quantum physics. This Field is far more involved than what we can scientifically detect in the visible universe. The frequency of visible objects can't be the source and frequency of Mind since our physical plane is easily explained by simple physics.

Mind will only be accepted by most people as being outside the brain when a convincing test like a PET scan somehow shows Mind external to neural activity. Science has long accepted that matter and energy cannot be created or destroyed ($E=mc^2$), and **everything is either matter or energy** (or it is Void). Therefore **information** is energy (or matter) and it **cannot be created or destroyed,** only **transformed.** If information permeates the entire quantum field, it can bridge Mind and matter in physical aspects. The universe is in constant transformation. Creativity is just another form of such transformation of energy. *Energy is information* in the sense that all chemical or electrical charges store polarities (like binary digits).

These energy packets contain information and are shuffled forever in the Quantum Field. This suggests that the Universe is self-aware—aka Universal Mind. That is consistent with current scientific findings and cutting-edge theories of physics and consciousness. The self-aware "extended Mind" explains how thinking can occur outside the brain. Therefore, the Universal Mind is a dynamic field of infinite information undergoing infinite transformations, and ideas survive in the field as memories. You and I are really accessing quantum memory when we think we are accessing our brains. This explains the phenomena of psychic mediumship as scientifically demonstrated in *The Afterlife Experiments* by Dr. Gary Schwartz. Consciousness, memory, and thought survive the physical body into other energy dimensions, and are transformed—or perhaps *consciousness is actually transferred intact*—into another energy frequency of existence.

Memory actually persists on a nonphysical level, at higher frequencies that we can currently detect physically, and quantum physics is just starting to confirm this. Medical PET and MRI brain scan images are only maps of brain activity which show the circuitry and electric flow in the "TV receiver" (the brain), but not the program—the content, idea or emotion experienced in consciousness. Science can never prove that the brain *is* the Mind.

Memory is probably a field effect. Brain functions act as a field, coordinating many events simultaneously, but we know the brain isn't actually a field. It's a receiver organ made of lifeless chemicals. Therefore, Mind is the controller of the brain, and the *mind field* is sending signals so that brain cells arrange firing patterns in response to what the field says. Our brains then construct "reality" as a hologram, implying that we may truly live in a holographic universe. The material world and its physics could be, therefore, an illusion, a projection of energy from frequency-specific wave forms of information.

A condition trained in brainwave biofeedback is called *neuroplasticity*, the brain's ability to change and be flexible and responsive to new learning, thoughts, will and intention. Learning with brainwave biofeedback may physically change brain cells—certainly their firing patterns and operational processes. This is consistent with the concept of Quantum Mind—Mind belongs to all of us simultaneously.

It is easy to comprehend how we *share* the same mind field. The brain processes only a small amount of the information it receives. It receives billions of bits of data such as sound, light, X-ray and gamma radiation, electromagnetic energy, Psi waves, and other electrical and chemical input from the environment. We only experience, notice and respond to a small amount of this. The brain filters information so we have a sufficiently narrow experience to retain a stable identity as an individual with personal memories, beliefs, intentions, and perceptions. We automatically filter out huge amounts of information, but injured brains may have limited ability to be so selective. Normal people who have brain tumors, neurological disorders and injuries (even lightening strikes) may have sudden new capabilities (including "paranormal" ones) or new artistic abilities. The brains of savants have abnormalities, often in the right temporal lobe—a special processor of conscious awareness. Those who are geniuses probably have special access to the Mind Field—ie. Einstein and Beethoven.

The brain is the receiver of Mind, not its creator. It connects our physical body to **infinite consciousness**. We filter out much of the Mind Field, but we can learn to access it more. Learning neuroplasticity with brainwave biofeedback is a beginning. The brain contains the potential for almost any mind ability known to man. You can adopt an infant from a less "advanced" culture into a higher learning environment, and that child can excel in math, science, music, and other sophisticated pursuits which would never have occurred in the original culture. Children have wonderful imaginations and greater access to the Mind Field. With training, we can access some of those capabilities we "lost" with our childhood.

The Axis

The concept of our "axis" is best explained by invoking a visualization and sensory perception of the flow of the brain's activity. Along this electro-chemical path, neurons carry information throughout the body to the central nervous system. See your axis as a "flowing circuit of light." The spinal cord is the pathway of all communication between brain, organs and cellular structures. Besides physical anatomy, the spine is also the location of the central energetic meridians. This vast ocean of energy contains Chi that is sent out to the various meridians. At least three sources of *energy* converge in the axis:

- The metabolic processes of the physical (electrochemical) nervous system
- The movement of the respiratory and cardiac cycles, which send Chi throughout the meridians
- The activities of Chakra energies, which are totally different from Chi.

The physical body sends electrical currents among nerve cells and promotes the chemical regulation of neurotransmitters throughout the spinal cord. The meridians contain and move different energies: Yin, Yang and Chi. The latter is derived from the respiratory cycle and the essence of our food. Western scientific research supports the Eastern teaching that Chi helps balance the chemistry of the immune system, hormones and autonomic nervous system. Eastern teaching also tells us that it is in the area between spinal vertebrae where the larger Chakras (the vortices) make connections with the physical body, emanating rhythms facilitating reception of *information from other dimensions*. They maintain the essence of the person while allowing qualitative changes in his/her energies.

We use the central Extraordinary Meridians in connection with the Axis. The foundation of the Axis is light, flexibility and warmth. Flexibility and warmth, two of the three, depend upon the Chi of the Governing Vessel (Du) and the Conception Vessel (Ren). The third, light, comes from photons via the light force and is related to Chakra energies. The Axis extends from between the eyes, over the middle line of the skull down the back of the neck, back, and sacrum. Furthermore, if one has accomplished energetic practices in the three-legged position, the tail can extend into/to the ground. The Du and Ren support this central pole energetically, while the other Extraordinary Meridians move in a *torus shape* energetically extending out from the body.

We call the interface between the Chi of the meridians and the energies of the vortices: *assembler points* or bridges. They have structural representation in the physical body, but also energetic expression in the other realms of being. Assembler points can be considered similar to holograms that contain, emanate and synthesize the three basic aspects of our presence as beings: form—matter, function—energy, dynamic flow—forces. Assembler points will be discussed further in a later chapter.

Creating the Inner Key to Our Axis

To discover our energetic *axis*, we focus on multi-sensory perceptions using smell, taste, hearing, touch and sight, leading us toward a pure state of Awareness. We utilize all our senses in a network to achieve a profound perception of our own unique *axis*. We define the color, form, movement, texture, sound, aroma, and taste of our axis in order to create a unique, personal Inner Key. The *axis* is used with the primordial concept that it is our "safe place," a space of peace, which can expand to create the joyful state of *being our essence*. When we recognize this and re-direct our outward focus inward to include deep, wholly introspective work, the true self is revealed.

Your *axis* will provide you with a beautiful inner dimension of unlimited enjoyment, forever. When you achieve such an internal focus, you will be linked quickly and readily with your more complex energetic human potential. Efficient learning requires an environment of security, peace and concentration without fear. We must assure our unconscious mind that everything is safe, and there is no threat from the new information or experience. The unconscious mind cannot be convinced with words, but responds most easily to symbols.

Axis as Analogy

The *axis* is an image analogy of our *essence*. We can engage in an inner attitude of self-nourishment, in such a way that others are unaware of what we are doing. The exercise called *three-leg position* reinforces our ability to stand on our own, not being influenced by outside pressures. The *axis* allows intention of maintaining physical awareness; we can use this 3-leg posture to transform daily life by allowing us to anchor ourselves and recharge our energy. The *axis* is a bridge for the physical body to synchronize with other dimensions beyond the limits of sensory perception, but it needs the information provided by *all of the senses*. It is a paradox in the context of linear thinking because it has a very complex energetic physiology with multiple roles, incorporating the actions of organic life on the earth and in the inner work of human lives.

Visual-sensory work with our *axis* allows the senses to communicate among themselves and act as bridges connecting areas of the brain. These zones are more efficient when engaging as a web. Individual representative brain areas may be responsible for certain functions; however, with brainwave biofeedback training, a proportion of each zone becomes better capable of interfacing with the others. The following are examples of the functions of different areas:

- Frontal Regions—abstraction, values, ethics, perception of aromas, mirror neurons that reflect actions, intentions and emotions of other people
- Occipital Zones—visual, memories, inner silence, magnetic balance in cerebellum work
- Temporal and Parietal Areas—language, reading, singing, listening, learning
- Hypothalamus, Deep Nucleus and Amygdala—emotions, memories, modulation of space-time environment

The higher integrative functions of the senses interface with the physical body, creating a web of information. They work best in balanced proportion to each other—not with any one dominating the others, or inhibiting the reception of more subtle messages. When sensory perceptions are experienced in this relative manner, pleasure is increased and joy nourishes the body. For example, when we see wonderful things, our physical autonomic network modulates the information and expands it to the emotional, mental and energetic realms.

All these achievements are steps toward freedom because volitional regulation of our physical, mental, and energetic systems gives us the power to be what we want to be, without dependence or need for drugs or intervention of others. We are in charge, and with our self-responsibility we can maintain our state of Awareness.

The Three Inner Forces

In working with the *axis*, you will focus on three keys to achieve deep energy work: *warmth, flexibility* and *light*. Use all the five senses when accessing the *axis*. In this way, areas of the brain can work together and create powerful sensory memories, thus facilitating the retrieval of Inner Keys. *Warmth, flexibility* and *light* are the terms used to describe the 3 basic characteristics that we can develop.

The concept of *warmth* is easily grasped. It is a sensation calling the subconscious mind into a safe place, thus reducing the stress response and helping the autonomic system reach balance. The goal is to expand that *warm, safe* reality into all parts of the brain and body. By doing so, the whole being becomes surrounded by waves of safe, nourishing, grounding energies.

Flexibility is the ability to shift quickly from one state to another; this is an essential concept for the bridging of our physical and energetic aspects. Flexibility is also the personal perspective of operating from free will. It is a deep feeling that gives the physical body a "taste" of impermanence. With flexibility training, we begin to get a sense of the universal flow of life; we are able to move beyond the ego and being stuck the way we are. Nothing that we claim to be *stable* truly is. Everything is constantly active on the planet, either in a state of *growth* or *decay*. Our bodies are in a continuing state of flux as well. Our entire skin renews itself every seven years, our red blood cells every three months, and the lining of our digestive tract every 24 hours. We can *remain in a state of growth* when we discover the ability to flow in the shifting river of daily life, without becoming caught in the decay of despair or fear. Manifest a warm ocean of impermanence, converting what we perceive as crashing waves into joyful opportunities to surf—that is *flexibility*!

Light is the visual and energetic expression of the billions of electrical connections running among neurons, but it is much more than that. *Light* is the energy of Awareness. Science accepts photons as the vehicles of manifestation; they move constantly in a dualistic reality, between particle and wave. Ancient wisdom considered *light* the food that supports the spark of life. EEG sensors on cranial meridian points improve the amplitude among brainwaves in Phi ratio, and the electromagnetic field of the Light Body of the learner becomes a Torus shape. Torus is the mathematical formula for the universe (the Einstein-Eddington: hyper sphere) and will be discussed in the last chapter.

Sleep and Dreams

Many years ago, Freud called dreams the *royal path to the unconscious.* They are another language of our multifaceted being, a useful tool on our inner journey. Scientists know that sleep and dreaming are vital and complex states, regulated by circadian and ultradian cycles, modulating the rhythms of wakefulness and rest in relation to days and nights. The cortical brainwaves during sleep are characterized by slow frequency with high voltage, and reveal two states: REM (rapid eye movement) and NREM (non-rapid eye movement). The normal biologic sequences of sleep progress in stages from relaxed wakefulness to early light sleep, and then to deep sleep. These cycles (light, REM and deep, NREM) repeat four or five times during eight hours of sleep. REM sleep usually follows each state of NREM, and the dream content is often recallable if the subject is awakened in the light period.

Sleep deprivation can have a dramatic impact on physiology and behavior. Not getting enough sleep is a lifestyle issue. About half of Americans are operating their lives *in sleep deprivation.* Lack of 6 to 8 hours of sleep for adults may be responsible for the apparent increases in clinical depression and stress in American society. We all know that diet and exercise are important to health, but we often forget that sleep is just as important. Most children do not receive the minimum of eight or nine hours sleep per night that their bodies need. Inadequate sleep can result in overeating, irritability, fatigue, and poor attention, which may express itself as hyperactivity in children. A regular sleep routine is important for pre-teens.

Sleep experts have observed teenagers in sleep labs and measured their levels of melatonin (the hormone that helps regulate the body's sleep cycles). They agree that teens' body clocks run on a schedule incompatible with the early-to-rise routine that is common. If they followed their *natural biorhythms,* most teens would tend to sleep from 2AM to 12noon, rather than from 11PM to 7AM. Unfortunately, most high school schedules suggest educators have been slow to get the message; sleep researchers would prefer to have adolescents start school at 10AM, since teens may not be completely "awake" during their first few classes.

The human brain's suprachiasmatic nucleus acts as master clock to control daily body rhythms. Light detected by the eyes suppresses the secretion of melatonin by the pineal gland. Modern society and culture today is immersed in light pollution (TV on all night in the bedroom, night lights in an infant's room, etc.). Our health is dependent on the natural circadian system, and many symptoms (such as depression, cognitive problems, memory loss, mental deterioration and some psychotic episodes) can be related to consequences of abnormal sleep not producing enough melatonin due to light exposure during the night. Some researchers reported that 6 hours of night work by women for 10 years doubled the chances of breast cancer.

It is imperative that we experience the proper quality and quantity of dreaming in order to maintain bodily homeostasis. Infants need 16 to 18 hours daily, but this is reduced to 6 to 8 hours of sleep for adults. Sleep and *dreams* provide us with access to the world of the *collective unconscious Mind Field* and *other dimensions*. We can then further our development based on the knowledge and wisdom garnered there as we recharge our energies nightly in another dimension. Sleeping and dreaming cease to be solely products of human physiology, rather they become an inner path of learning.

To Transform—an analogy

People can be likened to a drop in the ocean. Some never realize who they are. Others are lost in the chaotic waves of perpetual motion. Very few of them have the intention to understand the meaning and the direction of these movements. A few discover that the sea has ocean currents—inner rivers—that travel from pole to pole. When a drop of water is exposed to the frigid temperatures at the ice caps, the drop becomes frozen for a long time. This is the analogy of having *form* or physical bodies, and Chi energy binds the molecules together. But, in the ocean of *impermanence,* there is another kind of river of life, where the flowing water can be transformed by the warmth of the sun into vapor and clouds, which even travel to other dimensions.

We have two types of freedom. One is to come back in material form, to be alive, to participate in the recurrent movement of waves in the ocean of life forces. The second freedom is to experience the different states which our essence can attain.

Chapter 3

WESTERN AND ORIENTAL MEDICINE: TWO HALVES OF THE WHOLE PICTURE

A rabbi was asked to mediate in an argument between two people. After listening to the first person, he shook his head and responded, "You are right." He then listened to the second person present their case and responded, "You are right."

Both individuals walked away secure in the knowledge that they were each right.

The rabbi's wife who had watched and listened to both petitioners said, "That is crazy. Both those people were arguing completely different points of view."

The rabbi responded, "You know, you are right."

Eastern and western science and medicine have different "explanatory models" for the human organism—different ways of viewing mechanisms and accounting for the same scientific phenomena. As complete medical systems, they offer information about how to maintain health, diagnose and treat disease. Though the Eastern and Western paradigms differ, the *integration* of these two apparently opposing explanatory models is occurring more often. Along with that, the tendency to blend Eastern and Western science is progressing, mostly with Western science accepting those aspects of Eastern science which are measurable, reproducible, and fit into a scientific theory. Given that most Westerners have a basic science education, it is important to have some concept of the approach of Eastern sciences and philosophy so their application to everyday reality has meaning. This chapter offers an abbreviated overview since "they are both right." Oriental and Western medicine both have physical and energetic bodies as part of their paradigm, but the *foundation* of Oriental Medicine is the energy body, while that of Western medicine is the physical body.

Overview of Western Medicine

Experimental science, comprised of controlled and reproducible studies, has played a central role in Western Medicine for the last 100 years. The diagnostic and treatment system of Western medicine is built upon the ability to quantify events and manipulate physical attributes. Although the science of diagnosis using the health history and physical exam is balanced by the "art" of medicine—the experience of the diagnostician—still, blood pressure, heart rate, blood chemistry and other tests are scientifically measured. Treatment is based upon algorithmic paradigms. Drugs fit into specific receptors. Tissues that are multiplying out of control or are not functioning are removed. Broken bones are pinned, degenerative joints are replaced. Genes are altered or supplemented.

The physical body, when perceived from this mechanistic view, can be dismantled and reduced to its constituent parts: from individual systems to organs to tissues, cells, intracellular structures, biochemistry and the electrophysiology. Each level can be measured, quantified and analyzed thereby discerning its nature and function. This reductionist view allows Western doctors to pinpoint a diseased organ or tissue as a faulty component that can be repaired or severed from the body and discarded or replaced. Within this frame of reference, human bodies are considered to be similar to machines, systems that are governed by mechanical and other physical laws with the purpose of reproducing and doing work. These concepts are congruent with the laws of Newtonian physics. (The astronomer and mathematician, Isaac Newton, first outlined the cause-and-effect method of explaining the material universe.) This logic formed the basis for the 'scientific method,' which established the principles behind the protocols that are used in Western research and controlled studies today. The *randomized, controlled, double blind cross over study* is the gold standard in Western medicine.

Western medicine has a scientific approach which cannot be surpassed in understanding of the intricacies of:

- Metabolism
- Neurotransmitters, hormones and other endocrine and exocrine glandular secretions
- The structure and function of special cells or groups of tissues
- Specific nutrient requirements
- Microbial and viral causes of disease
- Surgical, laser and other invasive methodologies of treatment intervention
- Gathering, reorganizing and assessing clinical information according to organ systems

Who could imagine the knowledge that has been accumulated about the genetic code, let alone the fact that it can be manipulated? When it comes to the development of precise metabolic and organ-oriented diagnoses and trauma care, there is nothing like pure Western medicine.

Many improvements in health care can be attributed to advances in technology, but many others can be attributed to other causes. The decline in the rate of tuberculosis in the United States is due more to improvements in housing, nutrition and other public health measures than a specific treatment. The decline in the rate of heart disease is due more to the population choosing to decrease their consumption of tobacco and a high fat diet and increase their physical exercise. The limitations of a strictly measurable and biological approach to health are becoming recognized by practitioners, patients, medical educators and policy makers. Emotional, mental, social and environmental factors are now recognized as significant contributors to one's well being.

Western medicine is slow to embrace and integrate other paradigms and disciplines where scientific explanation is incomplete or when most experience is empirical. The assumption is that physical truth can be defined only by enough controlled studies and measurements. A faction in Western medicine states that it is not any specific modality that promotes healing, rather the relationship between provider and patient; many aspects of that relationship cannot be measured. According to the Journal of the American Medical Association, over 40% of Americans seek some form of complementary health care. Acupuncture, as practiced by Western physicians, is one example of how Eastern and Western voices can be brought together to create a better system.

APPROACH	EASTERN	WESTERN
Philosophy	Dynamic holism, Energies	Structural reductionism, Organ system diseases
Principle	Restore body, mind, emotion, and spirit	Repair physical body
Goal	Care	Cure
Intervention	Balance	Control
Focus	Preventive	Reactive
Techniques	Body work, Breath control, Meditation, Herbals	Surgery, Anti-medications
Time Frame	Long-term, life-long	Short-term
Efficacy	Chronic problem	Injury, Acute Infection
Presumed healing agent	Prana, chi, ki	Biological
Locus	Right brain	Left brain
Organizing Units	Five Elements	Biochemistry, Pathogens
Informational Basis	Yin/Yang	DNA
Mechanism	Meridians	Receptors
Causes	Implicit, Contextual	Explicit
Psychology	Emotionally-based imbalances	Separate from physical dysfunction
Health	Living a life of internal & external balance	Diet, Exercise, Avoidance of toxins, Stress management
Emphasis	Being inwardly connected to the Tao and actualizing Virtue	Individual initiative
De-emphasis	Personal development for the sake of achievement and recognition	Personal relationship to the creative forces

Comparison of Eastern and Western Healing Paradigms

Five Elements

The philosophical foundations for Eastern medicine were created over three thousand years ago in an agrarian society. The images are based on observations of the natural world. The organizing principles in Eastern medicine include: Elements, Tao/Virtue, Yin/Yang, Chi, Meridians and other "secret wisdom." For Eastern sages, the universe is divided into Five Elements: Water, Wood, Fire, Earth, and Metal. They have both physical and energetic qualities. Health applications include an understanding that an individual is more likely to suffer from certain physical or emotional conditions, imbalances or diseases during certain times of the year. Individuals have elemental "constitutions," and are more likely to be subject to a particular illness or set of symptoms when stressed or out of balance. For example, in response to stress, a woman with a "fire" constitution may be more likely to show heart palpitations, whereas a woman with a "wood" constitution may have migraines.

The five elements (matter), five senses (expression of spirit), and five primary emotions (interaction between matter and Qi / spirit) are all derived from *levels of existence far above the physical plane*—closer to what is called *Virtue*. All three aspects are expressed in an organ/meridian system as emotions, both unbalanced and balanced.

Examples or organs representing emotions in this system are:

- Heart: Joy, unconditional warm regard, touch or vibration sense
- Spleen: Sympathy, thinking, inner contentment, taste
- Lungs: Grief, detachment, non-possessiveness, smell
- Kidneys: Fear, hearing, courage to be who one really is
- Liver: Anger, forgiveness, assertiveness, vision

When the senses are cultivated and balanced, the Sheng or nourishing cycle of the Five Elements and their respective organs and meridians is reinforced. This may be referred to as the "path of natural expression."

Tao / Virtue

Eastern philosophy's approach to health and living is based on a creation myth that the *source of all is the eternal, unknowable Tao*. It permeates every aspect of reality, yet in and of itself does not change. Heaven and Earth are polar and complementary manifestations of the Tao. Yin and Yang in all sentient beings are a reflection of the relationship between Heaven and Earth. The attraction and unifying energy force between them is Qi. When the two are balanced, unified and elevated to the level of Ki, these qualities of energy plus High Will and Awareness are then tempered in the Fire of Interaction, and they can return to the One. In general, humans disrupt the natural harmony and spontaneity of the Tao by creating civilizations, closing doors of self-expression, obstructing the flow of Ki and trying to control nature—thus revealing a disconnection from one's indwelling state of being or True Self.

All things arise from Tao. They are nourished by Virtue. They are formed from matter. They are shaped by environment. Thus the ten thousand things all respect Tao and honor Virtue. By Virtue they are nourished, developed, cared for, sheltered, comforted, grown, and protected. Creating without claiming, doing without taking credit, guiding without interfering—This is Primal Virtue.

—Chapter 51 of the Tao Te Ching

Yin and Yang

Yin and Yang are terms used to describe the opposite and complementary aspects of reality. They are a constant reminder of the profound principle that everything changes. When any quality reaches its maximum, one will find the seed of the opposite characteristic within. Everything can be perceived as having characteristics of being *predominantly* yin or yang, but not totally—each changes into the other periodically. Yang is often a quality of reality considered more masculine, and Yin is considered predominately feminine. Relative *balance* between them is crucial to maintaining health. Yin arises from the Earth and creates Yang. Yang descends from the sky and penetrates earth, recreating in turn Yin. Even a solar system eventually becomes a black hole, as is expected when our sun burns out. The entire universe is constantly changing.

Within the human, solid organs (Heart, Spleen, Pancreas, Lungs, Kidneys, and Liver) are considered Yin, while the hollow organs (Small Intestine, Stomach, Colon, Urinary Bladder and Gall Bladder) are considered Yang. The actual function of an organ is seen as somewhat different than that in Western Medicine, although there are some similarities.

Chi, Qi and Ki

Chi, Qi and Ki represent three different qualities of energy. Although the rough translation in English for **Chi** is energy, inherent in the word is an understanding of transformation. Ted Kaptchuk says Chi is "matter on the verge of becoming energy, or energy at the point of materializing." Lonny Jarrett in *Nourishing Destiny* adds "Chi is the quality of the Tao that supports the emergence of any functional relationship at a specific moment in time . . ." "Chi is the basic substance by which all changes and mutations of all phenomena in the universe arise . . . It is a fundamental constituent of the body. The movements and changes of Chi explain all physiologic activity . . ."

Qi is that aspect of the Tao which supports the activity of the material plane; it is the awareness of that activity. It eludes our attempts to measure or precisely define it. In Chinese medicine, Qi also has multiple aspects or qualities depending on its association with animate life or the elements as they cycle through time. Qi flows throughout the whole body. It is in every cell, fluid and structure at all times and is created by fusion of three other forms: "essential Chi" of the kidney; "Chi derived from food" by the spleen's movement and transformation; and "Great Chi—Da Chi" taken from the qualities of air via the Lung.

There are specific Qi responsibilities:

- Retention—holding organs in place, keeping the blood in the vessels, fluid in the body, and holding one's center in the midst of turmoil (safe place).
- Movement—both conscious (walking, dancing, playing an instrument) and unconscious (growth, breathing, and the beating of the heart).
- Protection—an emanating field (second skin) that surrounds a healthy individual.
- Warmth—all physiological processes depend upon heat. Qi allows creation of physical and nonphysical warmth.
- Transformation—in the upward spiral of evolution beginning at the simplest level, to the joy experienced in self-regulation, to transcendent states of being.

Qi, when deficient or stagnated produces physical weakness, malnutrition, stress or aging. Stagnation often occurs early in the manifestation of disease resulting in moving or localized pain, distention, or feelings of oppression. *Axioms of Medicine* posits: 'When Qi gathers, the physical body is formed; when it disperses, the body dies.'

Ki is comprised of balanced Chi augmented and strengthened by High Will.

An analogy to describe the relationship between these energies is to see *Chi* as flour, High Will as the water, the *Qi* is the yeast, and the inner work we do is the act of kneading them together to make dough. To produce bread, *Ki*, we need the fire of our Highest Intention and personal purpose. We can view *Chi* as a bridge between matter and energy. *Ki* is seen as a like bridge between energy and pure movement as a spectrum of forces.

Organs and meridians

Chi is distributed through the body by channels called meridians. The twelve principle meridians are named after the organs. In addition to being assigned to one of the five elements, organs are also described as being either yin or yang. Again, the solid organs and their respective meridians, Heart, Spleen/Pancreas, Lungs, Kidneys, Liver, are considered Yin, while the hollow organs, Small Intestine, Stomach, Colon, Urinary Bladder and Gall Bladder, and their meridians are considered Yang. Two additional meridians, called Pericardium and Triple Heater, are found under the fire element. These are sometimes compared to the sympathetic and parasympathetic nervous systems (the two opposing components of the autonomic nervous system). The Pericardium is assigned yin qualities, and the Triple Heater is assigned yang qualities. Yin meridians flow from earth to sky and traverse the front of the body and the inner surface of the limbs. The Yang meridians flow from sky to earth traversing the sides and outer limb surfaces, and back of the body. The twelve principle meridians form three larger circuits that flow from feet to hands and hands to feet, covering the front, side and back of the body.

In Western medicine, an organ function is described by the *physical* work it performs—producing hormones, filtering blood, digesting food, etc. In Eastern medicine, the organs also have *energy* functions. Feminine breasts are the organs for emotions, parathyroid glands for the power in the voice, and marrow of the bones are viewed as source for the Inner Song. The respective organs work together, allowing total integration of the body's physical structure and function with nutrition, energy level, hormonal balance, immune system, emotions, senses and environmental influences.

An example of the oriental perspective is the functioning of the Kidney. It contains Kidney Yin, Yang, Chi and Essence (Jing), the latter being considered the root of life (congenital constitution). To visualize the interrelationship of these substances, picture a kettle containing Yin (water) and Essence (tea) over a Yang (fire) with Chi evolving as the energy of steam.

Eight extraordinary meridians

In addition to the twelve meridians associated with organs, there are eight special ones. They are called Extraordinary Meridians because they are more primordial and provide the formative structure for fetal development. The Extraordinary Meridians do not have a continuous linking pattern nor are they associated with a specific organ. They are closely related to the uterus and brain and can influence other structures. Surplus blood and Qi are taken up from the twelve principle meridians, held, and released when needed. Lonny Jarrett envisions these eight "meridians" as oceans, whereas the other twelve are like rivers. Many combinations of points related to these meridians treat problems of the brain, hormone axis, spinal column, especially stiffness, flexibility and overall balance from side to side.

The twelve organ-titled meridians regulate the activities of Chi. The *Eight Extraordinary Meridians are more like force fields* with a *torus* form. Until the person is evolved, this centripetal force is directed toward the middle of the body much like a pressure cooker holds in steam or a cocoon holds in the butterfly until it is completely transformed and ready to fly. When a person has developed High Will and Awareness, the Eight Extraordinary meridians allow *eight esoteric wings* to open at the Assembler Points where chakra—light and Ki energy—interface. Two small wings are located in the anterior temporal lobes, two above and medial to the scapulae, and four posterior to the ankles corresponding to points Bl-60 and Kd-3. The appearance of *the mythical wings* means that the person's autonomic nervous system is well-regulated, and yin, yang and the central axis are all balanced. Then the four horns, Powa point (Antaskarana), third eye and four legs are all communicating smoothly in a torus configuration; the senses have synergy with the axis of the heart, and there is sufficient High Will and Clear Intention for the individual to jump (or fly) to a new level of Awareness. These concepts will be elaborated later.

Philosophy and Practice

Shingon is a mantra sect of Buddhism, as well as Zen. In Shingon, it is taught that the body-matter existence (rupakaya) and ultimate reality (dharmakaya) is the same. The body is represented by a triangle which symbolizes the physical, mental and spiritual componants. A quadrangle in different colors (shaped like a square) represents the objective world composed of the four elements: earth, water, fire and air. The ultimate reality (dharmakaya) is a circle, the formless form. Many Buddhists and Hindus hold a dichotomous view of existence: form = rupakaya, and formless = arupa. Even with the concept of matter and energy, they believe that two aspects of a dichotomy must contradict each other and be mutually exclusive. However, Shingon, Zen and all the sages purport that form is formless and empty, and that dichotomies are actually identical beyond their dualistic natures. It seems a paradox, yet it appears to be a scientific truth being demonstrated by modern quantum physics.

For acupuncture practitioners, the highest calling is enabling others to fulfill their destiny. In the Eastern sense, fulfillment of destiny involves actualizing the potential virtues present in our constitutional endowments given to us at birth in the form of Kidney jing (*Nourishing Destiny*, L Jarrett.). In general, practitioners of Oriental Medicine take a broad, integrated, poetic view of health and disease. It is somewhat like the difference between looking at the stars on a clear night with the naked eye versus a telescope from an observatory. The former gets a big picture and can see interactions over a period of time while the latter focuses on the details in a particular segment of the sky.

At one time in China, the practitioner knew the whole family and it was his duty to recognize and correct patterns of disharmony early, before an unbalanced state progressed to the level of overt physical disease. However, at later periods in Japan, an oriental medical doctor was highy respected only if that doctor took responsibility to be present with people nearing death in order to make that transition painless, calm and peaceful. For each professional, every night people lit a candle for each patient that the doctor cared for in this life: the more candles, the more respect.

Harmony in Life and Oriental Treatment

Eastern diagnosis and treatment rely on the perception and manipulation of subtle energy. The assessment of pulse as a part of a comprehensive history, examination and evaluation, is based on the principle that the health and functioning of an organ's Yin, Yang, Chi and blood can be detected at the radial arteries just above the wrist. This form of evaluation is like a snapshot of a person's current condition, and assists in directing the course of treatment on a day-to-day basis. To regain harmonious functioning in early phases of imbalance, more gentle forms of treatment are utilized such as suggestions to modify attitudes that are no longer useful, and life style changes including revisions in daily diet and exercise, acupuncture treatments, tuina (physical therapy), and possibly herbal formula and massage.

Disease is seen as the result of violating natural laws, of falling out of harmony. "Losing the Way" refers to loss of inherent ability to adjust readily to changing environmental and social circumstances. "Failure to adjust" causes constrictions and energy blockages making one vulnerable to disease. In Oriental Medicine, attention is given predominately to the treatment of the causes, rather than the symptoms of disease.

Oriental methodologies may be incorporated in brainwave biofeedback training protocols and contribute to achieving a state of enhanced optimal performance and the expression of our True Nature. Thermal or EEG sensors are applied to acupuncture points to assist in learning self-regulation of the autonomic nervous system, to release hidden traumas, and to create a synergistic interaction among the various levels of our being.

Acupuncture in Western Medicine

Acupuncture is only one modality from the complete system of Oriental Medicine. A great deal of research has studied its mechanism of action, safety and efficacy. This research has opened the door for acupuncture to be integrated into the clinical practice of medicine in the United States. Over 10,000 practitioners of Oriental Medicine that have been certified by the National Boards and more than 5,000 United States physicians have received training in acupuncture.

Acupuncture can help in achieving and maintaining a balanced state through the redirection of energy as it travels through the meridians. New research is verifying that these meridian channels exist just as they were marked out on the bronze statue of a man over a thousand years ago. Radioactive dye has been observed to travel along meridians after dye injection into acupuncture points. In contrast, when the dye was not placed into a recognized point, it simply spread into the surrounding tissue.

Since all of the meridians in the body are linked to each other, using a point on the Lung channel of the arm can affect a Spleen channel symptom on the leg. Functional MRI and PET scans are showing that needling of a single acupuncture point can modulate activity in the brain. Z. H. Cho, Ph.D., used functional MRI brain imagery while stimulating a specific acupuncture point (Urinary Bladder 67) in twelve subjects. The MRI showed that this acupuncture point caused the visual cortex of the brain to be activated in a way similar to how it would be activated by light striking the eyes.

Most of the Western applications of acupuncture rely on knowledge of anatomy, the musculoskeletal system and neuroanatomy. Controversy exists as to the exact anatomical structure of an acupuncture point or meridian. In general, these are areas that are near blood or lymphatic vessels and nerves. Some researchers have noticed decreased resistance to electrical conductivity at acupuncture points. The primary meridians described in Chinese medicine tend to lie over muscle divisions (fascial planes), which are rich in interstitial fluid.

One area that has not received much investigation, yet is frequently observed by practitioners, is that of personal transformation. Clinically, practitioners often try to assist clients in focusing on their internal dialog, emotions and attitudes. The oriental approach has some advantages in achieving this. When a person is receiving acupuncture and is about to be punctured with a needle, their mental focus is usually inward, where a majority of their real work needs to be accomplished. Moreover, specific combinations of points can facilitate the introspective process. Emotions are most often addressed using some yang organ meridians, according to Iona Teeguarden, a Greek specialist. Stimulating some of these points generate an awareness of attitudes which otherwise would prevent the process of natural emotional transformation.

Acupuncture is an example of how the two very different medical traditions are becoming more integrated. The application of basic science research and determination of a mechanism of action with proof of efficacy for pain relief and nausea gave it an entrée into the Western medical toolkit. Western science is confirming that much of the clinical evidence gathered from the use of acupuncture over the last three thousand years shows value not only in the treatment of chronic disease, but in improving health and well-being as well as function to levels of optimal performance. The scientifically proven value and recent recommendation of acupuncture for back pain is an example of proof that results are not attributable to placebo effect (ref 3).

Energy Psychology

Neuroscientists and researchers in human behavior have established a new paradigm in Mind-Body Medicine. The old paradigm assumed that mind and consciousness came directly from the brain, but recent discoveries demonstrate that genetic selection and physical body alone cannot explain the origins of consciousness. The new paradigm is that mind is a form of energy which is different from electrochemical activity, and that mind has distinct causal power. In human behavior this new paradigm says that psychological and psychosomatic illnesses involve chemical, neurological, and cognitive components, but those are the results of specific energy information or configurations which are expressed as diagnosable psychological or physical symptoms.

Energy Psychology (EP) is part of Mind-Body Medicine and studies the mind as energy. Psychology is the study of mind and behavior, but EP is the study of mind/behavior as the results of bioenergy. Research is directed at the effects of energy systems (such as acupuncture meridians) on emotions and behavior. Therapy treats imbalances in the various bioenergetic systems. EP evaluation and treatment of conditions can include psychological and psychosomatic disorders. A traumatic event forms energetic fields, the perception of which further elicits the release of complex hormonal messengers from the limbic-hypothalamic-pituitary-adrenal systems which encode the sensory impressions of the event in a certain state of awareness. Conscious memory of a trauma may be short, but the memory is present at a deeper level of awareness—often with ongoing dreams of the event or psychological or psychosomatic problems associated with it. EP techniques isolate and treat destructive energy patterns which have become part of the body's physiological structures. Some of these techniques include acupuncture, Neuroemotional Technique (NET), Behavioral Kinesiology, Thought Field Therapy (TFT), and Visual/Kinesthetic Dissociation (V/KD). They often test the body's energy field for areas of imbalance. The subtle energy fields associated with acupuncture meridians or other morphogenic fields are effected empirically.

Applied Kinesiology (i.e., muscle testing) evaluates the energy fields and assumes that the body-mind is basically a biophysical, quantum energy-based generator which translates mental energy into physiological responses. Muscle strength is tested against resistance, and information from muscle groups correlates to psychological and/or psychosomatic imbalances, revealing the location of bioenergy information of traumatic events in the physiological structures. Partial reactivation of the information as cellular memory allows those memories to be accessed and perceptually reframed. The EP process is therefore an adjustment of the energy patterns associated with the event and a restructuring of cellular energy patterns. EP procedures often produce remarkably rapid results. Theoretically, these treatments achieve quick results from direct access at the interface between the quantum energy expressions of the brain-mind and the biochemical processes of the body. Eliminating destructive energetic information patterns at the cellular level is akin to eliminating a paralytic computer virus. Research into the subtle energy fields responsible for encoding information into the cellular structures of the body is providing valuable insights into the theories of Energy Psychology.

Transformational Procedures

Electromagnetic changes and energy shifts are the underlying process of all healing—both Eastern and Western. Think about this carefully. Creating change in one's nature and function using learning and flexibility is a goal which often requires effort in the face of resistance. This publication describes a model of what constitutes a hybrid transformative approach, using standard brainwave biofeedback placement points that measure physiologic parameters, and in addition uses traditional Oriental acupuncture meridian points. The biofeedback sessions are augmented by providing a person images and symbols to associate with the new state. Learners are also given physical exercises to combine breath and motion. These movements integrate the energetic and physical bodies, allowing for optimal transformation and growth. The blending of biofeedback-trained self-regulation and ancient wisdom enhances the capacity to remember and access innate programming.

"Now, before me, the dead trees come alive."—Zen Koan.

Chapter 4

ANCIENT WISDOM MEETS MODERN SCIENCE

Nasrudin's tomb was fronted by an immense wooden door which was barred and padlocked. Nobody could get into it, at least through the door. As his last joke, he decreed that the tomb should have no walls around it . . . The date inscribed on the tombstone was 386. Translating this into letters by substitution, a common device on Sufi tombs, we find the word ShWF; (sh=3; w=8; f=6). This is a form of the word for 'seeing', especially for 'making a person see'. Perhaps it is for this reason that for many years the dust from the tomb was considered to be effective in curing eye troubles . . ."

—Recompilation by Idries Shah

[Nasrudin is an archetypical Master in the Sufi schools who used extraordinary approaches to teach different perspectives. Stories (you will encounter here) were the instrument used by sages to teach *open perceptions.*]

The evolving person is ready to:

- *listen* **to new ideas that differ from those influenced by and learned from his/her culture**
- *see* **other models or paradigms and make innovative changes**
- *smell* **the spectrum of aromas that are part of the cycle of nature and its rhythms**

- *taste* **unknown "nutrients" that enhance a zest for life**
- *connect* **with others without prejudgment, being fully present with the entire spectrum of sensory perception.**

New information that changes people's lives is not easy to accept. This has been true all throughout history. When Nicholas Copernicus said the sun, and not the earth, was the center of the universe, he encountered a tremendous amount of resistance. Boundary-breaking ideas are never readily accepted by the ensconced sciences, ancient or modern, because the prevailing paradigms allow only very slow movement in their perspectives and modes of investigation.

Leonardo da Vinci's studies of human anatomy using dead bodies were considered sacrilegious in his century. He was forced to flee many times from the narrow frame of tyranny, repression and Inquisition rules. In reality Leonardo da Vinci's work is timeless. He had an extraordinary ability to implement his art in order to achieve the finished product. Creativity for him was an expression of a higher fine art, which can only be reached in the depth of our being. *Art* has always been a medium used by creative, innovative people of wisdom, to express and teach penetrating truths.

Planes of Evolution of Consciousness and the Soul

There is literally an infinite *energy spectrum* in the universe, and we are only cognizant of the parts we sense and are scientifically able to measure, only very limited aspects of it. We are rarely aware of subtle higher energies, but we contain them in our essence. You are familiar with the plane here of material things, but there are also different energetic (often called spiritual) planes (frequencies of existence). These different planes of energy represent different *frequencies of consciousness.* The **physical** world of solid matter is where all solid objects are actually made of invisible vibrations at a lowest frequency on a quantum mechanics level. (Remember that the *space* in solid matter composed of atomic particles is comparable to the space between the planets.) Many who practice finely tuning their consciousness by meditation or biofeedback can go inward and actually "hear" the vibration of many of the higher planes.

In the frequency plane just higher than physical is an energy field where we find clairvoyance, telepathy, and other subtle senses. In some schools that field is called the **Astral** plane and some teach that it is possible to find ghosts and spirits that are "stuck" there. Such disturbed souls remain caught between two worlds, since emotion dominates the *thought forms* at this level. Psychics and sages can more easily access astral planes than others, unrestricted by desires. You (your consciousness) spend a third of your life in lower astral levels—every night when you are asleep. You have a physical body and an analogous astral body that is also is called the **Ethereal** double by many.

When awake consciousness exists in the world of physical objects, its vibration is very slow and dense in relation to the total spectrum of energies, being limited by the physical nature of the body. Consciousness can go to a very high vibration at the level of *awareness*, with the wild mind quieted as it experiences a new quality of perceptions—of itself. The soul-consciousness can visit planes of vibration lower than itself. The evolution of the soul through lives is always to move up to a higher frequency-vibration by accomplishing every task in the life path of evolution and fulfilling promises in all the incarnations.

Personal relationships exist in the other planes of existence in the Quantum Field of life, just as they do in the physical. On these other levels, it means that you are vibrating in 'harmony' with someone else's consciousness and feel connected/attracted by feeling, unity of intention, and love. The relationship in this field of 'harmony' is not physical (e.g. sexual intercourse) since the energy of this part of the quantum field has only *thought forms* and *dream-like work*.

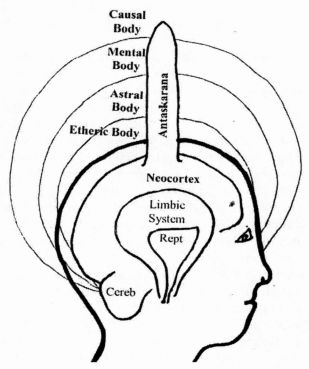

The planes of energy representing different Bodies of Consciousness as part of the Universal Mind and connected to the brain, presumably

through the Cerebellum. This Invisible Brain is said to operate at ultra high frequencies: Etheric Body at 10^{16} Hz, Astral Body at 10^{18} Hz, Mental Body at 10^{22} Hz, Causal Body at 10^{38} Hz. The evolved physical structures of the Triune Brain operate at lower frequencies (and memory capacity, bits): Neocortex at 10^{10} Hz, Limbic System at 10^{9} Hz, Reptilian Brain at 10^{8} Hz. Adapted from Seki, Hideo, PhD. The Science of Higher Dimensions: Qi and cosmic consciousness. p. 93, Sawayaka Publishing Co., Ltd., Hong Kong, 1995, referenced to Paul D. McLean, 1970.

The soul-consciousness-awareness continues to advance in its evolution to other higher, more refined energy fields (some esoteric schools call this next level the **Mental** plane), where knowledge, rather than emotions, plays the dominant role. We correlate this progressive wisdom with the concept of everything being a continuum of energies evolving in geometric proportion and therefore allowing further progress in quality and refinement. Evolution never stops, and one can eventually exist at ultra-high-frequency realms. Older teachings speak about such **Causal** planes. They say that consciousness has such a high frequency and subtle existence in those planes that there is no adequate concept or imagery for us to comprehend. We will know this level only when we are ready for it in our evolution, but we can move toward this aware state by inner work of self-regulation and self-discipline.

Theosophy and Anthroposophy

Theosophy, or spiritual science, originated with the philosopher Helene Blavatsky, and is defined as the objective science of all religions. It integrates principles of consciousness and spirituality taken from both Eastern and Western ancient religious traditions. Blavatsky's writings are a source of information about the spiritual attitudes and practices of many ancient cultures (but unfortunately included some racist ideas). They describe the multidimensional nature of human existence where we are understood as possessing multiple bodies, each of seven embedded within another. Some of he bodies include the physical, etheric (pranic), astral (emotional), mental (thought), and causal (consciousness), as well as spirit and soul (transcendental) bodies. These concepts are taken from the Tibetan Buddhist philosophy of the five interpenetrating sheaths of increasingly finer matter-energy that constitute a person. Blavatsky, Besant and Leadbeater wrote about these and also about karma and reincarnation. Theosophy represents a variant of ancient Tibetan culture and religion, implying that India had the most veritable religious concepts from which most other religions emanated.

Anthroposophy is a model of consciousness and spirituality arising from Theosophy using the scientific and philosophical theories of Rudolf Steiner on spirituality and consciousness. Carl Jung recognized these as energy concepts and suggested that some patients need *subtle body work*, referring to the etheric and astral bodies. Anthroposophy includes a method of child education, the Waldorf Schools. Anthroposophical medicine is a prototype of mind-body medicine. Humphreys successfully uses medical hypnosis of the different bodies using anthroposophical concepts. Anthroposophy does not come into conflict with existing knowledge and treatments within physical medicine—it is not in contradiction of current medical diagnosis and treatment of the physical body—since it involves treatment of the non-physical body. Unexplainable bodily phenomena are frequently explained through understanding the condition of the energy bodies.

Other Lifetimes in the Quantum Field

The concept of death from this lifetime in this body followed by transition to another state or dimension is both a scientific and religious concept. Please suspend for a moment whatever religious belief system you carry inside. Instead, consider the singular root of all consciousness, a timeless model of reality that explains the universe best, and bridges reality in terms of both mind and matter, which is a best fit for a Universal consciousness within current quantum physics operating in this universe. The Quantum Field continuity (aka Universal Mind, Quantum Mind, Mind of God, and Zero Point Field) extends backwards in time, but is also connected ahead to the future—a difficult concept to grasp.

This brings up the existence of an afterlife. We can consider this current lifetime in this physical body as a time away from our *real home*. We are here *for the purpose* of developing a new quality of nesting energies as well as learning skills which improve the collective evolution of humanity. Universal Mind—higher consciousness in the universe—is not localized, as we are in this body. It can not be identified in a specific location; this is a paradoxical concept: it is everywhere at every time. After death, our energy is no longer localized and directional, and we (as our energetic body) lose all our physical attachments and desires. Death ends money, taxes, sex, power, and physical pleasure, but provides an opportunity to grow and evolve further, widening our choices since we are not limited by this body. The miracle of death gives us access to infinite space and time, as well as the 'Intelligence' of creation.

It has been taught that being out of body is like entering a state halfway between sleep and waking. In this state, it seems like we are awake; all our senses are as keen as when we are fully physically awake—sight, hearing, even touch. The senses are actually better than they are during physical wakefulness. This is the state in which people have seen spirits and entities most vividly. It is the state of being out of the body, and for some, not knowing whether one is in the body or out.

The afterlife, inter-life, and all other non-physical dimensions are experiences in aware-consciousness. *Pure, unconditional love* has no need for a love object or other entity; it is a universal truth, and likely is the "magnetism" energizing the universe. There is the opportunity for infinite happiness, ecstasy, and even bliss. The soul remains the eternal memory of lifetimes experienced, and each lifetime (including this one) is recorded and added for the purpose of increasing Universal Wisdom.

Q: What is my real purpose for existing?

A: *to contribute to and increase Universal Wisdom.*

The Experience behind Reincarnation

Experiencing a 'Rebirth' is a natural capability of every person, and for another learning experience, one may repeat the physical life experience. There may also come a time in evolution to move on in the quantum fields of higher awareness and not be reborn on the physical plane. Everything solid and physical is transitory and transformational. We are, and the universe is, a product of change. The universe is constantly recreating itself, and we are part of that movement pattern. Remember that energy and matter are interchangeable. Everything is Matter or Energy. Consciousness and thoughts are Energy. Energy and Matter are neither created nor destroyed ($E=mc^2$). Thoughts are real, and consciousness is never destroyed, only transformed, purified, and evolved. We have evolved on earth, and we continue to "evolve in the unknown." The universe's system of rebirth is driven by the natural tendency for evolution. Each and every soul evolves in the soul's progress through experience, but not necessarily in a straight line (rather, *nonlinearity*—more like ripples in a pond from a rock). We are continually involved in our little part of the evolution of consciousness of humankind. Nature or the Universe somehow operates a mechanism of reincarnating consciousnesses. The afterlife experience of the soul is a transformational experience, similar to a caterpillar and a chrysalis, then the pupa inside reincarnates into a butterfly.

You may be surprised that all the world's religions have understood the concept of reincarnation of consciousness into flesh. Some Christian movements taught it until the 6th Century, and Chasidic Jews continue to believe in it. The Kabbalah and the Old Testament have evidence that reincarnation has always been a part of Jewish belief. Many Christian scholars know that reincarnation was completely accepted during Jesus' time and he himself spoke of resurrection—aka reincarnation. Of course, nearly all the Eastern religions have it as a basic concept.

Children who report past lives have been carefully studied, and this is the strongest evidence for reincarnation. It is common for toddlers and children up to ten years old to remember prior lives. It takes souls about 7 years to get adjusted to this life in time and body. Spontaneous recall of past lives is a natural phenomenon in children, not an illness. However, a quarter of all parents try to suppress this recall. Dr. Ian Stevenson examined more than 2,500 case studies of children who vividly remembered past lives. Carol Bowman reports that children often speak of their past life from the age of two and usually stop at age seven. They speak in a matter-of-fact tone about their last life and death, share amazing information and knowledge well beyond their current life experience. They may be scared of things related to a violent death. Dr. Ian Stevenson also studied more than 200 cases of birthmarks which clearly represented a violent cause of death in a past life.

Helen Wambach held many past life regression workshops and hypnotized thousands of people in groups who then completed questionnaires about their impressions and experiences. The data was organized and statistically analyzed, and the consistency in remembering past lives and the time periods represented were impressive and compelling. It is remarkable that reports of people who have had a Near Death Experience, children who remember past lives, and people who have had out-of-body experiences are all independently consistent with the concept of a standard process of reincarnation.

Certain repetitive compulsions or thoughts may be rooted in the unconscious or more deeply in the soul memory, and are not changeable through willpower. Accordingly, past life therapy is the only way to work through certain such memories from past lives (or *Samskaras* in Hindu language) whose source is in a record of the soul. They are transmitted through the subtle energy fields of the Mental and Causal bodies that are part of your soul memory. Your deepest thoughts are connected to other souls through many lifetimes.

Our thoughts are raw material (like dough) which need the fire of intention (energy) to transform that dough into bread. The new (reincarnated) "food" is always improved, more nutritional and tastes better. We can start this improvement process within our life now; renovation of thinking patterns today can elaborate a new quality of life here. Reincarnation is a renewal of consciousness using matter and energy that, according to physical science, can never be created or destroyed, only transformed.

About self-recognition: Is the physical body you? Is our physical aspect the only way that society accepts us?

"Nasrudin went inside a bank to the cashier to cash a check. "May I see your identification?" asked the employee.

Nasrudin pulled a mirror from his packet, looked at himself in it, and answered, "Yes, I am me."

—*Recompilation by Idries Shah*

Golden Proportion/Phi Ratio

Art becomes Beauty when the Golden Proportion is applied. It reveals a deep relationship between the fraction and the whole. Works from Leonardo da Vinci and Michelangelo have a harmonic resonance that flow with serenity and complexity, nourishing the meaning of this *pristine essence*—the Golden Proportion.

The Golden Proportion or *Phi Ratio* is a universal relationship between a part and a whole, and a fundamental expression of self-similarity and beauty. (The terms Golden Proportion, Golden Mean and Phi Ratio are used interchangeably here.) A line with any length can be divided into a smaller and larger part. When the relationship of the small segment of the line to the large piece is in the same proportion as the relationship of the large part to the whole line we have a Golden Mean. The unequal division 1 to 1.61803 . . . retains the primary unity.

From the archetypical expression of the Phi Ratio, a Golden Spiral grows in a telescoping image, remaining balanced as it expands. In architecture, art and nature the Golden Proportion is repeated in a myriad of ways: the Gothic cathedrals, 'David' of Michelangelo, 'The Last Supper' from Leonardo da Vinci, living things (nautilus shell, ram's horns, etc.), plants and in nature (profile of an ocean wave, vortex of hurricanes and tornadoes, subatomic particles, spiral galaxies, etc.), (ref 4).

Beauty and Fractals

Since the origin of the human race, men and women have developed specialized tools to improve evolution and inner transformation. Artistic creations are elements very much appreciated in the older paths of enlightenment. Aesthetic meditation brings pleasure and peace within. The deep significance of Beauty is being rediscovered in our computer-oriented society. Now, *fractal* mathematics use geometric designs to portray the universal relationship of part and whole:

- All fractal forms are duplicate-copies of an original with variations in the size of scale.
- The ordered complexity in natural systems has a Phi Ratio proportion.

- Phi functions are a quality of mathematical movements. They are found in both linear (arithmetic, algebraic, Western) and non-linear (geometric, symbolic, Eastern) constructs.
- Phi Ratio can be viewed as an essential energy with multiple levels of expression, which manifest as form in space and motion in time, producing a feedback loop in all dynamic systems (brain connections, fractals, etc.).

Crop circle formations around the world demonstrate this unique proportion seen in the geometry as a golden mean spiral, with fractals in the configuration of Julia and Mandelbrot sets (mathematical equations). The union of these powerful orders, perhaps by creating beauty in the mathematical proportion found throughout our cosmos, suggests that these circles represent a symbolic message of a harmonic universal unity in our culture.

The ancient Greek, Pythagoras, showed triangle sides were most pleasing when in the golden ratio, and found that the music scale reflects tones of strings subdivided in simple ratios of 2:1 or 3:2. Plato's study of Mathematics of Forms and Leonardo da Vinci's understanding of Vitruvius Man both found relationships that today's successful plastic surgeons call the "Golden Mask" (www.beautyanalysis.com)—a blueprint for the perfect face (e.g.: the nose and the mouth form a perfect acute golden triangle)

Human Nature

Take a deep breath, feel the warmth of the flow inside of you . . . enjoy for some time the sound of your heart . . . you are alive, exploring sage ideas that are vital in your awakening journey. It can be hard to fully understand new concepts the first time, but new meanings and reflective perceptions will flourish, giving you the power to integrate these concepts in yourself.

We are essentially stardust. Our material composition is similar to that of the planets and interstellar systems. Beyond the structure called the body, we are capable of thinking with *intention and will*, which connects all forms of life in higher awareness. From *matter* we extract *energy*—caloric, electric, chemical reactions—a physiology in flesh that forms the mystery of: What and who am I ? But in addition to our physical existence is another dimension: *awareness*. It is capable of transforming us and our environment using a deep and unique process which is beyond our knowledge being (mind), space being (body) and time being (soul). This quality of awareness emanates from our Highest Self.

Moses by Michelangelo

Merely observing outer form is not the same as inner vision. Everyday, many secrets of wisdom are offered to the individual who pierces the *depths* of art, beyond structural techniques and forms. When looking at the sculpture of Moses by Michelangelo, if we are not deeply transfixed beyond the limits of language, we have wasted an opportunity for growth. The sculpture of Moses discloses concealed information depicted by the placement of horns on the front, representing qualities of power owned by this leader. Moses inspires in others the faculties of penetrating self-observation, enlightened clarity and coherence in daily behavior. His insightful intuition and balanced state made a success of every endeavor toward fulfilling his mission. His frontal horns are a symbolic way of expressing his elevated awareness and connection to a greater dimension.

Brain scans have proven that emotional interactions between people are associated with changes in temperature and blood flow in frontal deep brain areas (the areas under the two *horns*). This takes place at the unconscious level. Social-affective transactions between individuals modulate each party's regulatory functions and homeostasis. These adaptive effects take place at the molecular level with the biochemical reactions of stress proteins, hormones and immune system involvement. These complex biologic processes are accepted in the scientific community as functions of the frontal-orbital-hypothalamic areas of the brain. Michelangelo's way of expressing that wisdom in the sculpture was in the form of *horns* extending from that zone. They are symbols of the unique esoteric qualities of awareness that Moses had, in contrast to the more mundane functioning of his peers in that environment and time.

The Hebrew word for horn is *Karen*, which is also the same word for a *ray*.

Two frontal horns in the statue of Moses by Michelangelo are found at the location of EEG points F3 and F4. These emanations represent forms of energy (thought and information) connecting humans and other dimensions.

Human Rays

We are comprised of the same atoms (and energies) as gigantic universe systems. We give off infrared radiation (detectable by thermography) and other components of the spectrum of energies (electricity from organs—heart, brain, etc.). We emanate an *aura* detectable by Kirlian photography. Phenomena in the universe influence our memories, habits, learning behavior, etc. Cosmic, social and environmental events affect what we emit; we can call these emissions "rays"—feelings of happiness, sadness, anger, love, etc. In turn, these same traits and attitudes impact our surroundings and other people. There is a continuous stream of interaction where these "rays" or *emanations* are intertwining several forms of energies between people: thought and information, feeling and emotion, intention, and neurochemistry affecting our immune systems, our will and our awareness. It all happens in the blink of an eye beyond conscious perception.

We mimic the phenomena of the universe. For instance, feelings are like pulsating stars. They flow out in waves touching others, who are altered, and who then send this transmuted energy either back to the source or further out, creating loops similar to the echoes of the stars. Thought can act like a supernova, illuminating the personal and social environment, or it can be like a red giant star, destroying and burning everything in its path. *High-Intention* in our life shapes its course, giving us new meaning and goals. Similarly, a galaxy sends out bursts of star formations, which are the new products in the universe, and *High Will* is akin to the light and energy of a quasar with its prominent emissions.

Awareness and Boundless Awareness

Awareness is the highest state that our physical organism can produce, and it arises in a manner comparable to what takes place in a black hole, where gravitational forces collapse all matter into an unconditional point of no return. Space/time sinks. Reality vanishes. Universes change, as does anything beyond our capacity to grasp with this limited mind at the present time. However, this can be a means of crossing dimensions to the unknown.

Awareness, when developed unconditionally, is supported by High Will and goes beyond the ego boundaries. Then, joyful enlightenment flourishes in the universal web of wisdom and the essence of humanity. The psycho-physiological field in a *state of Awareness* has multiple interactive components that transcend the window of science known at this time. The nervous system is crucial for changes that the body needs to accomplish—with the mind's intent to modify its own reality. The brain communicates by two kinds of signals: electricity in the cells, and by a chemical cascade of neurotransmitters, responsible for the feelings and emotions. *Glia cells* in the brain express direct electrical potentials that science now accepts as a language of non-localized signals and memory retrieval (ref 5). The cerebellum, the medulla and the spinal fluid are very important actors in the symphony of awareness, each with different roles including magnetic fields, movement of information, thermal effects, and other actions of the subtle energies. The immune system has multiple involvements with the quality and quantity of blood circulation, metabolic nutrients, hormone availability, intra- and extra-cellular toxicity management, quick responses of gases in tissues, and thermal balance. The immune system is paramount in the inception of a new state of higher awareness and optimal performance.

We know the body is a crystalline ionic water cluster of organic molecules with a high degree of coherence. This allows movement from a linear state of consciousness to a more elaborate shift in awareness states. The thermal threshold of 96.6 F to 98.6 F for Chi in meridians is (in the scientific world) accepted as the required condition for the metabolic shift, and this has also been observed in our research and practices for more than twenty years. The *neurological coherence* occurring after achieving this thermal state significantly increases the state of awareness, and has been called *Being Presence* in schools of inner wisdom. In the field of brainwave biofeedback, precise measurements allow trainees to see, in real time, the physiological condition which separates real *awareness* from hallucination, simulation or an abnormal mental state. These dynamic measurements are a documented fingerprint of the state. The signal is seen on high-tech computer equipment without artifact, demonstrating healthy self-regulation and the state of awareness called *Being Presence*. The dynamic display of this Traveling Brainwave state as an EEG signal has been presented at numerous scientific congresses by the authors, and is further discussed in Chapter 7.

We are a dynamic wave pattern of matter that interacts with waves of light, and also with the neurological chemical cascade. These substances are the amplifiers of certain states in the body. The attitude of *letting go* of attachments, addictions, habits, and degrading memories (content from the socio-cultural personality) is primary training for all those aspiring to reach states of higher awareness, according to both Eastern and Western sages.

Microtubules—the Anatomy of Awareness

At the microscopic (molecular) level of the cells in the nervous system are structures called *microtubules* of proteins folding in all possible shapes simultaneously, not overlapping themselves. Recent evidence shows they have signaling, communication and conductivity ability, and carry out classical and quantum information processing. The microtubules transform incoherent thermal and electromagnetic energy into coherent photons or soliton energy packets, which bring holographic, non-local perception into awareness. They are resonators capable of amplifying specific frequencies, causing an inner oscillation. They produce specific states of awareness (ref 6). Nano-pulses of light made in these tissues holographically encode information. The totality of the brain builds the objective reality that we perceive by transforming these energetic frequencies in projections.

A number of theories of cognition are grounded in metabolism and the soliton energetics of microtubules (ref 7). At Quantum Mind 2003 conference, Dr. Frank Smith said, "That is exactly what is implicit in the *microtubule model of quantum consciousness*. Not only can microtubule information patterns form thoughts, but they can also contain holographic information about how to organize new cell centers etc. In my view, the whole body (all of which has microtubules) can be involved in consciousness, not just the brain, although the brain has a neural organization structure that enables the thoughts to be expressed by muscles (vocal, gestures, writing, etc) whose activity is directed by the brain neural center, so that a naive first approximation is to consider the brain as the center of thought in the body. However, more nearly accurately in my view, consciousness is a whole-body holographic microtubule process." (ref 8).

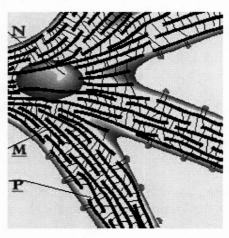

Microtubules found in the axon and dendrites of a neuron which carry out both classical and quantum information processing. N: nucleus, M: microtubule, P: microtubule structural protein.

When the microtubules' thermal threshold is reached (as in some meditation practices or breathing exercises that warm the spinal fluid), the energy becomes like a laser beam of resonant photons oscillating together at the same phase and frequency. The networks of microtubules emit intermittent pulses of coherent light-energies and vibrations which travel in the psycho-physiological realm, allowing for a merging experience of Oneness and movement to the unknown. Microtubule resonance in glia cells provides photon coherence that affects the cerebellum, generating signals of the non-local state of *boundless awareness*. With the cerebellum as director of the magnetic field, fed by High Intention, the resulting condition of Being is called by some, the *Mind of God* or the Zero Point.

The *direct current potentials of the glia cells* originate energy bursts at gamma frequency that touch the membranes of neighboring neurons. This allows the neurons to read the signal data of the field and decode the energy involved in the light resonance of the microtubules. As matter, our own physiology is subjected to electromagnetic fields and acoustic waves, which allow photons to produce this non-local dimension. The essence of our being can be free of the limited realities known by science today, those of matter-energy-antimatter. *Going 'home'* is reaching unity of life in form, soul purpose, and the essence of higher awareness—the realm of infinite possibilities—and transcending it.

Transformation

How does one learn to create boundless awareness? Long-term meditators can self-induce high-amplitude gamma EEG waves. After 10 years of meditative work, monks in monasteries are able to generate high gamma brainwaves, a state of open consciousness—enlightenment. The Laboratory for Affective Neuroscience, Department of Psychology, University of Wisconsin, and Keck Laboratory for Functional Brain Imaging and Behavior, studied monks of the Shechen Monastery of Katmandu, Nepal. The evidence was validated at Princeton University in August 2004 when they demonstrated that these long-term meditators self-induce high-amplitude gamma EEG synchrony in four areas during mental practice.

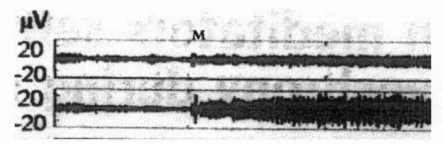

Self-induced high-amplitude gamma EEG synchrony in meditators. M: beginning of the mental practice.

In different eras, humanity has used several tools to help reach specific goals, but it is part of the human nature to explore new creative paths as opportunities for evolution. A knife as a tool is neither good nor bad; it depends on how it is used—a nice implement at the table or an assassin's dagger. Biofeedback can give us a shortcut to self-knowledge and self-regulation. Ancient methods take years of daily practice to develop an internal state of harmony. Mind training that takes monks decades to learn can be accomplished in a few months with biofeedback. We are lucky to be alive at a time when we can now synchronize so many deep philosophic constructs into our daily life in an efficacious manner. Psychology, physics, physiology, immunology, genetics and other sciences have contributed vast amounts of information for self-transformation. A myriad of methods are available.

Skeptical individuals may prefer fear and pessimism, saying, "There is insufficient scientific research and proof on this issue." They are actually uninformed of the recent advances in these fields. They prefer to rely on a handful of outdated papers indicating minimal or poor outcomes, most of them based on older technology incapable of registering more subtle information. Innovative research is accomplished by professionals with open minds that can tap into the deeper nature of things, using honest inquiry, modern scientific methods and new technology.

The Work of Sages is not Lost

Ancient wisdom involves no double blind experimentation. However, modern science over the past few decades now sees information and life in a more quantum context, and so we are now capable of visualizing a counterintuitive reality. Information from ancient wisdom accepted by western science is hardly impartial. Early materials from India (at the time of invasion by England) describe the basic chakra system, but to really conceive of subtle energies, we need education in and use of quantum physics as well as energetic physiology. Our two legs are bridges to communicate with the earth. Beyond these material forms, two more subtle bridges have been perceived by sages and those with inner discipline. We actually have four legs working in harmony to establish a geometric energy base in which the physical body is sustained, nurtured and creates an energetic process of self-transformation. Most people have only two-leg physical awareness. With real inner work and sustained effort, four legs become apparent. Martial artists, high quality athletes, and master sages in many lineages have sensed these conditions over eons.

Why do few people in Western and European culture have a sensitive, intuitive (perhaps "paranormal") ability? The physiology of the adult physical body needs to pass a threshold to allow this energetic ability to occur in us. (Many preadolescent children have these "special" abilities, but they usually become suppressed.) As we evolve, each lineage generates coded information in the genes (both DNA and energetically). The gene pool in Western and European Caucasians was depleted during the Inquisition in Europe and during witch hunts in America. Most people who were sensitives with such special abilities, with a physiology to transform energies (even Galileo), were killed—especially the young. With the genetic bank of the sensitives so depleted, few carried on these abilities in the West. Materialistic thinkers following the religious dogmas predominately bore children.

Though an individual atom of carbon cannot become magnetized, it is true that 60 atoms of carbon in a hollow molecular structure can be magnetized. Ancient wisdom teaches that it is *a small number of committed individuals who can change the world*, not by war, not by oppression, and not by imposing personal dogmas or beliefs. One can change the world only if first he or she changes the self. Then, together, we can provide the inner path of transformation to the entire population of humanity. The Hundredth Monkey Principle (reaching a threshold when knowledge or an understanding becomes universal) is real. These concepts are the distilled wisdom from different schools of thought. When the four legs are instruments of our intention from inner work, the four elements (earth, water, air and fire) become five (the subtle becomes perceived).

Even the most occult secrets of millionaires include, "As above—so is below." The Masons use this concept as a passport to levels of secrecy and awareness achieved. When Greek masters teach the *Sacred Mystery of Evolution* by 21 years of silent study, or one reads the antique Arquimedes' book, or when one enters a special state of awareness with a shaman teacher in the wild mountains (ideally without psychoactive drugs), there becomes a "seeing" or "perceiving" of dancing geometric forms in all the realms that we are. No space, no time, just Unity with the "*Original Smile.*" A recent discovery of the nuclei of cells in the deeper areas of the hippocampus reveals organization in a configuration of a geometric field of triangles; research with rats showed this to be responsible for a cognitive map of space in the environment and how the animal chose its movements.

Commitment and intention that transcends personal limitations (via honest inner work) engages three forces: *emotion with high will, clarity and silence in mind,* and *liberation from attachments and ego pressures.* They make the "cocoon of energies" melt away the older structure with persistent discipline, and they heat the energies to dancing the Torus form. Humanity wants to leap across the gap to an energy-sensitive, trained physiology, and the science of feedback technology can now help to achieve those results.

Nasrudin was walking to worship, being followed in back by a shoe thief. Nasrudin came inside, and sat, but did not take off his shoes, as tradition requires. The thief said in low voice, "Prayers with shoes on are ineffective." Nasrudin replied: 'You are mistaken; don't you see that it is very effective. I have my shoes, not you."

—Recompilation by Idries Shah

Interoception and Mirror Neurons

Research involving *interoception* (the ability to perceive sensations that arise from your own body) suggests that it is paramount for attuning emotional awareness and sentiment. The right frontal insula and anterior cingulate cortex of your brain are both involved in visceral (internal) awareness, important in your self-centering and your emotional cognition. Awareness of and following your heartbeat allows you to experience the full spectrum of emotions and has been shown to increase an individual's scores in psychological tests of empathy.

Recently, science discovered neurons in the frontal brain area that are called 'mirror neurons' because they are involved in learning copying movements in childhood—imitation (or mirroring) of what others do. These neurons increase the performance of the body's movements—particularly if it is in conjunction with empathy of care giving (from the mother or whoever has that role). Becoming emotionally aware of others has a physical basis, mostly in gray matter in the right frontal insula, and some studies suggest that when it is not used, neurons are lost. Autistic children have impairment of these neurons.

However, some practices (such as biofeedback) can enrich the neuronal connections. Training the receptors of internal balance in the skin, teeth, tongue, etc. by the practice of certain movements allows one to develop better maps of 'gut' feelings. A movement example is the tip of the tongue touching the inner front teeth. Many people unconsciously use this tongue placement when concentrating; it is known from oriental medicine that an important meridian point is located there, one which facilitates energy flows to the front areas of the brain for clarity and discernment. The right frontal insula is where physical sensation and emotional awareness merge. This homeostatic self-regulation center puts your internal sensations in context with motivations, ideas and intentions. Emotions are never truly out of decision making—they are the fire under the kettle in the "tea/elixir" of awareness.

Antonio Damasio, neuroscientist and director of the Brain and Creativity Institute at the University of Southern California, says that feelings contribute to most of the 'rational' decisions in life (ref 9). It is not possible to totally separate thinking from the emotions and more primitive aspects of the mind. When the fight or flight response of the nervous system is blocked by drugs or learning biofeedback, the fear that was *in your body* calms down, then the mind (and higher Being) can act and calmly perform in a more efficient way. We are, after all, a living system interacting with the entire spectrum of matter, energy and awareness.

Crescent of the Tide of Higher Evolution

For a Being to evolve, one integrates physiology, higher energy development and awareness into a transcendent releasing of the True Self, and develops the power needed to respond to a chaotic world, with intention, persistence and humor. *Education is the royal path to producing change*—both within and without. Ignorance keeps us slaves. We are capable of flying freely, since we can learn to use all the dimensions that we are (body, mind, and subtle energies) in a journey of joy.

Chapter 5

ACCESSING THE INNER SELF

A Sufi tale:

"*A stream, from its source in far-off mountains, passing through every kind and description of countryside, at last reached the sands of the desert. Just as it had crossed every other barrier, the stream tried to cross this one, but it found that as fast as it ran into the sand, its waters disappeared. It was convinced, however, that its destiny was to cross this desert, and yet there was no way. Now a hidden voice, coming from the desert itself, whispered: 'The Wind crossed the desert, and so can the stream.' The stream objected that it was dashing itself against the sand, and only getting absorbed: that the wind could fly, and this was why it could cross a desert. 'By hurtling in your own accustomed way you cannot get across. You will either disappear or become a marsh. You must allow the wind to carry you over, to your destination.' But how could this happen? 'By allowing yourself to be absorbed in the wind.' This idea was not acceptable to the stream. After all, it had never been absorbed before. It did not want to lose its individuality. And, once having lost it, how was one to know that it could ever be regained?*

'The wind,' said the sand, 'performs this function. It takes up water, carries it over the desert, and then lets it fall again. Falling as rain, the water again becomes a river.' 'How can I know that this is true?' 'It is so, and if you do not believe it, you cannot become more than a quagmire, and even that could take many, many years; and it certainly is not the same as a stream.' 'But can I not remain the same stream

that I am today?' 'You cannot in either case remain so,' the whisper said. 'Your essential part is carried away and forms a stream again. You are called what you are today because you do not know which part of you is the essential one.' When (s)he heard this, certain echoes began to arise in the thoughts of the stream. Dimly, (s)he remembered a state in which (s)he—or some part of him/her—had been held in the arms of a wind. (S)he also remembered—or did (s)he?—that this was the real thing—not necessarily the obvious thing—to do.

And the stream raised his/her vapors into the welcoming arms of the wind, which gently and easily bore it upwards and along, letting it fall softly as soon as they reached the roof of a mountain, many, many miles away. And because (s)he had had doubts, the stream was able to remember and record more strongly in his/her mind the details of the experience. (S)he reflected, 'Yes, now I have learned my true identity.'

The stream was learning. Then the sands whispered: 'We know, because we see it happen day after day, and because we, the sands, extend from the riverside all the way to the mountain.' And that is why it is said that the way in which the Stream of Life is to continue on its journey is written in the Sands."

—Recompilation by Idries Shah

Self-regulation and Self-realization

Integrating the development of an efficient, healthy, and happy life is a challenge. That is our daily struggle—to succeed and to attain our goals and purpose in life. Work from that theoretical background with an understanding that we are more than the sum of our parts. Individuals are a latticework in which *matter, energies and motion* are joyfully intertwined in such a way that our inner Being can be revealed as the transcendent dimension beyond our present narrow horizon. In learning self-regulation skills, one is lead by the *thought forms* from his or her higher Being. This brings the personal ego under self-control and allows self-actualization.

For the purpose of empowering people, we put together the ancient wisdom of the past with the speedway that scientific technology brings us. Respected schools teach students: to work with *perceptual flexibility* to open the inner frontiers of energies; to make cognitive, emotional and behavior changes; to let go of attachments to outcomes and their attitudes of suffering; and to recruit the direction of daily actions towards highly ethical values and virtues.

Ancient masters knew that physiological mechanisms can be associated with special meditations, practices, and exercises, which allow the body to learn and integrate new steps in awareness for every day life. Analogies, metaphors and movements can reframe emotional blocks and create skills that mobilize a new direction in one's physiology. This is where the instruments of biofeedback are such powerful tools for reinforcing, learning and increasing memories of previous successes, healing, and states of wisdom with positive expectation. The human being can be a model of fractal energy with self-regulation and self-realization, less effort and waste, and self-development in harmonic proportion to the world in which he or she lives.

Communication

Over the years, storytelling has been the primary means of transmitting wisdom from older people to younger generations. Listening, understanding and enjoying the many aspects of that practice (and visualizing internally) helped to develop the inter-neuronal connections from cavemen to humans of the industrial century. We created versatile images and personal approaches to the information that was given, stimulating diversity and imagination, the first steps of *intuition*. Storytellers and sages instilled in their listeners primordial truths and values at propitious times, presenting their physiology moments to assimilate and process the wisdom imparted. Today's technological explosion is changing that traditional path into an informational TV screen that facilitates mostly *linear thinking* and a high capacity for rapid retrieval of data (including immediate self-gratification). The Internet is a tremendous storehouse of available information; however, very few websites are developed that enhance the creativity and imagination of the visitor.

These techniques use both ancient and modern methods of communication:

- **Storytelling**: meaningful tales that precipitate lighthearted means of incorporating points of view from Zen, Sufi, Hopi, Hawaiian and many non-Western cultures, allowing integration of many aspects of personal reality.
- **Older analogies from Eastern wisdom:** promote grounding and flexibility in perceptions, and resilience in actions. They build self-esteem without getting caught up in competition or egocentrism.
- **Ancient metaphors:** used to release past experiences and/or frame perceptions that block the expression of a healthy psycho-immune state. These can promote the health of the physical body.
- **Sensory experiences:** provide keys to opening synesthesic appreciation (integration of the five senses). These modify the chemistry of neurotransmitters and neuromodulators.

· **Modern western analogies and metaphors:** help the transformation of physiological changes (thermal skin control, heart rate, respiration rhythm) to achieve states of higher awareness through personal cues that can be recalled at will: "Inner Keys."

Some common metaphors, analogies and techniques are:

· Axis: as a warm, flexible light path and a means of grounding to enhance balance and support forgiveness, through its three-legged connection with the earth.
· Counting during exhalation, while engaged in diaphragmatic breathing.
· Torus breathing technique.
· Releasing distress and unwanted memories via symbols: mountains, waterfalls, rivers.
· Opening symbolic doors: to re-ground or re-center meaningful individual information.
· The Bubble: as a personal safe place with self-nourishment and self-resilience.
· The Gray room: and the intent to acknowledge and experience freedom by transforming and self-processing energies.
· The Cocoon: as a progressive time path in the transformation (to butterfly).
· Self-healing in rainbows: perception of the new body with inner peace.
· Safe, beautiful, peaceful and joyful inner place.
· The Centaur: allowing deep connections, knowing beyond words the interactions of dimensions and their bridges.
· The Tunnel: preparation for transition movements in space-time dimensions.
· "Being" the breath: to integrate vital awareness in all realms.
· Dialogue with the allies: uniting the web of life forms.

Using the above techniques can help to balance the autonomic system at the meridian points and increases the flexibility of healthy responses and chemistry on demand, without wasting energy in explosive and disruptive behavior. We become the owner of our monkey mind, feelings and reactions. We are no longer slaves to our environmental conditions, attachments, or our personal hot buttons. Exercises, movements and body postures facilitate 24-hour access to efficient behavior, as energies needed for action are kept ready and available.

Synesthesia

Synesthesia is the ability to perceive multiple sensory information. A person with this capacity hears a bell and, at the same time, detects its primal odor, the color related to the quality of the sound, the texture or vibration of the experience, and may include a taste for that stimulus. Thus the senses of hearing, smell, vision, kinesthesia, and taste are being received at the same time. The capacity of synesthesia transcends the purely somatic attributes, and when appreciated, opens new channels of deep transformation. Human beings have the capacity for multi-sensory experiences beyond usual psychological reference frames of modern cultures.

Synesthesia is a new word for many people, but not in the National Institute of Health in Bethesda, Maryland where Dr. Grossenbacher and colleagues were the vanguard, studying this new frontier of multiple human sensory perceptions. Dr. Grossenbacher teaches in a private university in Boulder, Colorado. Researchers in Germany, Israel, Australia, France, Scotland, England, Canada, and Finland have made it very clear that the sensory experiences of a particular reality are not the same for everyone. People around us may receive different impressions, and we cannot dismiss their observations. Studies suggest that this ability is more prevalent in women than men.

Individuals with the gift of synesthesia are no more vulnerable to mental disorders or illness than the general population. Famous writers, artists, scientists and musical composers have enjoyed this natural gift. Sean Day, professor at Taiwan National Central University cataloged 19 forms of *synesthesia.* This capacity for multiple direct perceptions is enduring, and is found more in family lines, suggesting a genetic component, but environment and culture modifies responses. Cognitive scientists can scan, evaluate and stimulate humans with this ability; Positron Emission Tomography (PET) has suggested that individuals with *synesthesia* possess unusually high anatomic connectivity between sensory areas of the brain, especially at the interface between the cortical zones and deep limbic centers. These links might play an important role in use of metaphor information, which blend sensory elements of language (e.g. bitter cold). This is a technique of education in many ancient cultures (e.g. the "storyteller").

Most children at six months of age have responses similar to *synesthesia,* but selective cell death and reversal of circuits during infant development create sensory islands. When the synaptic bridges remain, we retain synesthesic ability as an adult. *The capacity to enhance our sensory awareness can be increased.* A new organization, The American Synesthesia Association, helps doctors, clinicians, educators and health professionals understand the part of unusual sensory experience that is Synesthesia.

We can change brainwave signal patterns with learning. Studies with rats suggest that they use a portion of their brain to learn a new habit, but once learned, the rats seem to know how to anticipate the challenge. Another part of the network of cells is responsible for the application of the habit. In humans, the interpretation and memory of incoming sensory information is strongly affected by emotional arousal. The proper integration of the pre-frontal cortex (planning), thalamus, amygdala (significance), and hippocampus (cognitive map) can be disrupted by a high level of stress, creating dysfunctional disorders, which are stored as phobias, panic attacks, and depression. Living systems can improve self-regulatory capacities if they receive appropriate information. Biofeedback acts as a mirror to provide an accurate picture, essential to learning and developing real skills that improve performance and higher potentials in many dimensions. *Repetition of experiences* preserves and *imprints* the latticework of synapses.

When the precision of modern biofeedback technology is joined with awareness exercises distilled from ancient wisdom, the Golden Proportion is reinforced in our bodies. This is a primordial program of transformation, and each of us has the ability to discover the full spectrum of the potential dimensions that we are.

Much Knowledge and Little Wisdom

This period in human history far surpasses all prior periods in levels of Knowledge, but there has not been a similar increase in Wisdom. Wisdom includes a sense of proportional judgment: the ability to understand all the important aspects and implications of a particular issue and to give each its appropriate weight. This is more difficult now because of the vast increase in scientific and technological knowledge. Scientists may have little time to consider all the *effects and implications* of their work. A prime example: In the last 50 years, science has come to understand the atom from a knowledge point of view, yet has created a means of destroying the human race. The pursuit of knowledge may create consequential damage if not combined with Wisdom.

Wisdom is the sense of *complete vision* in the pursuit of knowledge and understanding. Being complete and thorough alone is not enough to constitute Wisdom. There must also be an awareness of means as well as the ends. One could say the completeness that is Wisdom also includes not only intellect but also the quality of feeling emotion. It is common to find those whose knowledge is broad but whose emotional repertoire is narrow, based only on habitual body chemistry created by the culture and time of which they are part. They lack real Wisdom.

Not only in public, but also in private life, Wisdom is needed. It is needed in the *choice* of ends to be pursued and in liberation from personal prejudice. Pursuit of an unattainable goal is simply unwise. Many have devoted their lives to a search for the elixir of life. If they could have found it, it may have created great benefit for mankind, but their lives were simply wasted. Wisdom is also emancipation from tyrannical thinking. But our emotions, sight, sound and touch are part of our bodies and cannot be removed. An infant feels discomfort and is aware only of its own condition. Over the years, the view broadens, and thoughts and feelings become less concerned with personal states. That is growth of Wisdom by learning impartiality.

Some Wisdom can be taught. However, such teaching needs more reality-based understanding than has been found in usual morality instruction. The disastrous personal results of hatred and narrow-mindedness need to be taught and become common knowledge. The teaching of knowledge and the teaching of responsible morals and ethics should not be separated. Specialized knowledge required for various skills has little to do with Wisdom, but it should be supplemented by education of wider views of all human activities. Technicians should also be good citizens of the world. With increases of knowledge and skill, Wisdom becomes even more necessary. Every increase augments our capacity to realize our goals, and also augments our capacity for harm if the goals are unwise (e.g. computer-games that desensitize our youth to the concept of killing). The world needs more Wisdom now than ever before.

Collective Consciousness

In spite of the rise in religious fundamentalism, the "professional" skeptics who will forever cast doubts about experiences of reality, and media news spoon-fed to the masses, you can still notice a true shift in global collective consciousness and a heightened spiritual awareness in this millennium. More people now have "access" to the Quantum Field. Intense spiritual experiences are now common for those who are not even pursuing them. About a third of Americans have had a "paranormal" experience or an intense spiritual one, which is far more commonplace in less westernized cultures. One in seven Americans says he or she has seen a UFO including Presidents Jimmy Carter and Ronald Reagan as well as many reliable airline and Air Force pilots. Indigo/star children and the new plethora of psychics are just some of the indications that the collective mind of humanity may be approaching a point of convergence and is nearly ready to make a leap. The Hundredth Monkey Principle holds that when we reach a threshold, we can expect a leap in the consciousness of humankind and an acknowledged connection to other dimensions.

Our Pasts, Past Lives and Concepts of Time

Many people talk about remembering past lives. But, time is a human creation. *Time* may be defined as "duration of movement through space" and therefore has a vector or direction. Measurement began when people decided to start counting time (Gregorian, Mayan, Chinese, Hebrew calendars, etc.). Accordingly, time puts order into daily living, giving us days for work and for play. Time is in constant movement in the here and now. We are that movement. We are time travelers. What people call *consciousness* is a singular self-awareness within the framework of the incessant movement of life energy. But it is only a snapshot, only at that moment. *Awareness* is a pristine identity, a real 'who I am' in one's dynamic never ending fulfillment.

People register memories and store the sequence of what happened, with its emotional context. Thus builds a personal history of this lifetime. Many people have a collection of dark, painful memories that influence moods, indirectly creating depression, hate, anger, or resentments, which destroy the capacity to be free. These repressed memories require energy to hold them in the closet of our mind, creating a habit of self-preservation dedicated to "forgetting" or ignoring these events. Releasing the suffering of our life's dusty old recollections is a key to liberation.

Our journey becomes much more joyful when we learn to share the good and happy events. It is a change, but it is the way to regain our power. Every moment we allow our monkey mind to continuously parrot back the bad things that happened to us, or recount long lists of awful memories, takes away our power. (Some situations may need psychotherapy with a specialist capable of really helping a person to move beyond being a victim.)

One grows with a *capacity to let go* of deep material repressed in layers of the mind which affect daily behavior by creating recurrent failures and, frustration. Various verbal approaches are used in western psychology and eastern schools to facilitate healing with a mental process of "letting go." Symbolism and the archetypical forms may be used in the resolution of unconscious topics, with a delicate recreation of traumatic past events for liberation from emotional and neurochemical patterns. Therapeutic movements used by some schools of wisdom (e.g. Tai-Chi, Hatha Yoga, Bakua, and in the West such as Gurdjieff dancing & Tensegrity) have proven to be helpful to reach a state of *inner clarity, free of attachments and dependencies.* This letting go results in a new freedom, but only after long and disciplined practice of these movements-exercises-dances. Brainwave biofeedback applied at the right front brain (EEG point F4) produces similar results, and quickly restores personal freedom.

We also store memories connected with impacts of past-life experiences. Many of these are painful, dramatic, carry intense emotions, and pressure us to forget and dissociate. Not everyone needs to recall those past remembrances in detail; however, our evolution has a lot more power when we recognize ourselves as the sum of our multi-life history. With some training and collaboration, we can reconnect with the wisdom garnered in previous lives. This past knowledge can be accessed and applied to our present experiences to facilitate our higher creative expression. Understanding the lessons of past experiences in the light of day can stop the suffering and enhance our current situation tremendously. You have the power to recover the sage that lies within you, without rituals or dependence on others. There is an internal resonance that occurs when a person recovers his or her own important memories.

The profound metaphor from an ancient wisdom school of India at the beginning of this chapter about the stream in the sands of the desert can be used as a guide in pulling together one's personal history. One moves back to the fetal state and crosses over energetic bridges to reach lives before birth. It is a personal, individual journey that opens and decodes the meaning of information stored in our past lives, and recovers that wisdom.

Mystical vs. Experiential Spirituality and Roots of Learning

Spirituality is usually based upon **faith** (in an unseen world and creator) rather than **attainment**. Few of us feel we are "mystics" capable of an actual experience of spirit. Two things prove that many of us do have the ability of deep spiritual realizations that are potentially life transforming. "Near-death" experiences of those people who have physically died and are then revived, reveal a group where their consciousness remained totally intact and was given new perceptual abilities as well as access to *a transcendent understanding* that neither occurred before nor was enhanced after that experience. Another way some have experienced an awakening of the "sleeping mystic" is through medical hypnosis when a client spontaneously experiences a state of consciousness and gains access to the transcendent self. Other approaches such as spiritual regression or past life regression can allow a person to explore "super-conscious" dimensions. Importantly, there is great consensus and similarity in reports of spiritual realms and experiences.

We know that the practitioners of ancient mystery schools used to stimulate some points in the head and backbone as a way to achieve clarity and release inner power. Their training drew from music, mantras, visualizations, touch, massage, needles, rhythm percussion, moxa combustion and other techniques. Every culture and epoch also has established methods for obtaining the information about special body places (assembler points, chakras, etc.) and practices. Ancient wisdom may be hard to discover since it is often wrapped in tradition and subtle language meanings.

The aware and enlightened brain is not chaotic, but has areas with certain kinds of specificity. There are centers in the brain for speech and for visual interpretation, and secret schools consider those deeper structures (amygdala, hypothalamus, pituitary, etc.) related to basic responsibility, and other areas of the brain to be keys for Awareness and higher states of Being. Such characteristics can be studied in those who have achieved these states—Zen Masters, Lamas, Sufi Teachers, etc. We can call the key zones "the five horns."

Anatomy of the Five Horns

The five horns are like secret doors where biology interacts with the internal energy paths. The five include the unicorn horn, two horns above the hairline in front, and two other horns toward the back part of the head. The statue of Moses by Michelangelo was previously discussed as it relates the anatomic areas of two frontal horns seen in art. We are able to recreate the conditions for manifestation of the horns. The force / energy that occurs at these specific scalp locations are not Kundalini. Yoga masters can develop that quality of fire, but what we are describing is a different layer of energy which acts as a bridge to integration of subtle energies. Laya yoga (an ancient teaching related to sound and primordial manifestation) has clues for attaining the reality of the horns. With the use of colored light or thermal feedback in specific areas (in acupuncture called the "4 gates points" located in the legs and hands), the five horns can be developed very quickly.

In the front part of the head, is the *unicorn point* at the central meridian (in most people just below the hairline) where, with special pranayama breathing exercises, one can facilitate electromagnetic *perception*. This relates to the pineal gland, bridge (the Antaskarana), the pituitary medial lobe, and third eye chakra. The symbol associated with the area is an upward pointing triangle; we call this *unicorn*.

In the left front horn area (EEG point **F3**) near the parietal bone, the lateral meridian (Gall Bladder) has a point where we often train the EEG frequencies above 14 Hertz. The ancient symbol for the left frontal zone is an area for developing *discernment*. It is the capacity of *discernment* in subtle senses, sounds, images as information, and data from the environment in quality and quantity; also it is the redistribution of the data in the network formed by the assembly of physiological and energetic fields.

The right front horn area (EEG point **F4**) is where some eastern wisdom schools describe the infinity sign in constant motion, and it holds the triggers of habits, reactions, unconscious moods and primitive programs from childhood. Learning to *let go* of some of that baggage, without repressing the information or denying the inner pain, helps one to be emotionally healthy. Techniques to transform deep-seated emotional baggage can relieve some of the pressure of one's personal life, while improving the *flexibility* of one's Being and releasing the new chemistry of joy and freedom. Many people need to *let go* of attitudes of self-pity or selfish personality traits before they are ready to move on to deeper self-development. The right front area facilitates the *discharge of attachment* and is used to *let go* of excess or disturbing memory information, and to focus and equilibrate the conscious, subconscious and unconscious data. For some, it has been a point of the access to infinite non-linear time.

In the same meridians on the head are two points in back. The left back horn area (EEG point **P3**) is a *powerful coordinator* of rhythm in the autonomic network system (breath, pulse and facilitating the techniques of Chi Kung and pranayama). It is the key to self-regulate personal *Inner Power*, being aware of the coordination and the harmony among heart rate, breath, and the gamma brainwaves in synchronicity at the four areas of the head. It modulates the extra meridians—second skin (subtle structure of the electro-magnetic body in fractal design with Torus movements).

The right back horn area (EEG point **P4**) is a point trained for *quieting* the physical and energetic structures (soul/spirit). Inspiration, creation and originality in common sense are powers that flourish at this point. It is the key to self-regulate *silence in the mind.* In metaphoric words, it is seen as a beautiful star of five points emerging in sparkling lights. It is the space for coordinating electro-magnetic signals as a field of sounds without words as expressed in the Inner Song—a personal vibration of deep calm in a safe place.

Within a state of intention and awareness these two posterior points function as bridges between:

- Highest ethics with self-esteem, being in harmony with the environment,
- Art as a learning process for personal enhancement,
- Universal philosophy and ethics as inner wisdom.

From research came an interesting phenomenon that we call the "dance of the horns." When the brain reaches this higher state during brainwave biofeedback, the computer record of the session can pinpoint the areas with maximum electrical power. Regardless of frequency, an unexpected order arises in the wave amplitude. When the points of highest voltage are registered, and the lines in the graphic image connect the sequences of locations around the head, the resulting brain maps take on the form of mandalas, configurations of perfect Phi Ratio geometry. Here, ancient wisdom meets modern science. During this millennium, new technology will open the frontiers of perception in *subtle energies*, and a new generation of scientific research will expand knowledge of our potential and abilities.

"Though the grease burns out of the torch, the fire passes on, and no one knows where it ends."—Zhuangzi

Dance of the Horns

The activation of the five horns is by way of discipline and practice (music, meditation, visualization, biofeedback, etc.). Neurons learn to produce higher power brainwaves in Phi Ratio among the EEG frequencies. The oriental master, lacking technology over the millennia, observes with his or her *inner power* the fractal activities in the electromagnetic fields in the areas of the horns. This activity is what we call the "dance of the horns"—the harmony in Phi-ratio of the areas that express a self-adjustment in every band. In the EEG spectrum signal it is possible to see this progression.

An advanced state can be achieved by consolidating the newly learned pathways using the *perception* of three-dimensional movement inside the mind (designated as: right-left, front-back, up-down). These movement paths in the three directions allow the "monkey mind" to wander about, while the higher level energy remains in the areas of the five horns, manifesting warmth, light and flexibility. The energies of these five areas may synchronize together during the highest practice of the discipline, and when combined, direct themselves in summative energy vectors based on specific intention.

Intense discipline and exercises are needed to extract a strong force called *High Will*. It is different in quality and quantity than the ordinary concept of will. "High Will" is a special level of power and awareness that changes one's perceptions and lifestyle forever. Every high Lama, Swami, Zen Master, Christian mystic, or enlightened person is living proof that this quality of brain/body interaction is possible. They are examples of flexible functioning for all, beyond the influence of race, age, sex, culture or other factors.

Ancient wisdom acknowledges that immune physiology and the autonomic nervous system have a deep inner connection with the real 'essence' of the human being. The cortical brain and intellect are related to the personality and motivating functions. For most people the mind is forged in the mold of social culture. Those who wish to transcend these limits and seek real inner freedom can refer to the sages. The masters teach about secret doors (the five horns) where the biology interacts in flexible ways with the internal paths. However, these older forms of practice take many years. Scientific technology (biofeedback) now gives us the possibility to more rapidly access this power. This is a process for learning and embodying the psychobiological tools that transform us into *multi-sensory light beings in freedom.*

Five horns and the tunnel of time

The five areas can, with training, activate new clusters of neurons when precise inner disciplines are accomplished. These results will change a perspective to the extent of "the ability to see the universe in a grain of sand." To understand how past life connections and unfinished business can affect the here and now, here is a anecdote:

At springtime, a soft breeze expanded the aromas of new flowers in the garden. Late that afternoon, Ariel was invited by her friend to a new group, researching past lives. That evening, she found the spacious house had a decor that inspired broad-minded vision. The subject of investigation in that night was analysis of how and when people can call to mind memories, glimmerings from past lives, and re-identification with forgotten information from a previous life. The topic grasped the attention of Ariel, and from that day forward, she was a committed participant of that group. After only a few sessions, she became freinds with other participants. One man there, Vincent, an engineer from Italy, was handsome and also committed to this kind of inner work. Their common culture and easy dialogue led to a 'spring time' melody of romance between them. When summer arrived, the group leader proposed to her to engage a different level of learning, one where all the information gathered in group will be expressed as a living journey in a time dimension. Ariel accepted, and for months she was involved in the psychophysical exercises of preparations for the moment when she would join that extraordinary journey.

There was a three day closed retreat in that house with nine participants, and Vincent was one of the invited travelers. After a rather long technique, everybody was in a state of awareness ready for flying through the tunnel of time. When Ariel "took off," in front of her appeared a dark, spiraling tunnel, like a wormhole with millions of sparkling stars falling and passing her at high speed. Some appeared like shooting novas, and as Ariel peered into those luminary orbs, she saw scenery, faces, and situations which she easily identified as past forgotten experiences. Her mind remembered all the information. For a while the pictures came and went quickly, but at one moment everything changed, and Ariel knew, without doubt, the image of an arch of heavy rocks was part of the Roman coliseum where gladiators battled and Christians were put to death by beasts. Ariel recognized that she, as a young girl, came to that place because a gladiator was to appear there. He would bring a big piece of bread, and she was quite hungry. He walked through a dark corridor, and offered the food with a smile on his face. Ariel knew that was Vincent. In a glimpse, she understood the next image. A Christian girl was tied on the back of a furious bull, and this same man, seeing how she was to die on that animal, took the horns of the beast in his hands, and freed that young girl from a cruel death in the arena. And the circus continued for the Roman Cesar.

Ariel returned from that journey moved by the implications of the relationships between her and Vincent. The group's rule was that each of the participants would dialogue in private with only the teacher about the journey, in order to protect private information and avoid contamination by sharing details. The teacher allowed Ariel to clarify her experience, then asked if she and Vincent wanted to share their experiences. When they did so, the correlation of the expereinces was astounding. Vincent and Ariel had a relationship in a past life, which brought both into a current romance. Both saw from this new perspective of wisdom that they needed to revaluate their path together. Life is a learning field where opportunities pass us and may return. It is from a position of inner wisdom where choice can help one to evolve. Ariel evolved, and Vincent was a "dream of the past," realized for her in this life-incarnation.

"Awakening is possible only for those who seek it and want it, for those who are ready to struggle with themselves and work on themselves for a very long time and be very persistent in order to attain it. For this, it is necessary to go out to meet all those inner sufferings to which we are connected with the sensations of contradiction."

—*Gurdjieff*

Chapter 6

THE MIND—FROM MATTER TO ENERGY

Dogen (a Zen master) said: "You may suppose that time is only passing away, and not understand that time never arrives. Although, understanding itself is time, understanding does not depend on its arrival." Some say not to search, but don't postpone this moment as the only one for awakening our true nature.

Matter—Energy—Realms

Society has a tendency to see only the polar aspects of reality: matter/antimatter; day/night; woman/man; off-on binary computers, etc. This division and classification of the universe produces linear and categorical ways of thinking. Beyond this black and white view is another dynamic, spiral perspective of reality that is circular and encompasses life. At least three components constitute the unfolding process of the reality of life. How and where they interact in the infinite space-time dimension is the inherent wisdom of life itself and a universal principle.

The whole living universe is manifested as states of matter (solid, liquid, gas, plasma, etc.) or a spectrum of energies (light, solar wind, microwaves, gamma rays, ultraviolet, etc.). Furthermore, Einstein, through his famous $E=mc^2$ equation, shows that matter and energy are interchangeable. Everything is in a constant movement or state of vibration or flow (in waves). Our senses show us just a very small portion of this reality of many dynamic systems interacting. We usually only perceive those portions of reality that activate the narrow bands of the sensory receptors and their associated nerve and brain cells.

However, we also have learned that the telescope, microscope and television can make the invisible visible as radio makes the inaudible audible. We know that some portions of the enormous spectrum of reality that exist beyond the limits of normal perceptive range of our sense organs can be made sensible through the intermediary use of technological tools. The ordinarily imperceptible or "subtle" can be made perceptible. This suggests that there can be many "subtle" realities or other dimensions which possess life forms—probably most in energetic rather than physical forms. Such life forms are sometimes detectable by animals (e.g. infrared by snakes, magnetic fields in doves and migratory herds, and our pets likely detecting entities).

The "spiritual" realm, which lies outside of our range of *ordinary* perception, may be one of these "subtle" realities. Furthermore, Oriental thinking and Western religious paradigms assert that our body and Being is capable of perceiving the extraordinary with the cultivation and training of our inherent senses, and without the use of technology.

The Mind in Motion

In the average person's daily life, mundane features dominate. The "monkey mind" governs thoughts. The deep thinking mind is trapped, lacking control, in the chaos of our ideas, which are occupied with insubstantial topics, habits and entangled feelings.

The anatomy of matter overlaps, bridges, and links the flow of the physiology. Metabolic processes, immune responses and healthy internal feedback are complex interactions between a variety of chemical reactions, energy flows and rhythms, personal cycles, and movements—which represent *motion*. Mind is analogous to the onion, having layers. In the core, the *unconscious* materials push our emotional chemistry buttons, using a lot of energy in creating repression and frustration states. The *subconscious* layer is a direct link to the entire library of memories, education, and time-space where we develop our life, belief system, and "the way I am." What people call the *conscious* mind are the few moments of waking thoughts, between the longer "naps" of everyday life. During most of the journey, our life is driven by the *automatic pilot*, that aspect of the mind that takes care of and modifies our internal psycho-physiological states, allowing us to use "the mind" to think or daydream.

When a baby is born, all the potentials are in that body—the physiology to be a Buddha, Christ or Messiah, a perfectly balanced being. We have a pristine (original, pure) program impressed in our DNA and in our Being that says: "I am healthy, efficient, and happy; and I want to live long and successfully." Then what happens to us? How do we become reprogrammed into what we are today? It is a long story, but perhaps the human race will some day recognize the importance of educating people to become parents, the value of prevention versus healing, and the birthright of all humans to be respected as individual miracles of life, in freedom and peace with all other forms of existence on this planet.

There is a *search for meaning* in the depths of the hearts of all individuals, whether awake or sleeping. This drive for knowledge is likely the primary driver of human existence. When we give up that search, "we die." Environmental and cultural conditions change the way in which we perceive the world. However, it is the awakening mind that is capable of thinking beyond the limitations imposed upon it, while asking meaningful questions.

The *subconscious mind* hypothalamic frontal-orbital network of the brain is impressed from early childhood with experiences and emotions that can facilitate healthy, growth-enhancing behavior, or conversely, can lead to unhealthy, destructive behavior. These experiences have been scientifically shown to affect the very anatomical structure and function of the brain itself (ref 10). For example, when children are not guided to develop personal boundaries and self-discipline, a subconscious pattern emerges with manipulative tendencies that can instigate thoughtless, capricious behavior with immediate self-gratification as the main objective. Children then want their own way and can become tyrannical.

For mental health professionals, the biggest mystery is the *unconscious mind*. In recent history we have started using psychoanalysis, psychosynthesis (Assagioli), art, music, dance, dream therapy and modified states of awareness to explore our deepest psychology. Many of these developed from ancient wisdom, which gave valuable tools for accessing the unconscious. Physical and meditative exercises blended with intention and specific breathing patterns for heart rate variation have been used for centuries. Advanced technologies combine brainwave biofeedback, multi-sensory methods and leadership techniques in physiologic teamwork to quickly create beneficial changes.

Memory and The Automatic Pilot

When the mind learns information, it sometimes remembers and sometimes forgets. But, when it is the deep autonomic network body-mind that learns, one is able to recall or coordinate ingrained movements or information for a lifetime (e.g. walking, driving a car, riding a bicycle). Every person can create these patterns in the automatic-action center of the mind through repetitive movements with intention and multi-sensory input.

The autonomic network of the nervous system is comprised of areas interconnected anatomically and functionally, which receive and integrate information about fluids and other substances in the body (blood, minerals, biochemicals, etc.), about the visceral body organs and systems, and about environmental conditions. This network has specific functions and multiple pathways to the:

- Endocrine system (via hypothalamus-pituitary-peripheral endocrine organs)
- Sympathetic and parasympathetic system into visceral body organs
- Motor (movement) centers and pain control centers (respiratory, sphincter motor neurons)

The most interesting aspect of the autonomic network is that it can modulate behavioral and arousal states such as sleep/wake cycles and focused attention, as it receives feedback to self-adjust to environmental demands. Drugs, traumas, disease and other factors affect the efficient balance and functionality of the autonomic network.

In 1971, a discovery by John O'Keefe and Jonathan Dostrovsky at the University College in London showed the hippocampus area in the brain was the nerve cell-based location of a cognitive map of the environment. When a person remembers a past event, it is retrieved in the spatial-temporal context in which it happened. Further, Edward Moser and May-Britt Moser at the Norwegian University of Science and Technology discovered a system of grid cells in an area of the brain (medial entorhinal cortex) that are arranged in an uniform latticework of hexagons composed of equilateral triangles. These grid cells are the key components of brain functions which update location, even in absence of external sensory input. The brain's medial temporal lobe and hippocampus are its system of cognitive representations of the outside world. The patterns of brain cell firing are calibrated by sensory input, but they do not depend on external signals. When they are combined, memories have the quality of rich experiences, and this vital process is the foundation of the personal history (ref 11).

Immune System and Neurotransmitters

> *"By defining and defending the self, the immune system makes life possible; malfunction causes illness and death. Study of this system provides a unifying view of biology."*
> —*Sir Gustav J.V. Nossal, MD*

Immunology is the science of the Immune system. It involves many components: molecular and cellular systems, protein chemistry, neurobiology, endocrinology, cardiovascular physiology, and more. It is an instructive model of unity, and shows how all these aspects affect the organism as a whole. The burgeoning of scientific investigation over the past century has lead to the development of numerous medical specialties and subspecialties. As a result, we know much more about all of the biologic processes of the body. This library of knowledge is so vast now that it is impossible for one person to understand all its aspects. So, teamwork has become a necessity in modern science, and similarly, our body also uses teamwork among its living cells. Research has proven there is a dense communication network that interfaces the central nervous system with the endocrine and the immune system in numerous two-way feedback loops. Every cell in the physical body has on its surface thousands or even millions of receptors (protein scanners) capable of shape-specific binding (selecting one shape to which it can link).

The immune-hypothalamus-pituitary-adrenal system is active in the regulation of tolerance to or rejection of substances precipitated by emotions, menstrual cycles, stress, infection, etc. The immune system has a dynamic relationship of reciprocal interactions with exterior environmental conditions and interior psychological states. It is modulated by many factors including exposure to humor (Dillon, 1985), seasonal light (Kasper, 1991), marital conflict (Kiecolt-Glaser, 1993), physical fitness (Roth, 1985), and even odors (Cocke, 1993). Stress hormones like epinephrine decrease immune response. Depressive episodes cause immune suppression at the cellular level, reducing natural killer cells and allowing growth of cancers.

Neurotransmitters are chemical substances made by the body and have reciprocal communication within the central nervous system (CNS, brain and spinal cord), peripheral nervous system (PNS, nerves related to structures outside the CNS), immune system, and autonomic network. Neurotransmitters regulate and alter most activities in human physiology. We can visualize a receptor for these neuromodulators as a door with a keyhole, where only a specific key opens it, allowing the passing through or transmission of information. There are four basic types of biochemical "keys:"

- Neurotransmitters—many are simple amino acids, usually carrying information across the synapses (the space between neurons). Some neurotransmitters are: Serotonin, Dopamine, Norepinephrine, GABA, Acetylcholine, and Histamine. They modify mood, bio-psycho-emotional states and turn on and off secondary biochemical reactions.

- Steroids—hormones having cholesterol as a basic chemical structure. They are produced in the adrenal glands, gonads and placental tissues through metabolism. The homeostatic balance of these regulates receptor responses of emotional expression, stress and physical activities (violent, sexual, etc.) and many other responses of daily behavior.
- Peptides—small combinations of amino-acids that travel across the synapses (the gap between neurons) through the extra-cellular space. They travel long distances (as biochemical messengers) through blood and by other means causing complex changes in the body. Substance P, Y, endorphins, and more than fifteen other peptide substances are present in the brain, gastrointestinal tract and endocrine glands. They have analgesic properties and behavioral effects, and may be involved in certain states of consciousness.
- Neurosteroids—remarkable molecules with diverse biological specificity, synthesized in the neurons and glia cells of the brain. DHEA, DHEA-S, Pregnenolone and Progesterone cause change and growth in neurons and astrocytes, as well as glia cells in the CNS and Schwann cells in the PNS.

The work of Schummer in 1989 (replicated by Kang in 1991) showed that significant differences in natural immune cell activity are correlated with right frontal brainwave deactivation. Increased low frequency brainwaves in the right frontal lobe and high frequency brainwaves in left frontal lobe facilitate a healthy balance. Self-regulation though biofeedback is one learning process that accomplishes this rather quickly.

Beyond Mind

Society values the importance of the mind, mental activities and processes. On the other hand, we have a tendency to ignore the purpose of our life and our true state of being. The brain as an organ is correlated to our thoughts, but the Mind encompasses more than biochemical and electrical connections. In the brain, some states (awake, asleep, etc) are correlated to the electrical brainwave patterns observed in the moment. However, the energies involved and their interactions with subtle forces also create changes in wave amplitude and observed behavior. There is a group of frequencies that are best used for inward focus, but the special state of "doing nothing" or "empty mind" is the result of different levels of work in complementarily synchronized areas involving more than neurons.

The relationship between the mind and brain is not a direct linear one, because the brain's *plasticity* (an inherent functionality, also called flexibility) intertwines with energies when it is working in diverse vibration states, including those of dissimilar forms and circumstances. When people think of "brain" (the usual association), it is that organ in the skull as *tangible matter*. However, we are very complex entities, and that brain is only the organic component. There are other components of "brain." There is a "water brain" which flows in all the tissues of the body in liquid form, and there is also an "electro-magnetic brain" that transcends the boundary of the human skin. Dr. Emoto's experiments with water suggest that even water alone can hold information. The human body (and brain), being a 80% water-based crystalloid-protein emulsion, may also hold information and consciousness on levels of which we are not yet aware. One example is that heart transplant patients sometimes manifest verifiable memories belonging to their donor. It is theoretically possible that acquisition of information will be facilitated by imbibing a "programmed learning solution" whose crystalloids are "charged" with knowledge. We could swallow a math pill, and we may eventually share useful knowledge and attitudes using solutions or other subtle electrochemical technology.

Excellent mental results can be attained by practicing specific techniques, meditations, and exercises with Chi energy and movements. All these can facilitate the release and flow of emotional chain reactions. Longer exposure to inner awareness practices will also show results in the capacity to dream. Both Eastern and Western cultures know of specific movements and tapping techniques to increase what we call the *second attention*, or *dream body*. In the first part of the night's sleep we generally process that day, which can be called "junk." We can develop the condition of being in dreams, interact with them, and even change the outcome. After extended practices, some students may bring back knowledge from other locations of consciousness (the School of Dreams) or interactions thought to be in different dimensions.

Respiration, Physiologic Rhythms and Nasal Breathing

Respiration is one of the basic functions that can be optimized. The manner in which people breathe influences brain functions. Scientific research has shown the relationship between nostril dominance and brain hemisphere asymmetry. We have many different respiratory rhythms and capabilities. Most people breathe with the chest. This is the least efficient form of respiration and provides less nutrition and oxygen to the body than more relaxed abdominal breathing. Shallow breathing into the upper chest is often in response to fear and acute or chronic stress. It is the most common method of breathing when one is engaged in light physical work and mental activities. This method may fulfill the physical demands of the body but will not increase vitality and strength.

Athletes are taught to do diaphragmatic breathing, with the most movement centered at the lower edge of the rib cage. This method provides additional fuel for the increased demands of physical activities. Abdominal breathing is not like the sitting meditation where one follows the breath in the microcosmic orbit—inhaling into the lower abdomen chakra (Dantien), charging it with energy, and exhaling up the backbone to the sky. This method increases nourishment from the breath, but unless one is closely supervised in this technique and has proper intent, the result can be to only achieve a state of frontal EEG dissociation.

An average adult breathes 16-18 times per minute, with heartbeats occurring four times with each breath, a pulse rate of 72 beats per minute. This pattern maintains life but does not transform it. Modern science and ancient schools of wisdom advocate a reduction in the rate to six abdominal breaths and 48 heartbeats per minute. This combined effect gives you an energy level that we call *#48*. This allows one to move into resonance with high awareness when the frontal areas (2 of the 5 horns) are in Golden Proportion. This facilitates the accumulation of knowledge, expending less energy for greater gain. One of the most important processes teaches increasing vitality and strength as part of the synesthesic perceptions at sunrise or sunset. This "Exchange Exercise" is performed with breathing and heart rate in harmonious rhythm with brain activity. The intermingling of our red base Chakra color with the golden sun is an archetype representing the linking of our life energy with the essence of the sun as a cosmic photon fountain.

It is known that we breathe from our nostrils in different proportions in alternating cycles. Every two hours one side has greater circulation than the other. At the time of change over, there is a ten minute period when both nostrils have equal amounts of flowing air. Viewed scientifically, the inspiration process is completed in the alveoli of the lungs where blood gases are exchanged. But what we breathe is more than oxygen. We "digest" the air from the atmosphere and energies from the stars by bringing it in deeply through the nostrils. In eastern traditions, it is said that how we breathe leads the inspired 'cords of light' beyond the lungs and diaphragm into the lower abdomen. The 'cords of light' that come into the body with the breath are the densest aspect of energy and the lightest, most refined aspect of matter. A filament of rainbow color enters the right nostril, passes down the right side of the backbone, charges the Dantien and root Chakra, and then flows to every cell in the body. This is thought to exhibit characteristics of the solar, yang positive energy. The left nostril transports lunar, yin energy and moves along the left side of the backbone.

We know that each hemisphere of the brain modulates one aspect of the body. Left-brain dominates in men and manages the physical right side.

Testosterone, during puberty, gives muscular development, beard, voice, sexual attributes, and masculine behavior. In women, the right hemisphere is dominant and coordinates the left side of the physical body. Female hormones are responsible for breast development, cyclical changes in the uterus, giving sexual attributes and feminine behavior.

In the ancient teachings, the physical body is similar to a teacup that contains the 'tea' or Qi energy (the higher refinement of Chi). The right side is the more masculine *at the surface* while the left side is considered to be more feminine. However, at the energetic level *inside the body*, the left sided pulse is more masculine and the right-sided pulse is more feminine. This is another example of the yin / yang complementary system. The cords of light, which originate in the pristine source of all life force, nourish the *exterior material body*. The vital energy and energetic atmosphere of our planet nourish the *interior energy body*. When both the right and left filaments of rainbow-light reach down to the level of the fourth lumbar disk, they merge with the Chi energy. Together, they expand and travel up the front of the backbone and are distributed throughout the entire body.

The ancient schools teach that in order to heighten awareness, three different forces will effect in the inner work:

- *Chi (vital) energy* has been studied by the University of Peking, China. They place Chi in the energy spectrum after infrared and before microwaves. It is the basic constituent of the *soul* and is the vehicle of time and *memories*. Inner work transforms Chi into more subtle qualities such as Qi and Ki.
- *Transcendent Light* is found in the energy spectrum at the ultraviolet range. Our skin is affected by both of these bands of energy—ultraviolet (tan and sunburn) and transcendent light (immune response). Transcendent Light nourishes life and originates in the Primordial Life Source.
- The *Force of Integration* is the hidden power that reflects reality back to humans as broken pieces of lives in divisiveness. When a person becomes whole through inner work, he or she participates in the transmutation of a fractured society into the multifaceted gem of healthy humanity. These deep qualities of existence as pristine movements are possibly related to gravitational forces and photon pathways. The Force of Integration nourishes the True Self, using awareness as the vehicle, and comes from the Absolute Unified Pristine Field.

When we experience these three forces converging into our deep, flowing river (the Axis), and use abdominal breathing in a *torus* pattern, our whole being transforms into a perfect unity of self-regulation. Heart, mind, intention, immune system, High Will and Chi change into Qi, and come together in awareness. This does not happen by chance. It is the result of deeply committed work in the optimal place and appropriate time, producing a centered state that radiates as a fractal from the heart. We can then achieve inner wisdom and resilience, functioning in high awareness with High Will, clear intention without inner contradictions, and accomplish an individual purpose and meaning in life.

Pristine Movement

The human being is a complex reality of matter, energies and "original pristine movement /motion." To understand this sentence, one must leap beyond words into a pool of common sense that links life, vitality and awareness together. Wisdom, as real knowledge, is experiential. We are also a harmonic melody with an Inner Song that flourishes within us in the form of specific notes. Ancient traditions used mantras, chanting, music, or sacred syllables. These are the glue holding our parts together, which can be separated through life's conflicts and problems. When used with an attitude of respect, they help us to reach an inner silence and self-healing. Our unique sound is 'what we are' and is an expression of pure wisdom, light and awareness. When the uplifting energy of our Inner Song is fertilized by contact with the *original pristine movement*, and integrated, the two become one. We can then go 'home' to a state of unconditional presence and awareness.

Glias and cerebellum

There are at least five glia cells for every neuron in the brain. These cells not only nurture and protect neurons, but also fill the space between neural circuits. Since the late 1990s, the many functions of these glia brain cells are better understood; they record and recover memories, help with spatial and time orientation, are involved in paranormal abilities, and are one of the first electrical signals in many brain nerve pathways. The cerebellum (the small, lower back part of the brain) has more glia cells than both of the two upper hemispheres of the brain (ref 12). Many ancient wisdom books and Eastern schools describe the doors of higher enlightenment states as opening from back to front. The high masters' experiences often describe a force that comes in the spinal cord, making a torsion field in the back of the head, creating the perception of light or an infinite and a-temporal vacuum.

As described previously in the section on Boundless Awareness, it is apparent that glia cells are bridges to the highest human potentials, and cerebellar cells act as a designer of new pathways for awareness states and optimal performance. In physics, all matter of this universe (including amino acids in the human body) is built of Molecules, molecules are built of atoms, and atoms are built of particles. The new "**M** theory" sustains a rather complex physics: that multiple dimensions exist as strings vibrating in specific shapes and frequencies, which are unique for each particle. But the human body has organs, tissues, skin, cells, and metabolic process, which are all present in energetic and electro-magnetic fields. Beyond what is known or theorized by science today, there are certainly aspects of the human being which have developed over thousands of years and remain beyond our awareness.

Every discipline of inner work will be accomplished with some degree of involvement from the cerebellum. Brainwave biofeedback rarely measures and utilizes cerebellar data, but the *slow waves* generated there are receiving much more attention by researchers. A deeply connected mind is based in the cerebellum, allowing infinite transformations. If there is a location, it is probably *the cerebellum where the quantum field is connected to humans.* The director of the symphony of inner work is the cerebellum, with all the cells of the nervous system as beautiful instruments tuning into the melody of an a-dimensional awareness. Infinite potentials are there. What is only a dream today, can be an unlimited future, with infinite options of free will.

Flow of Spinal Fluid

The brain is composed of soft tissue immersed in a lake of cerebral spinal fluid that extends down the spine. The ancients called this fluid *the path of life.* Electrical frequencies are the voices of neurons in dialogue with each other and the body, but it is in the spinal fluid and its flow where the deep *subtle energies can be felt* rising and opening the way for personal metamorphosis. Some psycho-emotional exercises, mudras (hand movements), tapping and acupressure at meridian points, as well as specific backbone vibrations can create waves causing the spinal fluid to flow upwards in a column. Such exercises can modify the flow of subtle energies.

One breathing exercise in particular (ref 13), which employs pulsed Valsalva breathing probably forces more blood (and therefore, oxygen) to the brain and likely hypercirculates the spinal fluid. This may be able to facilitate the production of the Traveling Brainwave phenomenon discussed in Chapter 7.

Joyful High Will

Each of us can become endowed with Joyful High Will, which is distilled from the energies generated though the practice of precise exercises. Then, individuals are able to attune their personal attitudes with appropriate *intention.* They can expand into a sense of self-love and embrace altruistic endeavors.

High Will allows them to become a center of magnetic focus, generating peace in the chaotic arena of life (personal, social and beyond), and transforming this chaos into a harmonic fractal of value, building joy in their communities.

"Whoever said that a small group of concerned, committed individuals
cannot change the world?
In fact, it is the only thing that ever has."
—*Margaret Mead*

Peace is desirable, yet it comes with the responsibility to communicate cooperatively with the majority while respecting diversity. We can develop a society in which everyone is part of a flourishing team doing their best in the areas where they are most suited. Every business knows that optimum production is achieved when people work in a friendly environment, feel safe, and have personal motivation for community improvement. The slavery of the past millennium and the multinational economic and political pressures of the last century could never engender peace and happiness.

Sustaining *coherence* among the multifaceted roles of life creates the challenge of recognizing the Golden Proportion in every situation one encounters. Only an impeccable warrior survives this challenge. We are progressing when the moments of despair and mistakes become shorter in duration and less intense. However, any being in human form, the highest Lamas and Masters included, have moments of sadness and emotional stress, and this is a natural part of life. But we can become free if we achieve Total Awareness deep in our bone marrow, via our Inner Song, and at the same moment it manifests in our second skin.

Heisenberg's uncertainty principle claims a perfect vacuum can't exist, and this 'quantum foam' of virtual particles pops out of nothingness everywhere and at any time. Particles only exist for a trillionth of a second and vanish; but the power is enormous. Energy flows only from a place of greater energy to a place of lesser energy, and to make a *quantum foam energy flow* requires below absolute zero conditions, where atoms move slowly and nearly stop.

Can we, as human beings, reach this universal power? . . . beyond the difficulties that the challenges require? Realize that *we are that quantum foam / pristine nature / universal field.* That impermanent, constant transformation is our Original Smile. Always in movement, always alive and crossing dimensions, we are the intelligent form/shape that 'decided' to be human. Many of us in the process of intention to be part of this space-time forget about this ultimate reality. New generations of humans may solve this equation with new pathways of envisioning, thinking and doing. The bridge is open, choose to cross . . . or close the door to the passage. It is your birthright.

Chapter 7

BIOFEEDBACK AND A UNIQUE APPROACH TO BRAINWAVE BIOFEEDBACK

Principles of Biofeedback Training

Biofeedback training is a non-drug intervention used by a growing number of health care professionals to help people better understand and self-mange a wide range of psychological and medical problems including attention deficit disorder (ADD), mood swings, learning disorders, depression, addiction and anxiety disorders. It is also used by coaches and educators to help people become empowered and simply function better. Optimal physiological functioning may be limited in people for innumerable reasons. One of the most common is not realizing when some physiologic system is not functioning at the best level for a particular situation. For example, many runners do not use optimal breathing patterns for sustained running. Many people get headaches because they keep muscles in their jaws too tense for too long, either because they don't realize their jaw muscles are tense, or because they don't routinely relax their muscles after the need for tension is over. Physiologic training techniques such as biofeedback can be used in the realms of sports, education, medicine, and many more.

Biofeedback records physiological signals (such as muscle tension or brainwaves) and displays them to the learner in real time. This information is used to help the person learn to actually change and control the physiology. Training works by teaching people to recognize how their bodies are functioning and to self-regulate patterns of physiological functioning. For example, biofeedback for urinary incontinence works by helping people learn to control the pelvic floor muscles, which prevents unwanted urination. Migraine headache treatments and tension headache treatments teach people to modify blood flow and muscle tension patterns which cause or start headaches. ADD treatments help learners change brainwave patterns associated with the severity of these problems.

Electronic biofeedback devices are designed to record physiological functions non-invasively. Most record from the surface of the skin. The information recorded by surface sensors is sent to a computer for processing and then displayed on the monitor and/or through speakers. The learner and a coach who may be present can attend to the display of information and incorporate it into whatever improvement process they are performing. The device does not send anything directly into the person being recorded. The loop is completed only when the learner attends to and the brain uses the displayed information.

Brainwave biofeedback (aka neurofeedback) is how one learns how to modify his or her brainwave activity to improve overall functioning. It is a painless, non-invasive treatment approach that allows the learner to gain information about his or her brainwaves and use that information to produce changes in brainwave activity. Much research indicates that individuals with certain conditions have too little of certain types of brainwave activity in some areas of the brain and/or too much of certain other brainwave activity in comparison to those without the condition. Individuals are also trained through the use of computerized biofeedback to change their brainwave activity and make them more "flexible." Who can benefit from brainwave biofeedback ? Anyone who desires to understand and improve the performance of their brain. "Peak performance" biofeedback training is currently used in military academies, pilot training programs, Olympic and professional training programs, performing arts programs, and by many professionals and business executives. Those who seek to improve meditation training often gain better insight of their experiences through such training, and the advanced techniques described in this book are useful for empowerment and personal transformation.

How is brainwave biofeedback performed? Brainwave activity is measured with an electroencephalograph (EEG). The equipment is connected to the learner with sensors that are placed on the scalp and ears. The sensors are safe, do not puncture the skin, and are painless. After adequate connection to the scalp and ears is made, the individual's brainwave activity can be observed on a computer monitor. A coach will help the person learn to change his or her brainwave activity. The learner does not need to know details about biofeedback to be effectively trained. Learners are taught to change computer screens using their brainwave activity, since changes in brainwave activity are fed back through visual and auditory information from the computer. One example is a game where a person moves a figure through a maze (similar to the popular pac-man game). The figure does not move because of the person's motor activity (e.g., pushing a button or moving a stick). Instead, the figure moves whenever the learner produces specific brainwave patterns. When desired levels of brainwave activity occur, the *learning is reinforced* because the figure moves through the maze. Subsequently learners also practice maintaining learned brainwave states when engaged in school—or work-related tasks (e.g., reading, writing). This will help them use what they learned in their daily activities, and it can begin to operate in "automatic pilot."

Brainwaves

The neurons in the brain generate electric currents, which can be measured. These currents vary in frequency (cycles per second, or Hertz) and amplitude (amount or energy in the current strength per cycle). Science generally accepts that the EEG—electroencephalographic waves recorded from the surface of the scalp—represents the electrical potentials generated by cells on the surface of the brain, in response to rhythmic discharges from the deeper thalamic nuclei. Changes in deep brain structures alter the surface EEG. Brainwave biofeedback, which facilitates shifts in EEG patterns, can have intended effects upon these deep brain structures, as brain maps have proven.

At the beginning of the century, the range of the electrical frequencies in the brain was divided into four-Hertz segments classified as:

- 1 to 4 Hertz—delta,
- 4 to 8 Hertz—theta,
- 8 to 12 Hertz—alpha,
- 13 to 15 Hertz—SMR,
- 15 and above Hertz—beta.

However, newer technology and research have more recently given professionals the ability to observe the *raw signal* (view of the amplitudes of all frequencies in a linear, analog display spectrum form) as continuous dynamic patterns. With this new configuration, it is clear that every frequency seen in this EEG raw spectrum, and its location in the brain, has actions that are relatively specific. Modern computer technology has elevated brainwave science and given new meaning to the physiology of the nervous system through observation of continuous movements of electrical signals among brain cells. These can also be viewed like intelligent dances of bio-electro-chemical signals. The more this is studied, the more it becomes clear in the EEG map that every frequency represents individual messages. The location on the cortex where the frequency is measured changes the significance. Some people who train consistently can display a higher order of wave congruence in Phi ratio than the average person dealing with daily stressors.

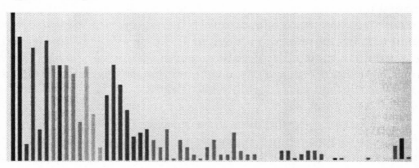

Histogram display of EEG frequency spectrum from 1Hz to 60Hz at a particular scalp location

Standard Applications of Brainwave Training

The scalp location where the training is done and the frequencies used can modify results. It is well known that routine biofeedback therapy provides results using these points:

- Cz point with SMR frequency helps to calm down stress, and regulate insomnia, impulsiveness, anxiety, fears, hyperactive behavior, panic, obsession, compulsion and chronic pain.
- Cz point with beta frequencies for attention and memory
- Fz point with beta frequencies for lack of motivation and attention deficit disorder
- C3 point with beta frequencies for depression, language problems, PTSD, social anxiety, anorexia, bulimia, PMS, chronic fatigue, temporal epilepsy, and addictions.
- Pz point with alpha frequency on parietal-occipital areas enhances the immune system.
- C4 point with SMR frequency for aggressiveness, autism, type A, bipolar disorder, cocaine addiction, masochistic behavior, fibromyalgia, and temporal epilepsy.

- C4 with beta frequencies for paralysis, shyness, and severe depression.

Time/space awareness is the first thing to disappear when one is moving into an altered state. We see 6 to 8 Hz in high levels at Cz point. Then there is a rapid shift to the temporal areas, also increasing higher frequencies. Skin conductance shows variation when the high amplitude waves shift to the temporal areas. We call this experience "the opening of the wings." The caudate nucleus does not develop well functionally until we start to open ourselves to a deep state of awareness with expansive feelings, instead of cognition. It was expressed years ago by Dr Edgar Wilson: "Those who can produce Fibonacci/Golden Mean patterns make low frequencies with high amplitude across the head." We have seen this, followed by an escalation of waves, with a flow of harmonic wave patterns.

Alpha frequencies act as inhibiters in shifting toward transcendent states, because they ground us in time/space reality and daydream states. If alpha is too high, people get stuck in unhealthy thinking patterns or intense emotions (common in closed head injury). When we decrease alpha, we go into a more immediate awareness of what is in the moment, not what we expect it to be. Research has proven the following about brainwave frequencies (EEG):

- 3 to 5 Hertz elevated at central areas are associated with primordial fear, confusion, loss of ones' center and presence.
- 5 to 6 Hertz high in parietal occipital areas are associated to rumination and obsessive-compulsive disorders.
- 7 to 8 Hertz increased bandwidth occurs for those with creative and flexible minds. These frequencies allow one to receive more sensory input and new ideas, enhance visualization, and resolve problems in dream work. They are the basis of the big waves of enlightened states. Depending on where it is located in the brain, the state reached varies. For example: high 7/8 Hertz in the occipital region enhances the visualization abilities, and in the frontal areas is related to dreams and creativity.
- 9 Hertz is also a classic state in which many people think: "I am meditating." Only years of meditative practices can help the person to change that mistaken thought, but a few minutes of EEG feedback can do that.
- 10.5 to 12 Hertz is associated with a feeling of being grounded and enhancement of focus. For most people, with EEG in 10 Hertz at central regions, reflective thought, self-observation and peaceful self-healing is experienced.

- 11 to 12 Hertz increased at central and frontal regions helps most people to focus outwardly with grounded and calm thoughts and feelings. Contents are meaningful and memorable.
- 14 Hertz in central regions helps individuals grasp information (attentive) in a multi-sensory manner. This integrates the body, predisposing the capacity of leadership. (A transformation can occur in the Inner Self so that a series of harmonic waves occur. Feedback at acupuncture points can be used to facilitate this process.)
- 11 to 16 Hertz at the central point of the scalp increases and empowers mental and emotional flexibility. These frequencies provide a grounding foundation for training in higher frequencies such as high beta (40 Hertz). They also help many people to develop the ability to have transcendent experiences, as well as development of optimistic approaches to daily challenges of life.
- 13 to 15 Hertz, when reinforced in biofeedback training, helps fine motor skill, develops coordination, and at Cz point is used for insomnia, ADD and fibromyalgia.
- 21 to 23 Hertz are frequencies that relate to empathy for others, and increasing those facilitates improvement of compassion and the connection with altruistic feeling, reinforcing inner strength, and encouraging a sense of humor.

When meditation is done in Tibetan Buddhist groups, it is common to see in beginners a decrease on 8-10 Hertz at all locations in the brain. As they advance (over 6 years) they increase that band, as well as 6-8 Hertz at all locations. This does not indicate a state of enlightenment. Other meditative practices, such as observing the flow of the breath, increases 9 Hertz at frontal areas, which is experienced by the person as 'calm.' This quality of inner work does not give them tangible changes in daily life. Many people become attached to the sensory perception that develops, but the objective results observable by others show nothing real or practical, since inner power coming to full bloom in this manner will require about 10 years of daily practice for more than 30 minutes.

Abnormal mental conditions should be identified and addressed before one undertakes a transformative journey. A person may claim to have transcendent experiences, but the EEG map reveals much. A paranormal episode can be caused by an aberrant event (e.g. head injury, drug use, high fever, etc.) as well as through self-discipline with simple will power. The former cannot easily be duplicated at will and does not help new inner development. However, EEG patterns of self-regulation as a result of the individual's transformation can be duplicated.

When everything in the physiology of the body is performing optimally and energy is flowing in all of the meridians, the kinetic awareness of one's personal electromagnetic field is noticeable. We can touch our 'second skin' through physical exercises, such as the 'Clock Movement.' It is performed with harmonious regulation of the breath and heart rhythms, allowing one to develop more pathways of the synesthesic capacity, called the *neurochemistry of internal joy.*

Thresholds Used in the Biofeedback Training of Brainwaves

In brainwave biofeedback training, thresholds are used that are like fenced-in areas of frequencies selected for that session. They are limits within which an audible sound can be stabilized or changed in relation to the goals of the experience. If the intention is to enhance the brainwave frequency, the trainee receives information only from the amplitude achieved above threshold—they will hear a pleasant sound. This disappears if they go below the threshold. As the trainee becomes more efficient, the threshold or fence is altered accordingly.

If a frequency needs to be diminished, the audio signal is set up so that if the brainwaves go above the threshold a discouraging sound is heard. If the trainee maintains low amplitude of the frequency that needs to be decreased, the sound is not heard. Establishing thresholds requires some professional skill. As a rule, they are placed so the listener hears the pleasant sound at least 80% of the time. This method incites a more competitive relationship between the activity of the brain and the feedback sounds. The person is learning to use conscious attention to modify physiology. There is gradually a more natural increase in amplitude with the cooperation of the unconscious mind and the autonomic network. Subsequently, the unconscious, subconscious and motor minds will automatically maintain the correct frequencies. The conscious monkey mind is kept busy during training with music, metaphors, imagery and internally focused awareness in the rhythms of the breath and heart rate.

In some cases where one band is being increased and a second band is inhibited, the person may experience some difficulty in increasing that band. Then, little attention should be given to reducing the 'inhibit frequency' because focusing on that may limit the ability to increase the band that we are training. Human physiology is a web of energies unparalleled and unique, where dynamic processes overlap. During the biofeedback training, the attention of the conscious mind is redirected by eastern metaphors, analogies, music or mathematical sounds (Fibonacci scale), breath and heart rhythm, and with symbolic language. Here the threshold goal is not the primary concern; the purpose is to learn while enjoying the process. The visual display on the computer screen may seem similar to a video game, but it is not a competition where we are driven to succeed or arrive at a goal, rather the joy of making the journey.

A Unique Approach to Biofeedback Training

Biofeedback is a learning process of self-regulation. The use of scientific equipment described in this book facilitates rapid modification of one's psychophysiology to an optimum level. Different biofeedback techniques such as measurements of skin resistance, temperature, heart rate variability, respiration, hemodynamic response and brainwave biofeedback are used simultaneously to promote more efficient biological and neural functions. Science has revealed that when we reorganize the electrical activity of brain cells, we change neuronal pathways, thus affecting physical and emotional states. Our approach is not intended as medical treatment or therapy for a disease state and includes the following:

- Measurement of brainwaves (EEG, electro-encephalography) and the amplitude of these frequencies determine what is unique to each person in line with his or her goals. Frequency patterns are increased in amplitude in a natural ratio in harmony with other brainwaves, at EEG acupuncture meridian points on the head.
- Multiple biofeedback sensors are applied to acupuncture meridian points on the body, and scalp. These allow an individual to access and balance sympathetic / parasympathetic nervous systems and self-regulate metabolism. This multi-sensory style facilitates the flow of information through biologic as well as energetic pathways. The use of meridian points promotes the healthy interaction of the neuro-endocrine and immune systems. In addition, it permits other forms of subtle homeostasis to occur. The physical aspects of the body as well as the yang and yin energies can be balanced, as is done in the acupuncture/acupressure style and energy therapies.
- Simultaneous multi-sensor brainwave biofeedback addresses mathematical patterns—the Fibonacci sequence in the brainwave signals. The amplitude (voltage) of each electric frequency (brainwave) is strengthened by training with another mathematical proportion called Phi Ratio—the Golden Proportion. This relationship is easily seen in the dynamic graphic of the human EEG signal. This style of brainwave biofeedback is combined with physical and integrative mental exercises to produce changes in brainwave frequencies and amplitude, and also in the configurations among the frequencies.

- Analogies and life-enhancing movement meditations are combined with respiratory feedback, heart rate variability and brainwave biofeedback recorded from specific meridian points. These cause electrical changes and often result in neurotransmitter modifications, enlivening the disposition and enhancing cognitive functions.
- Mathematically proportioned auditory and tactile stimulation organized into mathematical vibration patterns, harmonious with natural rhythms help recall and reinforce optimal psycho-immune functioning.
- Auditory and visual multimedia are used to provide scientific information clarifying concepts and reinforcing specific goals, while shaping a new understanding of self-regulation.

Specialized Techniques Used in Brainwave biofeedback

Metaphors, heart rate resonance, hemodynamic response and physical movements incorporating intention, respiration and pulse detection are combined with brainwave biofeedback. These form new neural and energy pathways, modify the amplitude of the brainwaves, and enhance self-regulation.

Four kinds of *metaphors*, many from ancient wisdom of both Eastern and Western origin, and their integrative exercises are used to:

- Ground—to stabilize and nourish
- Open Inner Spaces—to promote flexibility and resilience
- Release and Transform—to release past experiences or perceptions (which block the expression of optimal psycho-immune processes) and improve the quality of personal energy
- Access Higher Consciousness—to attain a transcendent level of awareness beyond usual mental states.

Feedback from cardio-respiratory rhythms (*Heart Rate Resonance*) in the context of ancient wisdom metaphors with brainwave biofeedback at meridian points on the head facilitates a physiologic higher resonance. Much current research on Heart Rate Resonance has proven its utility in stress management, psychological improvement, and optimal functioning.

Selective training to improve blood circulation in the front part of the brain (*hemodynamic response*) before starting brainwave biofeedback can expedite the learning process of self-regulation, and the quality of the amplitude of brainwaves is also improved.

Physical *motion (movement) and exercises* combined with *heightened intention* and modulation of the breathing can facilitate the balance of energy within the body. Strong intention, High Will and disciplined training in all the above techniques propel the individual to states of higher awareness.

Specific and uniquely-selected tools and procedures are normally utilized based on each individual's assessment and goals. No one standard recipe can allow everyone to mature, become resilient and healthy, increase efficiency, and establish a joyful life. In determining which methods to employ, one must consider that the human mind has unconscious, subconscious and conscious layers that function together in a network. Each layer has its own wisdom, timing, awareness, and doors of access. People strive to create a healthy flow of interaction among physiological functioning, mental activity, energies and the full spectrum of perception. Such communication allows the monkey mind to become a helpful assistant in carrying out our daily activities, not the decision-maker it believes itself to be.

EEG Spectral Dance—and Drugs

Individual frequencies of the raw EEG spectrum signal show rhythmic increases and decreases in height (power). This is a harmonic movement, a dance, in different locations. In addition, the information as a whole displays a beautiful wave in Golden Proportion, like an experience in the higher states of physiological awareness or enlightenment. The healthiest brains show a fingerprint of personal dancing patterns. In a concert, all the instruments need to be tuned to a frequency to be in harmony; there is only one director who takes responsibility for making the melody flow. Our brainwaves are each one unique instrument, and what is called today the *dominant frequency* is the director.

This rhythm is not seen when one is under the influence of street drugs or hallucinogens, which decrease the highest brainpower of the person (and limit future potential). In the neurons, such psychoactive drugs tear down the usable receptors of neurotransmitters and neuromodulators, which allow the physiologic responses to quickly open new pathways. The use of street drugs generates more receptors than before, with the neurochemistry becoming exhausted and unable to fulfill so many new receptors. The person develops a craving and withdrawal symptoms, becoming a slave to the habit. Such substances destroy the bridges to the higher forms of energies and power. It is true that ancient schools and cultures made use of some hallucinogenic substances in deep ceremonial rituals. But they lacked today's high technology to improve physiology and human potential. How and why they used those ceremonial drugs differs completely from the habitual way in which people today consume street drugs. High Priests, Sibyls, Vestals, Incas, Shamans, Native Americans, etc. consumed specific drugs only on propitious days, after special preparation with long periods of discipline. They used these substances with respect, as tools for finding meaningful answers, never for pleasure, sexual intercourse, or for the purpose of avoidance or self-gratification.

Today, dynamic brain maps can be achieved in all trainees with disciplined practices and focused intention sustained for the period of time. Biofeedback technology gives us an exact mirror in which the individual can progress. Then, ancient metaphors bring those experiences alive. The quality of daily behavior in the individual releases the exact amount of energy needed in the journey of self-transformation.

> *"Our main function is to reflect and to clarify, giving authority back to*
> *the person rather than taking it ourselves"*
> —*Fritz Perls PhD*

The Quantum Hologram as the nature of Mind

Information is patterns of energy which flow bi-directionally to and from the observer and the object, with the observer having causal effects. *Perception* is the subjective experience of information, which involves both the object and the perceiver. The mechanism of perception is dualistic, including a space-time information component (the sensory system) as well as quantum information (a holographic function of the nervous system including a mind-brain-immune response). *Learning* is actually a whole body-brain process which integrates perception, evaluative cognition and memory, and provides the ability to intentionally make personal changes. Marcer, in 1997 (ref 14), proposed the concept of Phase-Conjugate-Adaptive-Resonance (PCAR) which is necessary for accurate perception of an object in three dimensional reality. PCAR is a reciprocal relationship that mathematically connects perception and attention between the perceiver and the object. However, this bi-directional path suggests that information from the perceiver is also available to the object.

The work of Dean Radin at University of Nevada suggests that *focused attention* can change a system from a state of randomness to one of reduced entropy and create greater order (ref 15). Randomness contains no *resonant information* for a perceptual system. Intention, belief and bias (prejudgment) can effect the outcomes of mind-matter interactions in double blind experiments (Princeton University). In 1809, Lamarck stated "evolution is a learning feedback loop with the environment." However, Darwin's random mutation theory became a consensus because of the prevailing mechanistic scientific point of view at that time. Pribram and others support a holographic mechanism for brain function. That is, information (as patterns of energy) is stored as holograms which are mapped by Fourier transformation equations. Decoding and memory is a reversed phase vector in space with matched frequency, phase and resonance of information.

Space-time information of the sensory system is decoded by synesthesic pathways (space in phase with cellular connections) which facilitate perception in a PCAR state. PCAR conditions are also present when the attention is trained in brainwave biofeedback. The concept of bi-directional actions is analogous to the phenomenon of two separate brainwave bands that are the duplication of one another as observed in the spectrum of frequencies of the EEG. A unique state of open perception occurs with training of both the brainwave 'fingerprint' and a harmonic 'duplication' frequency. *Intention* generated by a motivational storyline of content with engaging synesthesic details optimizes body-mind-energies and creates a state of resonance. This is a quantum holographic state of evolved self-regulation that produces a new energy physiology, a learned tool usable at will.

Some of these concepts are beyond the prevailing paradigms of science. All human physiological structures of mind-matter interface use the same microtubule process. The immune system is in a conjugal relationship with the electric-magnetic field in a mathematical wave form, and the endocrine system represents every step of evolution. Adaptive cardio-respiratory rhythms create new possibilities for perceptual energy, and thermodynamic metabolic resonance opens bridges to the non-local dimensionality of universal perception. *Focused attention* when engaged in inner work is accomplished by the cognitive components of the left hemisphere of the brain. However, other parts of the nervous system are operating simultaneously. When the intuitive right brain provides its common sense wisdom, this allows increased order for that person. Metaphors and analogies are excellent methods to communicate non-local information, often suppressed in some cultural environments, thus limiting intuitive perception.

Focusing attention on an object of meditation (or a metaphor storyline) together with repetitive biofeedback training produces an association between the deeper information that the object represents and the techniques used (candles, symbols, etc.). Attention focused on both a concept and the object thereby records that event as a quantum hologram, which can be detected by a phase shift in *the object's holographic field* (Aharonov-Bohm effect). The passive state of cognitive understanding of the meaning of a perception is then changed to *intention*, a pro-active state, where the person can now choose how to utilize that information. To create a PCAR condition, efficient learning without personal and cultural limitations requires integrated inner work that is neither isolated nor simply linear. *Intuition* can be learned, producing dominant physiological pathways which are usable at will. The intuitive mode of perception can evolve from chaos and becomes time-independent.

In 1998, Marcer found "the waves reverberating through the universe remain coherent with the waves at the source, and are thus sufficient to serve as the reference to decode the holographic information of any quantum hologram emanating from remote locations." Action on one particle creates an effect on every other particle that is entangled with it. Spin coherence of entangled particles is reciprocal, and the work of Berry (1988) and Anandan (1992) in geometric phase analysis of information indicates that quantum phase information can be recovered and used (ref 16).

The Zero point field and trans-dimensional nature of space is the quantum potential energy of unmanifest particles and antiparticles that arise and disappear spontaneously. Measurements by Van Flandern (ref 17) with GPS clocks suggests that Lorenzian relativity, not Einstein relativity, applies to the zero point field and explains instantaneous propagation of non-local effects. The astronaut, Edgar Mitchell, said: "Non-locality is the antecedent attribute of energy and matter which permits perception, and is the root of the consciousness, manifesting in the evolved organism existing in three dimensional reality."

The Traveling Brainwave Phenomenon

A rare standing wave can occur in the raw spectral EEG which appears to *maintain its amplitude,* and travel along the frequency bands. The amplitude of the peak at different frequencies is maintained in a golden mean proportion, a non-symmetric mathematical relationship. It is as if the brain is clearing the register of frequencies bottom to top. It can be bidirectional, and travel from low frequencies to high ones, often past 60Hz, but has also been seen traveling from high to low. One might wonder if this wave actually travels to the top of the frequency scale, perhaps to the multiple 100 Hz ranges, then travels back down the register.

The right timing, either universally or personally, along with the right state of mind from training seems to have much to do with the production of the traveling wave and replication of the phenomenon. We may want to call it the "blue wave of Shiva dancing," an image representing the healthy physiology of the "blue body" or electromagnetic cocoon (second skin and the inner space) that some schools teach.

"Throughout the night, I have been annoyed by the thought of Nirvana
and Samsara:
How exhausting the dream! Apparently I had been made a captive of
Buddha. "—Hotei Master

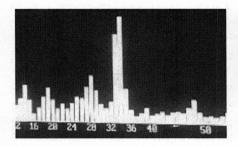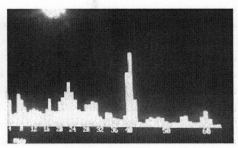

The Traveling Brainwave Phenomenon shown as a dynamic standing wave moving
very slowly to the right, up the EEG frequency spectrum. Note location at two different
times.

Biofeedback Results

Each method of biofeedback has its own focus and influence, such as:

- Increasing skin temperature creates the feeling of calm and safety. This thermal feedback is used to modulate the flight/fight response, and when used at meridian points, helps to quickly develop an effective power of self-regulation. The fingers disclose information associated with the meridians. The index finger relates to intellectual and mental activity, the middle finger to the immune system and heart, the ring finger to unconscious material, and the little finger to emotional issues.
- Skin conductance (GSR/EDR) fluctuations reveal the experience of several feelings such as fear, anger, and repressed emotions as well as peaceful emotions. It goes up and skin temperature goes down when we are in a state of distress.
- When frontal EEG is in the Phi ratio between brainwaves, in resonance with respiration and heart rate, a state is attained where the metaphysical anterior horns open and function. This sacred geometry is called the Star of David in some ancient schools.

Individuals who have received brainwave biofeedback training have reported improvements in school and work performance, social relationships, and self-esteem, as well as reduction in irritability and troublesome feelings and behaviors. Some individuals report increased relaxation, reduced stress, and a heightened sense of control over their bodies, thoughts, and feelings during or immediately after treatment sessions. Individuals should be aware that brainwave biofeedback can have a significant effect on seizure activity for those with seizure disorders. This effect, however, is usually positive (e.g., a reduction in seizures).

Lehrer at the University of Medicine of New Jersey studied the effectiveness of heart rate variability (HRV) biofeedback as a complementary treatment for asthma. In a controlled study of 94 adult outpatients with asthma, compared with the two control groups, subjects in both of two HRV biofeedback groups were prescribed less medication. Improvements averaged one full level of asthma severity. Measures similarly showed improvement in pulmonary function. The results suggest that biofeedback is a useful adjunct to asthma treatment and may help to reduce dependence on steroid medications (ref 18).

The potential side-effects of brainwave biofeedback are few. Unlike the use of medications for treating conditions, brainwave biofeedback rarely produces negative side-effects. In fact, lack of side-effects is a major reason for its use! To reduce electrical impedance, the skin may be cleaned on the areas where the EEG sensors are applied. Some individuals with sensitive skin may experience small breaks or irritation in the skin when the cleaning occurs. A very small minority of individuals have reported brief periods of negative feelings (e.g., anxiety, or frustration) or negative physical sensations (e.g., fatigue, dizziness, tingling sensations) while doing training. These negative side-effects are very rare and usually last for only a short period of time. They usually result from training in suboptimal frequencies or inappropriate scalp locations.

Some families experience a disruption in family roles and relationships after the family member who has received training changes for the better. The suboptimal role behaviors of the family member may have masked other family problems that come into the spotlight once the trainee changes. The anxiety levels of family members may increase because they have been used to focusing on one problem and now must find a new one. Sometimes new realities surface which require change or active adjustment.

Biofeedback technology is now superior in precision to human senses, and often more relevant than the content received from personal counseling. It provides the opportunity to learn the quantity and quality of inner nourishment needed for *an individual's* body-mind physiology on a moment to moment basis. Personal enlightenment is an individual path, as unique as fingerprints, voiceprints and retinal scans. The DNA genome has demonstrated that all people are quite similar, but also unique. Biofeedback is a personalized fast path to inner power—thanks to modern technology.

Just as we would use a car or airplane for a long journey, making most horse travel obsolete, the same applies to the use of brain technology on a path to enlightenment, rather than simple meditation.

To Regulate your Energies with Biofeedback

Biofeedback is a learning process of self-regulation, and *the deep structure of our Being is our reality*—who we are—not what we believe about ourselves. Biofeedback signals we receive about what is happening inside us are the mirrors in which we can see ourselves, without the cloud of our interpretations. Courage and serious intention will allow us to be what we want to be. A major step toward that goal is to strip off the *false appearances of self-importance.* Some classic arguments from those who are operating from a place of fear and ignorance, are "What can a computer teach me (I am far superior to any machine)?" Some may feel that results from a machine could not possibly have "spiritual value" because a master is not involved, or worse, that without "long suffering" this cannot be connected to a path of enlightenment.

Illustrative anecdote: Our biofeedback team met a venerable yogi, capable of many physical tasks, which proved his body mastery. This oriental master agreed to be hooked up to a simple biofeedback machine with only a frontal band of sensors checking the level of relaxation of the face and his muscles. His registered signal was very low, indicating his deep conscious control of his body. After ten minutes of continuous feedback, the master reached a far deeper level. In an honest declaration, he admitted that his entire life belief had been that a clue from the body told him when he had reached the most relaxed level possible (our first readings). The biofeedback signal further allowed him to recognize that an even deeper level was available.

Biofeedback technology can be used to accelerate the progress of learning to change the vibrations in our physical body by opening up to the next level of intelligent energies. Without the help of the precise measure/mirror received from biofeedback, it would take many years to develop the mastery that is possible to achieve in a comparably short time. Working with biofeedback and this neuro-integrative system increases the vibration (the amplitude of EEG bands), expands sensory perception in a synesthesic way, enhances the awareness, and puts all these pieces of the puzzle together in harmonic proportion to each other. This proportion is part of the universal Life force. The Phi Ratio shows us the relationship of the kind of energy needed and the work to be done to obtain the next level of awareness. Biofeedback technology is superior to our senses in receiving data from experience. It provides the individual the opportunity to perceive with clarity the quantity and quality of inner energy nourishment needed for best physiology and making changes in our lives.

Every human being is different, so a rigidly-set mantra, exercise or universal model for everyone is not realistic. Personal enlightenment is an individual path, and what works for one might not work for another. Biofeedback is not only a fast path, it is an individualized approach to quality work that humanity was previously unable to do.

> *Nature is the dark or light, the cold or hot, and the Systems of time.*
> *Situation is the distant or immediate, the obstructed or easy, the broad or narrow, and the chances of life or death.*
> *Leadership is intelligence, credibility, humanity, courage and discipline.*
> *Art is a flexible System.*
>
> —*from "The Art of Strategy"—Sun Tzu*

Chapter 8

FROM ENERGY TO MOVEMENT, ACTION AND RELATIONSHIPS

A Tale of Personal Motivation:

Froggie moseyed down the dirt road and enjoyed snatching up insects. Along the sides of the road was tall grass (about 4 inches high). As he walked along, he heard "rivet" "rivet." He looked around and saw no other frogs.

He walked a bit more, and it got louder; again he heard "rivet" "rivet." As he approached a rut in the road, there was his old acquaintance, Bufo, down in the rut, and he couldn't get out. Bufo said, "Extend one of you legs down, and I will grab onto it, and pull myself out."

But the dirt was slippery, and Froggie knew if he did this, he would fall in too! But he had the idea of looking for a big stick to put down into the hole for him, so he moved ahead.

As he walked down the road looking for the stick, a few moments later he heard "rivet" "rivet" again, turned around, and there was Bufo!

He asked him, "How did you ever get yourself out?" Bufo said, "Well, a truck was coming."

Subtle Energies

In ancient traditions, the human body has other layers of energy beyond the physical skin. These realms transcend the narrow view taught in our daily society. Different energies have different frequencies when being absorbed, sensed and processed. Our retina is capable of discerning red from violet, but other forms of life on the planet (animals and insects) are able to discern much more input in multiple ways. Eastern masters teach techniques to open new parts of our physiology. These methods usually require many years of dedication and training. Modern technology, in particular biofeedback, helps people to achieve those levels of personal development quickly. All the data are there, but because our machine/body is not yet able to detect the unseen does not mean that the unseen is not real. Being blind does not mean that color is not there, or that the planet is flat.

You will now learn the most important tools for transforming yourself. Knowing *how* to know, *why* the process has certain steps, and *when to* apply specific tools will make this journey joyful, faster and more precise. Every creature alive is perfect in itself when it embodies the entire spectrum of its capabilities. What everyone wishes to build is a true identity, fully expressing all of their potential. Then, the inner nature flourishes and emits waves of a wonderful aroma of spring flowers (if one works hard on the land to prepare the seed-bed, provide sufficient water at the right time, and develop the discipline and patience to sustain the purpose during the winter season).

Layers of Energy

Western science accepts that *we emit infrared rays* and studies these with thermography, binocular nocturnal vision, and Kirlian photography. This is analogous to the first layer of teaching in Eastern traditions. Most oriental schools consider two qualities of energies in the *first layer:* the infrared, and Chi (which is between microwaves and infrared). Beyond that is a *second layer* that has been naturally adopted by different cultures. It is your personal space: that area where you feel comfortable near other people, extending out a foot or more for some, perhaps less for others. This is your private zone, the place where you move without irritation from outside signals. When this is disturbed by loud noises, too many intrusions, and other beings, then animals and humans alike become unhappy and aggressiveness escalates. In the ancient traditions it is said that the individual's dimension is made from life energy. We can remodel the form and increase the quantity of energy with exercises and high intention. What the ancient wisdom spoke of as *life force,* we can also call the Inner Song, because with training we can hear ourselves in that dimension. This energy quality seems to be beyond ultraviolet, nearer to gamma rays.

A healer's persona has a natural abundance of the second layer. Once a student has learned self-healing, and has developed the internal vision with clear perception, he or she is capable of directing this energy from the two frontal horns to the eyes, intertwining with the force of the unicorn point. From there, it guides the healing power to an area of illness. Those who have that 'gift' (of subtle healing) don't necessarily even know that they have a special ability. They feel empowered within themselves, and their ego does not inflate. An impeccable healer does not proclaim his or her power, nor is there a need to impose beliefs upon others. To do otherwise is to exaggerate personal importance, and diminish one's growth. The outermost boundary is called the *second skin* (third layer). It is crucial that this zone remains healthy and maintains a delicate equilibrium with different energies. Any damage to this level produces a loss of life-force energy that translates into feeling tired, depressed and lacking incentive or motivation. Techniques and exercises allow greater awareness of these layers of energy.

Each body has a proportional relationship between the segments from the top of the head to the heart, to the distance from the heart to the bottom of the feet. That is the ratio of the personal Golden Mean. The physical body (of matter) must be in a state of self-regulation, with harmonized breaths and cardiac rhythm, active High Will, intention with clarity of purpose, and specific exercises to create a healthy second skin.

Techniques for Healthy Energy Layers

Thermal feedback makes it easy to learn modifications in the infrared emission at specific meridian points of the body, which is a powerful tool for diminishing stress and sustaining healthy body-mind balance. Breathing exercises with awareness and intention increase the capacity for metabolic changes in the Chi digestion (refining the quality of Chi to process Qi and Ki) and storage in the appropriate zone (e.g. High Will in the Dantien). Traditionally, Righteous Chi (a perfect balance of yin/yang) was formed from exercises like Chi Kung and Tai Chi as they were taught in many ancient schools. The extended discipline gives the practitioner great powers, but it is used in western competitions or tournaments many times only for physical actions (breaking wood or bricks). Righteous Chi nourishes the physical—material—space body; it also integrates (as a bridge) with the formative—soul—time body.

Breath is a powerful tool for the physiology, and the best internal sound. Listening to the heart rate in conjunction with breathing gives balance and flow to the immune system. The high intention to open ourselves to the deep synesthesic reality weaves together zones of the brain. The inter-link of experiences with the physiologic involvement of the physical body and the quality of awareness have resulted in inner transformations and an increased quality of subtle energies.

We can view the immune system as the 'water brain'—the interface where emotions, types of breathing, rhythms, heart rate and multi-faceted eastern and western tools take effect. Here knowledge is transformed into wisdom, a profound sense of recognition that emanates from the flesh of our bones. None of this process is linear or exclusive; it is interwoven into a complex, alive, dynamic network.

Exercises help maintain the health of the layers. They involve *aware intention*, synthesis of righteous Chi and *actions*. It is necessary for the collection of specific qualities of energy—High Will and others—to be stored inside of us. The exercises (e.g. Exchange, Tense the web) help in self-integration and enhance the quality and power of the will, making it capable of interacting with the electromagnetic body. That is what we call High Will. It transforms our daily conflictive mode to a more peaceful and joyful style of being. This new state of awareness expands our limits to allow deeper experiences of the recognition of our second skin (cocoon or energetic field). Exercises from different lineages and schools (e.g. Three-Leg, Clock, Lobster) improve its 'quality and radiance' and extend the frontier of this shining egg of light.

The quality of the second skin depends on the availability of *energy #48*—life as force. Radiance is the envelopment of awareness within common sense—this we call *energy #24. Movements* are one step deeper into the refinement of the energies and forces that *exercises* provide. Movements require discipline and most necessitate some energetic and biologic alignment before they are done. Ambient energies (e.g. waterfall, sunrise) can accelerate the process and attainment of goals. Movements like 'Dance of the Enneagram,' 'Fly in dimension' and 'Cross beyond unknown' are done at specific times during the year. Exercises, dreams, movements and sudden realizations (insights) give us the power to open bridges of communication between the realms within us. Meaningful work is to grow to the point where we understand who we are, what kind of wisdom we have inside, and how we can improve the efficiency and joy of our daily life.

The Chakras

The Chakras can be viewed as nodes on the Divine Antenna. We are essentially Radiant Beings with a boundary, somewhat spherical in nature.

As we progress outward from the center we encounter seven different energetic shells, each with its own informational texture. Chakras are usually pictured in books as small circles, or flowers, ascending from the lower abdomen up through the top of the head, with the highest, #7, being at the crown of the head, or even a foot or so above the crown. The 16th century Italian Master, Giordano Bruno, defined God as a "Circle, whose radius is Infinite and whose Center is Everywhere." (However, he was painfully killed in the Inquisition.)

Imagine a TV antenna, pointed towards the tower (which is often radiating circularly in a ground plane). This antenna may have several different elements crossing its axis, each a different length. Each element is activated by a specific frequency, or channel. All the frequencies occupy the same space without a problem! Once they are converted into TV pictures, however, each "set" needs a couple of cubic feet of space, or it will bump into the next one . . . humans, too! Each element can be said to occupy a node. Here are the top 3 definitions of node from Wikipedia:

Node (botany), the place on a plant stem where a leaf is attached.

Node (physics), a spatial locus along a standing wave where the wave has minimal amplitude.

Node (networking), a device connected to a network, such as a computer or router.

By taking a little bit from each definition to broaden our understanding: Consider a leaf (def. 1) as a device (def. 3). Why does it appear on the stem at a place ("spatial locus", def. 2) where the wave (plant) has minimal amplitude? Because it is easiest to introduce a new form or element at the point in a being (stem) where the being is least established in form. There is less resistance to change—the path of least resistance. Although a stem may not appear to be smaller where a leaf attaches, remember that Physical Form is precipitated from Etheric Forces, which may produce a minimum at the point of leaf emergence. A second point to consider is that the Plan for the plant (Mental plane or Body) calls for a leaf at that juncture. The blueprint indicates a leaf somewhere along the stem—the exact position is left to the Builder. And third—the Builder is aware of all the other plants, the soil type, the time of year—everything that goes into the surroundings of this particular plant and stem.

So if we now consider the leaf as an antenna, what does it receive? Leaves are a bit more general purpose than chakras, and receive many things: water, sunlight, and air, at the very least. If we consider these three things as bearing information, the multi-purpose antenna analogy holds. And even if a leaf sometimes serves as a landing pad for a bug, the bug is bringing awareness of itself to the plant, which may decide to mount defenses, warn its neighbors in response, or eat it (if a Venus fly trap). But we humans are a little more complex than plants, so we have evolved more discrete transducers in the form of chakras. Each chakra has a specialized function, like a computer or router as in definition 3 above.

Sexual and Creative Energies

In physics, *energy* is defined as "the capacity to do work." Other meanings are: available power, the ability to act, leading others or affecting things forcefully. However, energies form a continuous series, ordered in accordance with the magnitudes of common physical properties. In ancient wisdom, energy is an ordered sequence, sustaining all matter, and in some domains creating and dissolving reality while opening bridges into different realms—now recognized in western science as dark matter / dark energy. The word *energy* is vast, but let's address a "power" that moves our daily life: Sexual Energy. In most of the species on this planet, we see a division between female or male, and the spectrum of these energies is more than the steroid hormones that regulate the reproductive organs or stimulate the development of the secondary sexual characteristics. They are instinct, attraction and behavior.

One way to unify our language is to distinguish between (1.) Genital: the psychosexual development of humans where the sexual organs become the focus of pleasure; and (2.) Sexual: the state of awareness in a person with capacity to engage in sexual activity. But in ancient wisdom, sexual energy is Life Force in proportion to Light, Fire and Wind, and all matter is alive by the intertwining of Life Force. In this context, *everything has some quality of life* (rocks, plants, animals, etc.). But human beings have minds, capacity of thought, volition, and choice of destiny. Belief, knowledge, training, and information available are factors that program our will, desires and volitions. For most people, destiny as a spiritual being leaves the awareness.

How we select sexual partners is not related to education, environment or dogmas. It goes beyond those limits. Being in real inner connection with the Light allows clarity, focus without attachment, and respect for the freedom of others. It is not a blind hormonal chemistry that selects a partner; it is a river of resonance between to souls walking the same destiny. And *soul* is not defined by genital type. That connection can be a *pure, highest expression of human realization,* seen in both feminine and masculine bodies, in partnerships as woman and man, or even in those with same-gender body organs.

The two components Wind and Fire define most of what society calls falling in love. Wind is the perception/feeling of attraction for another person. It is a balance between chemistry and electromagnetic field that motivates us to establish a relationship with someone. It is the mind and the inner wisdom that allows us to select a partner (again, not genital definition). When the chemistry (hormones, feelings only) is the major attractor, the Wind pulls these individuals in chaotic situations where happiness rarely is the long-term result. Fire is a component that gives the person the passion, the courage to cross boundaries and obstacles, and the determination to persist into the process of accomplishing a mission to be one with a partner in that life, to surpass limitations to reach the union of the totality that we are as human beings (body, soul, spirit, awareness and beyond).

Our society emphasizes belief in our feelings (the direct result of emotional chemistry)—the same ones responsible of our addictions, emotional crises and distress. Look at your partner not from the chemistry of possession, being needed, insecurity or a victim role. Stop justification for the other person. Do not believe he/she will change for you. Approach each other with an open mind and intention of sharing joy and purpose in this life. Dialogue all the topics that are food for thinking together, and go deep in personal information and experience. Understand the physiological cycles each person experiences at different stages of life. Biological rhythms, hormone peaks and orgasms are different in each person. Culture, education and the personal story can become daily challenges in a relationship. Since every human being is unique, the personal story may be repressed in the depths of his or her subconscious, as a memory being ignored, and postponing happiness. To start a sexual relationship between two people is always the deepest experience any human being can have in the physical body. Honor and respect that interchange of essential energies. Share life, joy and the future. The inner power that sexual energy provides is an infinite fountain of creativity, efficient movements and self-joy. *A partner is a mirror of our highest being,* and as that, can share life and progress together in all the aspects of existence.

Sexual and creative energy can be used as bridges of transformation, spirituality and higher creativity. "The sacred unity of two in one" is the highest expression of human development and can be produced in us when our mental, physical and energetic maturity allows us to bypass deceptive emotionality and a judgmental attitude arising from fixed boundaries. The optimal energetic process is one of the entire psycho-physiology engaging in a relationship that two people share in love, commitment and respect. Spirituality is a way of living, not a goal or a destination. We are spiritual forms that made the decision to dwell in physical matter containers. Any actions, thoughts and words that we share with the environment are a spiritual discovery. It is an opportunity to explore our real identities. Being creative is the discovery of the path to our Original Smile.

Sexual energy is called the fire of creation because this special quality of energy is the *highest power* that human beings possess. It is seen as a *pristine Fire* that transforms anything and recreates—not only children, but also personal freedoms. This pristine Fire is what gives seekers enlightened states. It is in the *sacred Wind*, where one can fly in joy and health to unlimited potentials. Some societies and religious groups enslave others by regulation, mandate, suppression, and distortion of this wisdom of how we can use that inner power of sexual and creative energies to transcend. Above, we defined sexual-creative energy as Life Force in a Golden proportion with Light, Fire, and Wind. When Life Force is present, and Light participates in the Golden proportion, the quality of this human inner power is the highest and most subtle force in creation. These combinations can be seen as the personal, charismatic attitude that leaders display.

These qualities are also determined from another kind of more aware Mind. They select a partner as a personal choice, free of influence of education, environment, or dogmas. To be in real inner contact (with the Light) allows them clarity, the ability to focus without attachment, and a respect for the freedom of others. Such free choice relationships are thoughtful and not based on chemistry or hormones that induce blindness in such a selection. It is a river of resonance between two souls walking the same destiny. Thinking outside of the box of the environment is not an easy path. However, using the mind to understand what really happens moment to moment is the real route of freedom (with the least mistakes) for the spiritual person.

Start a relationship without knowing the attainable level of dynamic capacity to interact, and quality of possible communication will be self-destructive of healthy energy exchange. When both participants are not in harmony and relatively balanced, then sexual energy can become toxic and destroy evolution of the relationship. The sexual unwelcome relationship, or inadequacy of parents' parenting ability are expressions of an egocentric or enslaved personality.

Chronobiology is the study of cycles where partners may recognize unsynchronized timing, positive moments, and varied brainwaves and mood states. The physiology of women and men is different in various hormonal cycles. The timing of peak of orgasmic relationships are also different. For men, the sexual cycle is rather static, whereas in women, conversely, the sexual response is very cyclic. Ovulation marks peak desire and orgasm is quickly attained. The premenstrual phase is an optimal time for longer intercourse, and when menses are finished is a refractory time where women lack sexual interest. Mental illness and drug abuse can have a harmful impact in one's sexual chemistry, and attitudes learned from media, pornography and the environment can also affect sexual capacity. There can be difficulty in discerning what is intrinsic from what is due to the influence of education, religion, society, and even peers.

Our cells are constantly reproducing with our molecules changing and atoms vibrating. We are "Creative Beings" of courage and energy, and positive sexualty and creativity can help us discover our Original Smile.

Love as a force of evolution—storyline:

For this woman, he was her perfect partner, sharing similar language, a home, and many points of view in parallel. That was the ideal relationship of a force of evolution. Their bonds were a link for similar values, purposes in life and mutual admirations, which allowed both personal integration and evolution. The moments of physical love between them were best expressed as a rain of shooting stars. Energies intertwined in the fields of both physical bodies, and unconditional sharing in high awareness transformed and transmuted every sexual partnering experience in an unlimited expansion of two as one. All boundaries, time worries, and selfish attitudes disappeared in such open, giving and loving tenderness between their two beings. There was no judgment and no frontier to conquer. Their naked forms became so integrated that their essences naturally flowed between them. Dreaming together during the day and at night was common. So was knowing what the other person needed at any particular moment, even before words expressed it. Many times, without being asked, he would bring the cup of tea that she desired, and she would always open the dining room window before the meal only because he liked the smell of the flowers in the garden. Nearly every detail of everyday life manifested the most sensual and deep communication between their hearts and brains, with the totality of both in harmony and happiness. When their bodies vibrated in balance, is was like an aphrodisiac that magnetized charm and attraction, and renovated the relationship in a flow of joy.

Thoughts Become Things

We continually send out and receive signals from one another, and also from mass consciousness. Learn to discern those that are good and productive from those of greed, anger, and dishonesty. These negative thoughts can *attach* to our basic nature. The bombardment of lower-consciousness influences can infiltrate and begin to dominate thoughts of a higher nature for the masses. Healing thoughts and love (higher thought vibrations) are received by others, though not always detected consciously.

Science has shown such "Distance Intentionality" (DI, defined as sending thoughts at a distance) is effective. There are numerous mass email lists for sending "health intention" to those that are sick, and it appears to make a difference in outcomes. A study by Achterberg, using functional magnetic resonance imaging (f-MRI) technology, demonstrated that DI is correlated with an activation of certain brain functions in the recipients. Eleven distance healers each selected a person with whom they felt a special connection as a recipient for DI. The recipient was placed in the MRI scanner and isolated from all forms of sensory contact from the healer. The healers sent forms of DI that related to their own healing practices at random 2-minute intervals that were unknown to the recipient. Significant differences between experimental (send) and control (no send) procedures were found (p = 0.0001). Areas activated during the experimental procedures included the anterior and middle cingulate area, precuneus, and frontal area. It was concluded that instructions to a healer to make an intentional connection with a sensory isolated person can be correlated to changes in brain function of that individual.

Again, quantum physics states that Energy and Matter are interchangeable. Everything is Mass or Energy. Consciousness is Energy. Thoughts are Energy. Energy and Matter are neither created nor destroyed. So Thoughts Become Things. Thoughts *are* things . . . like the organs in your body. With what thoughts do you fill your mind? Positive and friendly, or negative and hurtful thoughts? Since thoughts are powerful, you must *pay attention to what you think about* all the time. Your life is the result of your thinking.

Seeing is enough to create. The "observer effect" in physics proves that seeing actually creates matter. The observer actually turns the invisible "energy state" of an electron into an actual particle state in a specific time and space. Before the observer sees the electron, there is none—only its statistical possibility. At any moment in time, there are infinite possibilities for the electron's location in time. Every electron that can possibly exist potentially exists right now. When we see it, we "create" it in time and space from pure possibilities—created by the act of looking. These facts used to be theoretical physics ideas, but are now proven. Everything is created by the observer, therefore *seeing is creation.*

Synchronicity, per Carl Jung, says that no coincidence is without meaning and cause. Your Mind is therefore shaping your Reality. *The thoughts that predominate in your awareness will manifest*—whether conscious or unconscious. Stated another way, "What you think about, you bring about." And another way, "To Think is to Create." Every thought you have carries a frequency that you send out.

Intention is Energy. Energy flows where attention goes. So, identify your Intention daily, and keep it in mind all day. You automatically act to fulfill that intention. As shown by Napoleon Hill's studies of the world's most successful people, and described in his books, *Think and Grow Rich*, success depends on a clear vision, determination and maintaining intention. Success thinking must include 1) a clear and strong intention, 2) a person capable of self-regulation of body and mind with 3) subtle energies balanced in both. This enables us to reach individual goals, and can create efficiency, intuition, focus, endurance, and emotional resilience. The transformative power of *intention with awareness* builds a self-sustaining force, maintaining personal integration, and much more.

Happiness as a Cultural Issue

Happiness is a relatively new idea. It is relative to where you are, not what you have. It has usually been associated with the afterlife, not on earth. Only when technology made life less brutal did we become aware of the "pursuit of happiness"—as suggested at the creation of the United States. Does money buy happiness? Not for long. If one doesn't have life's necessities, then money makes happiness, but in most undeveloped countries many people do not even consider their level of happiness. For those in developed countries, many people pursue their happiness with material things. However, most lottery winners find their lives turn quite empty after they have won big. No matter how much you buy, things will not make you happy.

One reason things do not make us happy is because people *adapt*. Having one level of wealth now requires new levels for more happiness—a bigger car, a faster computer—to re-juice the joy. Babies are usually happy playing with a toy. But those who are used to playing with 5 objects at one time are subsequently dissatisfied with only one, or their joy runs out of juice. The UN says the amount of money needed per person in America to fulfill consumption aspirations doubled from 1986 to 1994.

A survey of the richest people in America showed they did not rate themselves as any happier than the average American. With twice the incomes and twice the possessions than 40 years ago, surveys show that Americans are no happier now than back then. Successful people must worry about all the things they have to take care of, and about not losing what they have. The more money and possessions, the more complex life becomes (including the tax return). Complexity of life certainly does not make happiness. Could that be why monks divest themselves of material possessions?

Happiness is partly genetic, as shown in identical twin studies. The mood and outlook of twins raised apart in different settings is often very similar. Some people are simply born happy or unhappy. Certain babies smile more; they are born that way. The rest of their life they remain cheerful optimists with a positive outlook, and it can be seen as left sided frontal activation of the EEG. Dean Hamer at the National Cancer Institute suggests a genetic component that manufactures a protein that binds monoamines (which regulate mood—serotonin and dopamine, as well as those that cause mystical visions—mescaline and LSD) into vesicles that facilitate the transportation between neurons.

More leisure time does not make one happy. *Busy people are happier,* activity in the flow of life creates greater joy. Happiness comes from pursuing other things (vs. happiness per se)—it's a side effect of *activity.* People who are passive and sit watching TV are less happy than those that are actively doing things and accomplishing things.

How to increase your happiness

1) Practice living in the moment (here and now); enjoy the sensory experiences that synesthesic techniques given to you; focus your full attention in activities that are challenging and absorbing, creating a 'flow state.' Do not allow your wild monkey mind to dwell on thoughts about the past or the future.

2) Practice moderation as a way of life. It is not 'more' things that will bring you happiness; it is *quality and time to enjoy* that is more important than quantity.

3) Practice not becoming attached to results, goals or outcomes; it is good to have a focus for action, but remember *flexibility* is the way to reach the unknown, and the completion of the impossible mission.

4) Practice a state of self-centered contentment, free of regret, comparison and anxiety. Your safe place is the space of inner discernment where joy can flourish when you bring the 'water' of personal happy memories. Let go the judgment of self-pity.

5) Practice *gratefulness* work (e.g. volunteer some hours to your community). This renovates the *chemistry of gratitude* in you, appreciation for all the people, places, experiences and wisdom that you have received in this lifetime.

Coping with Anger, Fear, and Depression

Coping with problems by using your innate Fight or Flight response will include the unpleasant emotions of *anger and fear*. If we cope this way most of the time, we get angry or afraid, and we usually lose our battles; we get frustrated, then eventually *sad and depressed*. This is often the root of disEASE. The biological mechanisms of stress, distress, depression, and disease are a physiological continuum. The outward signs of depression are different by age and gender. "*Women get sad, and men get mad.*" Men more often show anger, frustration and discontent. Women more frequently experience worry, fear, and tears.

The *triad of anger, fear, and depression* is our basic set of *inherited survival emotions* and the common emotional denominator for personal problems. When we get angry and aggressive toward others too often, or if we continually *fear* and then *retreat* from others, then we can become upset with losing and will feel depressed much of the time. So, over-reliance on Fight or Flight brings on the emotions of *anger, fear, and depression,* which come from *aggression, flight, and frustration.* We get angry, fearful, or depressed because we are chemically, physiologically and psychologically constructed to feel these ways—it allowed our ancestors to survive harsh conditions.

Anger, fear, and depression *had survival value,* and are chemically controlled in the brain. Even though we have the human alternative choice to aggression and flight—that is, *verbal problem solving*—we will still *feel* the emotions programmed within us, no matter what we do. Learning self-regulation using brainwave biofeedback can help. There are times we will feel afraid and angry from our inherited psychophysiology, but we *can* assertively interact with others. Then we have the best chance of getting at least part of what we want, and the automatic anger and fear is less likely. If we are frustrated with something we cannot change, if we fail to use our innate verbal ability to cope with something we can change, or if we have not learned self-regulation, then we are more likely to feel emotionally depressed.

Depression had survival value to our ancestors. Being depressed causes us to slow down and do little except maintain necessary bodily functions (similar to hibernation). This was beneficial for putting up with harsh conditions in the environment—withdraw and retrench, conserve resources and energy—useful changes for survival until better times come along. Inversely, *depression is now a sedentary disease,* and physical exercise and movement can actively change the physiology of depression. Controlled studies in Canada showed that physical exercise (defined as a half hour of movement that increased heart rate and caused some sweating) done 4 times a week was as effective as Prozac in relieving depression.

In today's society, depression has little survival benefit. The way to lift depression is to cause (force) someone to get back on his or her feet, moving again, and *reconnect with positive life experiences,* rather than to sit out the course of the depression. One should make a list of things that were enjoyed when not depressed, and commit to indulge in at least two of these activities each week. It is necessary to *force oneself to get active,* no matter how depressed one is. Whenever one senses he or she is doing something poorly at work or socially, he or she must not repeat the *past habit of fleeing* from the situation by rehearsing the depressed feelings and withdrawing. Rather finish the job at hand or continue the activity, even if the immediate feeling is that he or she doesn't want to. One may feel miserable, but with exercise, positive experience and time, the psychological hibernation of depression lifts.

Neurophysiologic coping mechanisms of anger-aggression, fear-flight, and depression-withdrawal are not themselves signs of poor coping (or being at fault), they are just not much use to us any more. They rarely work or help our situations. Most of our conflicts and problems come from dealing with others, and our *primitive responses* are insignificant in comparison to our uniquely human *coping ability of verbal assertive problem-solving and learned self-regulation.*

Anger-fight and *fear-flight* actually interfere with this cognitive coping ability. When angry or afraid, your primitive lower brain centers will automatically shut down much of the operation of your new higher brain centers; the blood supply is actually rerouted away from your brain and gut to your muscles to prepare them for action. Your higher *problem-solving brain is now inhibited* from processing information. You do not think so clearly. You make mistakes. So remember, *you always have the right to declare a time out to think things over!*

Most people are trained as children to be responsive to manipulative emotional control. These psychological puppet *strings are attached to us* through *learned* feelings of nervousness or anxiety, ignorance and guilt, and by controls over our childhood assertiveness. This protected us from danger as children, but as adults these are *used by others* to get us to do what *they* want, irrespective of what we want for ourselves. Practicing *assertiveness* allows us to eliminate some of these learned emotions in coping with other people in the ordinary experiences of our lives. It takes practice to become aware of and in control of beliefs that allow others to manipulate us. These verbal skills are easily learned for everyday situations that enable us to enforce our rights as human beings and not be manipulated by others. They are discussed further in the next chapter.

Behind the Fear

High Love (not the chemistry of hormones) is a unifying force, and fear is the dividing one. We arrive in this world with all the 'impression-memories' of our past lives, and some people retain the real wisdom that they worked on previously. Sometimes the environment and the family in which they develop and grow up during the first three to five years of life does not allow that past knowing to be sustained and flourish. The information persists, but remains in a kind of storage code-language-energy that we may not learn to access if a real master does not arrive in our life. So we often remain that blank slate. As we grow up, we may learn to perceive reality based on the judgments and beliefs of others. If we lose connection to our true loving selves, we may become fearful with time. Fear is created in our minds and physiology. It is not real like our cells, but only a chemistry cocktail that circulates in our physical body and, with repetitive conditions, makes our cells even more susceptible to that fear chemistry.

Deceptive emotional fear comes from faulty impressions and illusions. *All fear is a primitive emotion in the evolution of human beings and is originally rooted in the fear of death.* There are real things to fear in the world, and with that comes our hard-wired survival instincts. As we grow through childhood, we have emotional fears programmed by events and experiences, and we may start to feel that life is a fearful process. We become afraid of anything that threatens us with *any loss* (and it is ultimately represented by death). Most fear is based on *other* people's issues, and we are untrue to ourselves when we operate within the belief systems of others (based also in the culture and time in which we are immersed).

Fear shuts down the inner wisdom of the soul. Truths that could remove the fear are then blocked from view. Fears can take control of our choices and stop us from appropriate risk-taking and exploration of this lifetime. Overcome *unnecessary* fears both by consciously thinking positively and systematically using subconscious affirmation processes. The subconscious "aha" gained from taking action to bust though and face your fear head-on is crucial, and many techniques can help this process of regaining the inner power of self-peace.

Since we create our destiny by how we think, replace negative thoughts with positive ones *by design*. You will then create assurance and trust, rather than fear and uncertainty. It also behooves you to be loving and kind to others. If you're creating misery, you will not generate happiness and joy for yourself.

What do you have to fear? Nothing.
Whom do you have to fear? No one.
Why? Because whoever has joined forces with God obtains three great
privileges: omnipotence without power, intoxication without wine, and
life without death.
—St. Francis of Assisi

Your Self-esteem

Much self-esteem is programmed by adolescence, but adults can gain self-confidence and self-esteem which will result in payoffs that last a lifetime. Confidence and independence require several *traits that can develop self-esteem*:

RESOURCEFULNESS—Gain resourcefulness by doing a lot with a little, without store-bought materialism.

IMAGINATION & CREATIVITY—Read, tell stories, and make up your own stories. Those with imagination are not television addicts who sit for hours staring at it.

DETERMINATION—Build determination by challenging obstacles and with plenty of self-encouragement. Determined people learn to tolerate realistic doses of frustration. This helps you overcome obstacles.

SELF-SUFFICIENCY—Allow yourself to make mistakes. Learn to stand on your own two feet by self-encouragement and getting support when things are tough. Do not let others solve your problems.

RESPONSIBILITY—Learn that success depends on what you put into things rather than what you take out.

RESPECTFULNESS—Demonstrate respect by learning from good examples. If your friends and family respect you and understand what you expect from them, all will have a better feeling of security.

AUTONOMY—Maintain your own interests. Learn to focus your talents.

Self esteem and self-confidence grows whenever a person succeeds at doing things, and learns to believe in one's own value and personal integrity. You can build your self-confidence as you see yourself as able to solve problems, find answers, and try new ways to do things.

If children live with encouragement, they learn confidence.
If children live with praise, they learn to appreciate.
If children live with approval, they learn to like themselves.
-Anonymous

Lighten Up and Laugh

"A clown is like an aspirin, only he works twice as fast."
—Groucho Marx

Why are we oftentimes so hard on ourselves? Have you ever spent time listening to your own "self talk?" It can be depressing. Most of us do not *take laughter seriously* enough. How therapeutic is a light-hearted attitude?

At a wellness conference in Philadelphia in April 1990, participants were asked to introduce themselves to the stranger next to them, and then vividly tell in one minute the three worst things that had happened to them in the previous 24 hours. For example, "My cab was held up in traffic and I missed my original flight; one of my suitcases is still missing; and I've only had four hours sleep." Then they switched, and the other person told their story. The next step was to describe with equal drama the *same* three events and *what was so wonderful* about them. For example, "I missed my flight, which gave me an extra three hours to read the novel I have been carrying around with me for six months; I lost my suitcase, so I went out and bought myself my first new suit in two years; and I discovered I am functioning better on four hours sleep than I ever thought I could!" You could feel the change in the atmosphere in the room. Ask yourself how, by focusing on the bright side of a recent event in your life, you could *reframe* a negative experience as a positive or useful one.

In addition to the mental-health benefits of focusing on the positive, a light-hearted attitude and humor can have physical benefits as well. *Vigorous laughter* produces a workout for your heart and exercise for your abdominal muscles. As the laughter subsides, your body relaxes. Some people claim that frequent laughter decreases their craving for unnecessary snacks.

Author Norman Cousins once described laughter as "a form of jogging for the innards." In his book *Anatomy of an Illness,* he tells how his recovery from a life-threatening illness was partly due to watching reruns of *Candid Camera* television shows (ref 19). When his illness was diagnosed, and his physician told him that his chances for recovery were about 1 in 100, he decided to take the management of his own case into his own hands. "I can do better than that," he figured. He checked out of his hospital bed and into a hotel. He hired private nurses to regulate his medications, ate wisely, spent an hour a day laughing at *Candid Camera* reruns, and he gradually recovered. Subsequently, he stressed the value of "positive" emotions such as festivity, love, faith, sense of purpose, and a strong will to live.

Here are some facts about laughter. It:

1. cuts down stress and reduces the levels of stress hormones.
2. strengthens the immune system and helps maintain good health.
3. is anti-aging and increases blood supply to the face, nourishes the skin and makes it glow.
4. is an aerobic exercise equivalent to any other standard aerobic exercise.
5. increases the levels of endorphins—the body's natural pain killers.
6. helps control high blood pressure by reducing the release of stress related hormones.
7. helps eliminate depression and anxiety.
8. makes us more creative and imaginative, and improves our sense of humor.
9. shrinks the hurts of everyday life to a smaller, inconsequential size.
10. helps people be more self-confident and self-expressive.

There is a practice of "acting happy," and it is a physical technique, not a mental practice. You do not need to have a sense of humor or even a reason to laugh. This laughter is returning to the childlike playfulness that we all had. A child laughs 500 times a day. An adult laughs less than 40 times a day. Laughter is contagious (so is fear). Controlled studies show those engaging in laughter had only an 8% chance of a second heart attack, compared to 42% of the control group. Laughers needed less beta-blockers and nitroglycerin. They also have a stronger immune response to flu vaccination. Optimists live 7 years longer than pessimists. If you are not happy by nature, *pretend that you are*, and you will get the same benefits. Health Rx: 30 minutes a day of laughter 4 times a week. Much of your happiness is located and detectable in the left prefrontal cortex, and it can also be improved with brainwave biofeedback.

Here are some ideas for making yourself more lighthearted:

1. Pay attention to taking yourself less seriously.
2. Learn to notice when you are being judgmental *of others*.
3. *Learn* to see and laugh at your own shortcomings.
4. Ask yourself if anyone else will remember in a year the fool you thought you made of yourself today.
5. Rent comedy videos.

6. Go to a magic or novelty shop, and buy something that appeals to your playful side.
7. Develop friendships with optimists, and spend less time with people who are pessimists or toxic personalities!
8. Remind yourself of a quote by Sebastian Chamfort, "The most utterly lost of all days is that in which we have not once laughed."
9. Contact a Laughter Yoga Club in your area: www.laughteryoga.org

"The flying dragon is in the sky."
—refers to the attainment of human greatness in the I Ching

Chapter 9

NURTURING YOUR RELATIONSHIPS IN THIS LIFETIME

So think as if your every thought were to be etched in fire upon the
sky for all and everything to see. For so, in truth, it is.
So speak as if the world entire were but a single ear intent on hearing
what you say. And so, in truth, it is.
So do as if your every deed were to recoil upon your head.
And so, in truth, it does.
So wish as if you were the wish. And so, in truth, you are.
So live as if your God Himself had need of you His life to live.
And so, in truth, He does.
—Mikhail Naimy, The Book of Mirdad, p.57

Know Your Relationships

How you interact with the world around you makes the difference
between having an effortless life or one with continual struggles.
Relationships strongly depend on trust—*complete and reciprocal trust.* They
also rely on openness, honesty, love and caring. Really think about whether
your relationship with each of these is centered on Trust, Openness,
Honesty, Caring and Love. Consider your relationship with your:

> *Self.* Are you loving, caring and honest with yourself? Are you
> trustworthy?

Spouse or Significant Other. Are you really there for them or just for you?

Family. This includes everyone—siblings, children, parents and extended family.

Neighbors and Friends. Those next door, across town, across the country and around the world.

Possessions. Are you too attached, or are you too distant and careless with your "stuff?"

Doctor. (Think about this one carefully.)

Job. Your coworkers, supervisor, and customers.

Higher Power. Trust in this relationship can be as challenging as the others.

Planet. It includes nature, the environment, and your carbon footprint.

Maintaining Emotional Safety in Relationships

We all want healthy relationships with those who are important in our lives. The level of emotional safety can be determined by the *quality of our conversations.* Here are some ideas for all your relationships, friendships, and working partnerships:

- Communicate your feelings in a responsible and thoughtful way. Do not use feelings to control. Do not blame.

- Be responsible for your own behaviors and hold the other accountable for his/hers.

- When there is a conflict, attack the problem, not the person. Avoid judgments and criticisms.

- Do not back the other into a corner with ultimatums or by making threats. They will backfire.

- Establish and maintain your own boundaries and limits.

- Give the other person space to have feelings and to be authentic. Accept who he/she truly is.

- Listen without interrupting. Hear what is really being said and what is not being said. Watch body language.

- Do what you say you will do. Honor your agreements and preserve your integrity.

- There is power in *forgiveness*. There is also *strength in touch*.

- The most powerful way to create emotional safety is *unconditional love*. Give it and you will receive it, but usually not from the same one you gave it to!

How to really Listen

One of life's great challenges is *to listen well*. Often, we *think about our response* rather than really listen. Or, we think we *already know* what the other person is going to say, so we simply interrupt or wait impatiently for our turn. Listening, *really listening*, with our whole being, is a skill, and it is the most important compliment we can give another human being. To really listen, you must do these things:

Stop Talking! One cannot listen and speak at the same time.

Put the other person at ease. Give space, time and "permission" to speak their piece. The way you look at them and how you stand or sit is important. Relax, and let them relax too.

Show the other person that you want to hear them. Look at them. Nod when you can agree, and ask them to explain further if you do not understand. Listen to *understand* them and their words, rather than just waiting for your turn.

Remove distractions. Real listening means being willing to turn off the TV, close the door, or stop reading the paper. Give the person your *full attention*, and let them know they are getting it.

Empathize with the other person—especially if they are telling you something personal, painful or disagreeable. Stand in their shoes, and look at the situation from their point of view.

Be patient. Some people take longer to find the right words, to make a point or to clarify an issue. Give the speaker time to get it all out before you jump in with your reply.

Ask lots of questions. Ask the speaker to clarify, give an example, or explain further. It will help them speak more precisely, and it will help you hear and understand them more accurately.

Watch your own emotions. If what is being said creates an *emotional response in you*, then listen more carefully, with attention to the *intent and full meaning* of their words. When you are angry, frightened or upset, you often *miss critical parts* of what is being said. (Remember the Fight or Flight response shuts down your higher thought centers.)

Be very slow to disagree, criticize or argue. Even if you disagree, let them have their point of view. If you respond in a way that makes the other person defensive or misunderstood, *even if you "win"* the argument, you may lose something far more valuable!

STOP TALKING! This is both the first and the last point, because all else depends on it. Nature gave us two ears and only one tongue, which is a gentle hint that we should listen at least twice as much as we talk.

Handling Angry or Negative People

We have all been confronted with someone who is upset with us. Self-regulation gives us the emotional control to do the right things in a situation. There are also useful ways to properly deal with such interpersonal situations:

Don't react! Easier said than done, you say, but that is exactly what your angry or negative other won't expect! Instead of reacting and saying the first thing that comes to mind, take a moment, count silently to ten if you need to, take a deep breath, step back mentally and create some space between you and the person.

Listen for the message behind the words. About 90% of anger is directed at the wrong person. Anger is often a function of *fear or frustration* about something that has *little or nothing to do with you* (or the current issue). Often, in or behind the words, there is a clue as to what is *really* bothering him or her. Listen for it with your senses and your intuition.

Acknowledge that you heard what was said. When you acknowledge what the other person has said, you *are not necessarily agreeing* with him or her. You're simply letting them know that *they have been heard.* Example: "I can see that you are very unhappy about this."

Ask a clarifying question. There are two reasons for asking a question: 1. It defuses the anger by causing the person to expand upon what he or she has said initially, and 2. it lets the person know that you are really interested in finding out what is going on. Example: "Can you tell me more about what concerns you?"

Repeat back what is said. This is the first of three steps designed to further *defuse the situation prior to looking for a solution.* Repeating back lets the other person know that you really did "get" what was said. Example: "If I understand you correctly, you are concerned that __. (Use mostly the *exact* words said initially by the other person.)

Expand upon what was said by getting in the other person's place, but go further. This lets the other person know that you really do understand and have thought about what he/she said. Example: "In light of your concern, that would mean __. Is that correct?" Ending with a question encourages the other person to confirm to you that he/she feels you are open to discussion.

Legitimize. As above, to legitimize does not mean *to agree.* It simply means that, based on where the other person is coming from, you can understand why he/she said that. Example: "I can certainly understand why you feel that way."

Offer *to explore* solutions—different from *offering* solutions. Most likely, if you *offer* a solution out of hand, you will be shot down. Better to ask *permission to participate* in the problem solving process. Example: "Would it be helpful to explore what can be done about this?" A "no" answer suggests that the *person really does not want to resolve it!* Notice that you did not say *we* explore what can be done. Putting it that way can place you in the position of assuming responsibility for the solution. Keeping the question neutral allows you to get more feedback about how willing the person is to assume responsibility for finding a solution.

Establish your boundaries. You have asked a reasonable question and you're entitled to a reasonable and courteous reply. If you do not get it, stand your ground. If necessary, point out that your question was prompted by your concern that this person be able to resolve the situation. Sometimes you need to simply ask: "What can I do to help?" Surprisingly, that can trigger an awakening in the other person that it really *is not your responsibility* to solve the problem.

Use as much force as necessary to enforce the boundaries you have set. Occasionally, you will encounter someone who just will not take responsibility. They return to the same issue and begin all over, or they make an accusation. You have listened, acknowledged, explored, legitimized and offered, but that just will not do. So, "I believe I understand your concern, and I have offered to help you reach a solution. What more do you want?" If the person becomes nasty after all this, you can simply say: "I am sorry. I do not believe that I can help you any further. If you're going to speak to me like that, I'm afraid you will have to work it out for yourself." You have to judge how far you want to go with this by observing the other person's response and if you feel the situation is salvageable.

How People Control You

Some pick you because you need something that they have, and then they keep you dependent, not empowered.

Some do not give complete answers to the questions you ask, so you to come back for more.

Some play your insecurities about yourself, causing you to doubt yourself.

Some keep you busy, directing your behaviors, focus and attention where they want it.

Some withhold or slowly dole out what you need most to make you feel overly grateful (like a captive does for food).

Some are on and off, which means that they are warm/interested/ nice sometimes and then cold/distant/mean at other times, with no explanation, warning or sensitivity. This keeps you off-balance and worried about what happens next.

Some seduce you by giving things and then think that this gives them the right to your life, energies and skills.

Some sulk or overreact to minor errors you make and cause you to get upset so they can blame you for overreacting.

Some put you in a dysfunctional role, usually that of a parent or child that *they* had a tough time with earlier in their life. You are triggered and guided to be this individual.

Some want to know everything about you, watch your actions, and need to be fully informed about everything that you are thinking, feeling or doing. When they ask too many questions and watch you that hard, then they are trying to control you.

Truthfulness vs. Honesty

Truthfulness is telling the truth: a transcendent fundamental or spiritual reality, or the body of real things, events, and facts. Honesty is adherence to the facts and also includes a refusal to lie, steal, or deceive in any way. But compare these three kinds of truthfulness:

* Caring and insightful vs. Rigorous and disciplined
* Whole brain, holistic vs. Left brain, linear
* Skillful vs. Blunt

As an example, she expressed her truth, when she said, "I am feeling upset about our relationship right now. You seem to be blaming me for our financial problems. Is that what you intend?" He was being honest when he said, "I am feeling angry, and I am thinking about giving up on our relationship because I believe you are blaming me for our financial problems." The key point is that *being truthful is stronger than being honest*, because it requires you to get beyond what you are presently thinking to that which you know, and then honestly present it. The benefit is that your relationships with both others and yourself will benefit greatly by appreciating this distinction. But notice two other related distinctions:

* tactful vs. blunt
* unconditionally constructive vs. critical

Assertive Communicating for Success

How you *communicate* and *respond* to people is important to your happiness and success. Getting across your thoughts, feelings, and desires *well* is not always easy. Practice using assertive words and sentences. Also *listen* carefully to others. *Keeping communication open will help create TRUST.* Listening *carefully* to what a person says cuts down miscommunication and makes the person feel understood. There are *three ways to listen*:

1. Agreeing with and believing everything—not smart.
2. Disagreeing and not believing anything—not useful.
3. Being Selective and Interested—This lets *you hear it*, get in touch with how *you feel*, and then step aside and ask yourself *WHY you feel that way.*

When you are *assertive*, you respect *your rights and the other person's rights.* You stand up for your rights by honestly and directly expressing your feelings, your opinions and what you want. There is no shouting, no put-down, and no name calling. Only a calm exchange of ideas. You *listen* carefully, and *accept the other person's feelings.* You courteously state FACTS, and WHAT YOU FEEL, without purposely holding back. You are more effective when you use assertive sentences like:

I AM ANGRY because of what happened.
I AM SCARED of what will happen.
I FEEL HURT when that happens.
I FEEL GUILTY because that happened.
I AM SORRY it happened.
I WANT you to help me with this.
I NEED to know what you think.
I WOULD LIKE you to stop doing that.
I WOULD PREFER to discuss this privately.

Remember that *you have the right* to:

* *Take time* to sort out your feelings and reactions.
* feel and express anger and other emotions.
* use your judgment in deciding your own needs.
* make mistakes (but not the same old ones).
* have your opinions and ideas get heard.
* make requests of other people.

* refuse requests from them without feeling guilty.
* not have them force their values on you.
* ask them to change what they are doing.
* tell them what your needs are.

There are 3 very different ways you can relate to others:

If you are PASSIVE, you are Silent and Hold back—you feel Hurt and Fear.

If you are AGGRESSIVE, you are Hostile and Dominate—you feel Angry and Guilty.

If you are ASSERTIVE, you are Direct and Honest—you feel Confident and Satisfied.

When we are *passive,* and give up our rights, we *teach* other people to take advantage of us. By *avoiding* or *denying* our feelings, relationships are *damaged,* or they never develop at all. Being *aggressive* creates enemies and ignores other peoples' rights. Relationships are also damaged when we try to *control* others with fear or guilt.

Being *assertive* helps all our relationships. By telling other people how *what they do* affects us, we are giving them the chance to change. Relationships become more satisfying when we *share our true feelings* with others, and we do not stop them from sharing theirs. When we *put down* people, we also put down ourselves, and everyone loses. But, when we stand up for ourselves and express our *real feelings and thoughts,* directly, courteously, and fairly, everyone benefits.

How to Forgive

For many people forgiveness is the hardest step of all in progress toward *freedom of spirit.* Yet it is essential. For as long as we are unable to forgive, *we keep ourselves chained* to the unforgiven. We give them rent-free space in our minds, *emotional shackles on our hearts,* and the right to torment us in the small hours of the night.

In a situation, ask yourself: What was done to me that seems so unfair ? How much hurt and resentment am I letting myself feel ?—and how much anger ? Think about the truth of the situation. You are both hurt and resentful because of what the other apparently did. You are disappointed because he/she didn't meet your expectations. And you are angry because it was not fair. And it grows into hate the more you replay it and the longer it goes unresolved.

So you are *resisting* each other and not listening or willing to talk—a big emotional barrier. You're totally disconnected, and pulled away *to relieve resentment.* Since this destruction of your love is emotionally and physically painful, you can see how you are emotionally drained and edgy, even fatigued and maybe even physically sick. Then some *revenge happens*—no winner in that.

Instead of *being right or winning the battle*—be *completely honest* here—confront yourself. If you justify, make excuses, it hurts more in the long run. Avoidance is simply dishonest, and makes your emotions worse. Use your strength of forgiveness to dump the negative stuff and accept his or her mistake—even if it seemed intentional. You can *get past your hurt and resentment.* That re-connection gives you back your strength and love. You must be willing to say, "I am really sorry about my contribution to the problem."

Holding onto resentment drains your energy, creates distance, and hurts you more than him or her. Sometimes your stubborn unforgiveness affects your other relationships too. Your power is really in your forgiveness, both in forgiving yourself, and in forgiving the other. It is a hard step, but you get back to your freedom of spirit. As long as you can not forgive, *you stay chained to the pain.* It takes up space in your mind, emotionally chains your heart, and torments you late at night. The Hate eats you up inside.

Who is being hurt by your non-forgiveness? He/she does not feel the knot in your stomach, or have the recycled thoughts as you repeat it all in your mind. You stay awake and rehearse in your mind what you are going say or do to 'punish' him or her. So, *the pain is all yours.* Understanding and forgiving does not mean you are giving permission for it to be repeated, or that it was OK to do. Forgiveness is needed for behaviors that were not acceptable and that you should not allow to be repeated.

Do not demand an apology as a requirement for your forgiveness. And do not demand to know 'why' as a requirement for forgiveness. Knowing why the behavior happened is unlikely to lessen the pain, because the pain came at a time when you did not know why. Occasionally there are times when knowing why makes forgiveness unnecessary, but they are rare. Do not count on it, and do not count on the perpetrator being able to explain or even know why.

Once you have released the pain, you will be lighter and more joyful, and you can go on without that bitterness. Use your love to dump your hurt, and use your forgiveness to get rid of the anger. Let go of all the mean things that have been said so far. You both already know what you did to each other. So pick up a coin, and flip it. The winning call gets to speak first, starting with: *I am really SORRY about my part of the problem.*

For the random act of violence from a stranger, do these things: Write a letter to the person (no need to mail it). Express forgiveness for the hurt. Allow yourself to express *all* your feelings fully. Do not focus only on the hurts. Create a ceremony in which you get rid of your hurt list and the letter, thus symbolizing the ending of the link between you. You may choose to visualize placing them on a raft and watching it drift gently away down a river. You may prefer to burn them and scatter the ashes. You may invent some other form of ritualized separation. Visualize the person you are forgiving being blessed by your forgiveness and, as a result, being freed from the behavior that hurt you.

Being Forgiven

Certainly, to be able to forgive is beneficial to the forgiver. However, within most religions there is a clear requirement for repentance by the perpetrator as a prerequisite to forgiveness. Repentance is *not* just saying you are sorry. (Unfortunately the "sorry" is often more about being caught than about regretting the original act.) Repentance also means communicating *sincere regret* and taking steps to be sure that you never repeat the action.

Search your heart to be sure that it is the *pain or harm caused to the other person* that you regret, not just *your* experience of your own consequences. Understand that, however much you want to explain, and however much the other person wants to know why, once they know, the *hurt will not change.* Decide what you need to do and what you need to change in order to ensure that you do not ever again make that kind of choice and cause others more pain. Make those changes in yourself. Until you have learned the lesson and *sincerely attempted to make the changes,* it is unreasonable to expect that the human heart will truly be able to forgive you, and it is questionable as to whether it should.

You must *acknowledge your part.* It takes two to mess up, and you do have responsibility. Accept that it was what you said or did that caused pain for him or her. No matter how much you want to explain, and how much he/she wants to know why, the hurt will still be the hurt. Reasons and explanations are *self-serving excuses.* If an apology is needed, you do it without excuses and reasons. Just make an apology with no strings attached. But being forgiven is not permission to do the same thing and repeat the same mistake. And if he or she is not ready for your apology, just accept this too. If that hurts, do not turn the pain into anger. He/she may just need time to heal.

Have the confidence to accept your fault and get past your fear of failure or having to *win.* The Win-Lose paradigm doesn't work—since we all fight to not lose. So, Win-Win means both of you come out better in the long run.

Dissolving Negative Emotions and Vaporizing Old Hurts

Life does not always go our way. People can be thoughtless or cruel. Things happen to which we over-react, often because they trigger *old feelings from our past* when we were helpless to deal with them. Sometimes we respond far more strongly than is warranted by the present situation. Neither we nor those around us may realize that most often our *reaction is not based on what is happening now, but on something that occurred way back in our past.* (Remember this!) As we grow within ourselves we learn to be less affected by such situations. Here are the 10 stages of progress you experience as you grow in self-regulation and this understanding:

- You respond furiously to anything that upsets you. You are convinced you are right and that your response, however strong and intense, is appropriate. The situation continues to replay in your head, and to upset you again and again, long after it is over.

- You become aware that you are feeling negative way beyond what is appropriate to the current situation, but you cannot stop yourself from expressing your fury. When the situation is past you are unable to stop yourself from recycling it in your mind.

-You come to the same realization, but now you manage to refrain from acting out. It still continues to bother you long afterwards.

- You recognize what past situation the anger was really coming from and why the present situation triggered it, but still have difficulty in not reacting inwardly.

- You become able to laugh at yourself as you look at the way your gut is churning, recognizing that it is really about something that actually happened long ago.

- Your gut no longer churns and you congratulate yourself on staying calm. However, the person stays in your head and you (calmly) continue to rehash what you really should have said and imagine yourself "winning" or being proven right.

- The person/situation remains in your head, but now you are able to consider your opponent's point of view. You may be able to allow the person in your head to present their viewpoint without inventing ways to verbally retort.

- When the situation is over, it is over. You are able to rid the person from your head as soon as the situation is over.

- You get that it was a lesson that you may have needed to learn, and you resolve to act upon that learning. You attach no blame to the situation.

- You get immediately that the situation is not important and it will not change your life. You do not allow it to distract your behavior or your thinking. You observe it, respond appropriately without interference from your gut, and move on.

You may have negative energy from your past, but that can be changed. In order to get past the past, make a deep decision to take responsibility to get over the hurts. Here are some useful **R**-ways to dump the hurts of your past:

Take Responsibility to heal your hurts.
Repair what was damaged.
Recover what was lost or what you gave up.
Reclaim what was stolen or what was taken from you.
Rebuild what was destroyed.
Remove what was damaging or what is no longer important.
Recreate what is truly important to have.

Responsible, Open Self-Expression (ROSE) of Thoughts and Feelings

As previously emphasized, everyday interactions and relationships with people can bring up old memories, which create thoughts and feelings. The way we communicate and respond to others will determine the amount of happiness and success in our lives. The ability to communicate thoughts, feelings and desires is not formally taught in school, but is usually a family default style. Some people are more effective than others at these expressive skills through practice. Like a foreign language, the words and sentences of *responsible, open self-expression* can be learned. If you master all the language in this section (and in the Appendix), if it becomes second nature to you, and you practice it, then your life will improve remarkably.

Things occur and situations happen all the time, every day. They may bring up *positive* subconscious memories of past experiences, often related to our parents and childhood. Some of these are memories of praise, attention and love. The subconscious images of these past positive experiences will influence how you THINK about what is happening in the situation NOW. This will happen AUTOMATICALLY, without you even realizing it, and it is beyond your control. The influenced thoughts will generate positive feelings about the current situation, and you will probably notice these FEELINGS first.

Other situations also occur which may bring up *negative* subconscious memories of past experiences, often related to our parents and childhood. Some of these are memories of putdowns, disapproval, and rejection. The subconscious images of these past negative experiences will also influence how you THINK about what is happening in the situation NOW. This will also happen AUTOMATICALLY, without you realizing it. These influenced thoughts will generate negative feelings about the current situation, and you will probably notice these FEELINGS first. They may REMIND YOU of the past negative experiences.

Problems occur when the feelings are negative, and we *automatically react* defensively by fighting, leaving, or covering up the bad feelings. If we are unwilling to communicate, we usually express them by a *Negative Reaction*. But we could do it by Positive Self-Expression. There are 5 major negative emotions: HURT and Resentment, ANGER and Blame, FEAR and Worry, GUILT and Self-Criticism, and DEPRESSION and Sadness. They often interchange and most people have a very hard time distinguishing between them when they are felt.

HURT & Resentment is:
The negative feeling about what you think someone has done to you.
A strong dislike for an injustice.
Disappointment and frustration because you believe what happened to you was unfair.
A feeling that can grow into Hate the more you replay it and the longer it goes unresolved.

ANGER & Blame is:
Frustration because you want or expect something.
Dissatisfaction of not getting what you want though you think you deserve it.
A sign of feeling inadequate inside.
The result of unmet expectations.
Directed at yourself and/or others.

FEAR & Worry is:
Suspecting that you will lose something important to you.
Concern or dread of harm.
The expectation of physical or mental danger.
Your biggest obstacle in life.

GUILT & Self-Criticism is:
Blaming yourself for bad results.
The feeling after doing wrong.
A sense of being unworthy and ashamed.
Feeling bad inside because what happened seems to be your fault.

DEPRESSION and Sadness is:
Grieving over an irretrievable loss.
Paralytic to mental ability.
Associated with physical inactivity.
A feeling of burnout from continual stress or any of the above 4 emotions going unresolved.

A *NEGATIVE REACTION* occurs when you are unable or unwilling to VERBALLY express negative feelings when they occur. There are four things that you do when you feel R*esentment* and you can not or do not openly express your feelings: *Resistance, Rejection, Repression and Revenge.*

RESISTANCE is:
Not really listening to understand.
Not having willingness to talk.
Turning off your positive self-expression.
Putting up an emotional barrier.
Closing up the lines of communication.
How you look when you cross your arms.

REJECTION is:
Emotional or physical disconnection.
Separating or pulling away.
When you have turned off to someone.
Pushing away to relieve Resentment.
Shutting down and refusing to pay attention or acknowledge someone.

REPRESSION is:
Emotional numbness and apathy.
When feelings are put away to simply make peace.
Too tired to feel the pain any more.
All desire to communicate gone.
Nice and polite, and seemingly happy.
No pain, no joy, no enthusiasm in a relationship.

REVENGE is:
Getting someone back.
Not always obvious.
The cause of permanent scars.
Fatal for communication.
Total destruction of trust.
An action with no winner.
Often the beginning of war.

These are the 5C opposite responses for these 5R negative reactions:

Resentment vs. Consideration
RESISTANCE vs. COMMUNICATION
REJECTION vs. COMPROMISE
REPRESSION vs. COLLABORATION
REVENGE vs. COOPERATION

When we are upset, we can *decide to NOT automatically react negatively,* but instead chose to replace bad feelings with a WILLINGNESS to communicate. We can verbally express negative feelings through Positive Self-Expression. It is telling the full TRUTH about your feelings. You are very good at hiding your true emotions from others *and* even from yourself. These techniques will help you discern between them even when you are hiding them. Negative feelings will heal when you SHARE all your true self.

But first you have to *discern* what you are REALLY feeling. The key is to learn to *search for and discern all five negative feelings when you are upset.* You can often find **hurt, anger, fear, guilt and depression** at the same time, sometimes conflicting. You will usually only NOTICE one at a time, while the others are temporarily buried. When upset, there are 3 questions to ask yourself:

- WHAT DOES THIS REMIND ME OF ? and
- WHAT AM I REALLY FEELING ? and
- WHAT WOULD I REALLY LIKE ?

Just like we learn a foreign language by *practice* of words and phrases, we can learn the language of *responsible, open, self-expression* the same way. There are only a few questions, 10 feeling words, and a few expressive sentences that start with "I." Before you can ever have real happiness, you must be completely honest with yourself. When you withhold, justify, rationalize, or deceive, rather than confront yourself, you harm yourself and others. False promises, avoiding, pretending, and ignoring are all dishonest, and they will destroy your positive emotions.

RESPONSIBLE Self-Expression respects the other person's rights. There is no putdown, shouting, or name-calling. Rather, there is calm, gentle verbal exchange, where each person carefully listens to, accepts, and respects the feelings expressed. Each person has the RIGHT to feel their emotions, and is given the TIME to sort out their reactions and feelings.

OPEN Self-Expression is tactfully direct, not beating around the bush. It expresses *facts* and *what you feel*, without purposely holding back. When you communicate openly, you allow the other person to explore your feelings with you, and you exchange feelings. When feelings are positive, we sometimes express them as best as we can, but only as much as we are able, maybe with a hug, a look, or in WORDS. When we do not express emotions, it is because we do not know what they are called, we do not know how to, or we are UNWILLING.

There are 5 major positive emotions: LOVE and Caring, FORGIVENESS and Understanding, TRUST and Acceptance, CONFIDENCE and Self-Worth, and HAPPINESS and Joy.

LOVE & Caring is:
Being gentle, kind, and patient to yourself and others.
Unconditional affection and giving.
A state of happiness, ease, and well-being.
What you must have for yourself before you can give it to others.
The most powerful emotion.

FORGIVENESS & Understanding is:
An important step in resolving negative feelings.
Your strength in excusing the mistake of another.
The one attitude that allows you to get past your hurt and resentment.
An emotional connection to another person that helps you regain strength and love.

TRUST & Acceptance is:
The willingness to depend and rely on someone.
A confident belief and faith in another.

Easy to lose, and hard to regain.
Needed for you to express yourself fully, and to stop hiding who you really are.
Necessary to receive love and appreciation from others.

CONFIDENCE & Self-Worth is:
Loving yourself and even your negatives.
Accepting your faults and going beyond self-criticism and fear of failure.
Recognizing your own abilities, merit, and value.
Your self-esteem knowing you deserve respect and self-satisfaction.
Needed for you to give love, gratitude and praise.

HAPPINESS and Joy is:
Freedom of your spirit to express itself.
An energy that comes from your essence that is pure and unencumbered.
Not possible when any negative emotion predominates over time.
Feels chemically mediated.

Responsible, open, self-expression will be mastered when you know the opposite feelings to draw upon when you are upset. Always remember:

> *Love overcomes hurt.*
> *Forgiveness eliminates anger.*
> *Trust decreases fear.*
> *Confidence replaces guilt.*
> *Inner Joy counters sadness.*

You have just experienced an important language tool and process ! If you express yourself Responsibly, Openly, and Honestly, you will be happy and successful. Remember to practice **Responsible, Open Self-Expression** (ROSE) regularly ! See the Appendix for learning the **ROSE** *process* and for *What Works in Your Life.*

This Lifetime in the Quantum Field

There is only one reality, that of the Universe, and we are not privy to all its aspects in the physical lifetime. Most of us have been mercifully given "Universal Amnesia" in this lifetime, so we can have a pure and new learning experience uncluttered by all our past experiences and emotions. The brain of a newborn baby seems blank, and learning progresses over years, then later we forget the first few years of this life. But our soul is the record (accessible by some) that reconnects us to our past experiences and wisdom, and ultimately back to Universal Mind.

You may feel that "life's not fair" since sometimes bad guys win and saints suffer. Evolutionary progress of the soul is not related to social position or amount of suffering experienced as some religions purport. Events beyond your control mold the circumstances within which you must make choices about your actions. And life is not a struggle between good and evil, but a complex web of experiences and actions. 'Good' and 'bad' are simply emotional connotations based mostly in culture, education, and time period. Life happens to us even if we are asleep, and it is *awareness without judgment of moral rules* and an ethical foundation of *universal respect for all life forms* that makes this life a path of wonderful evolution. We create who we are by our choices. *Choice* is the stuff that makes a person. The experience of reality just is (what Zen masters call: 'original smile'), and all the rest is clutter from illusion, dogma, or belief systems.

The Quantum Field Continuity (aka Quantum Mind, Akashic field, Universal Consciousness, Light Force) has a different definition in every culture and religion. It is the energy field of pure potential, so *you have infinite potential.* Now that you know your transcendent purpose (from the earlier discussion: to share experience with all humanity and increase Universal Wisdom), perhaps you would like to reconsider *who you really are.* To know this, you will need to focus on gaining an understanding of four of your individual aspects:

1. Consider where you are in the cycle of life in this lifetime, including your self-image and what memories shaped your mind.
2. Look at your expectations of what you want to manifest in this life, and the meaning you are trying to find through fulfillment of your goals.
3. Explore where you want to go, directions to take to get there, and any obstacles in your way (coming from both from outside or inside).
4. Examine your inner strengths, as well as your inner vulnerabilities.

These answers will probably not necessarily come to you consciously while sitting on the toilet. You will need to contact your inner wisdom, and that starts with a connection to your inner silence. Our inner silence is not a void. When you meditate deeply enough, thoughts disappear, and that leaves only the experience of silence. One could say that this silence is nothing, or emptiness, but there is great wisdom in such a rich silence.

Other aspects of your attitude will contribute to your evolution in daily life: Be righteous. Live in gratefulness and gratitude. Participate in nurturing friendships. Act cheerful, and be humble. Become aware of each of the five negative emotions when you have them, and do not tolerate any of these in yourself either: hatred, suspiciousness, self-criticism, irritability, and jealousy or envy. They are a biochemical cocktail to which your cells become addicted by repetition of the same habit patterns. You can choose to be different!

So, meditate daily, and this is not just sitting on a cushion! Every act of daily life *is meditation* if you are *present in awareness*, including simply cutting a piece of bread, drinking a glass of water, smiling to a friend. Use the internal skills learned in brainwave biofeedback. By aligning yourself with this Universal Consciousness, you have connection to the spiritual dimensions at a heightened and increased vibration. You can access different realms of consciousness. Allow silence to raise the level of your awareness of the Universal Mind energy within you. You will learn to maintain a very high vibration of awareness and love, and thereby can comprehend different levels of reality. With that inner peace, silence of the wild-mind, and *second attention* in the opening of perceptions, we share our life with this essence of Light Force. You can reach *Pure Awareness* being aware of itself. Here and now, *it begins with a silent mind.* There is a very subtle chemistry at the core of evolving life. Everything interacts and evolves you into a universal relationship with your true Being.

Focus on evolving yourself. Focus on Love, Truth, and Impeccability.
One can not be Loving and Truthful without being Impeccable.
—Gary Bate

Chapter 10

THE TOROIDAL JOURNEY FROM LIGHT TO ENLIGHTENMENT

*The nature of infinity is this: That everything has its own vortex,
and when once a traveler thro' Eternity has pass'd that Vortex,
he perceives it roll backward behind His path, into a globe itself
unfolding like a sun . . . Thus is the heaven a vortex pass'd already,
and the earth a vortex not yet pass'd by the traveler thro' Eternity.*

—William Blake, from 'Milton'

The Torus

A *torus* is a geometric shape of particular importance to understanding the nature of electromagnetic energy fields, evolution, consciousness, the heart and breath, and sacred geometry. It comes in many forms, the simplest of which is to picture a doughnut shape. The energy lines around the poles of a magnet and of the Earth are in the form of a torus. To mathematicians, it is important in several ways. Projective geometry deals with the study of surfaces, and the torus is the most complex shape. The surface bends around and comes back inside and through, so it creates deep structure rather than just a covering. It also takes seven points connected in a spiral to construct a torus. Each of the seven areas of the torus touches all of the others as they cascade and spiral upward from a central starting point, then outward and downward around the shape, returning inward and upward back to the beginning.

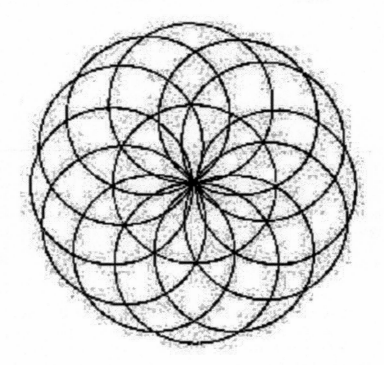

The geometry of the Torus, seen here as a doughnut with a particularly small center.

Sacred Geometry

A unique characteristic of the torus is that it can be molded or morphed, without changing its mathematical properties, from a doughnut into any shape with the two perpendicular circularities mentioned above. They will share a hole or center, like a cup, a pipe, the earth, an eye, and a tornado. The torus shape can also be constructed by drawing a circle with a central point, then moving to any point on the circumference and drawing another with the same radius. One of the two intersections of that second with the first you then use as the center of a third circle of equal radius. Continue like that until you have completed the pattern, which will emerge as six circles overlapping with a seventh in the center. This is known as The Flower of Life or the *Genesis pattern of creation*. When you rotate this around its central axis, you get a three-dimensional torus, also called "*the first shape.*" This is the only form that can turn inward or outward on itself.

The spiral of the torus is of great significance and a current controversy. It may be the logarithmic spiral known as the *Golden Proportion* or *Phi Ratio*. Or it may be the *Fibonacci spiral*. The Phi Ratio is the spiral proportion of 1.618 and is unending with no exact start or end. The Fibonacci spiral is the pattern in nature by which all things grow, by adding what went before to what exists now. Its progression is 0 1 1 2 3 5 8 13 21 34 55, etc. It has a beginning and is seen as Nature's way of modifying this ideal Golden Ratio to allow an individual starting point. Note how they soon come together. *The body* is constructed in (on average) the Golden Proportion and grows in Fibonacci patterns, as do all living forms in some way (e.g. the nautilus shell which shows the pattern most visibly).

The three-dimensional spiraling of the torus is unique since it does not go on forever in a linear sense, because it moves upward and outward, then down and around the outside, and finally the same spiral comes into itself turning upward to its source. We can see this is a little like throwing a curve ball into space and noticing how it slows as it goes further out; then gravity pulls it back accelerating its return. This completes a cycle of the torus; it moves through (or creates) space, then returns within itself to the starting point, to begin again. It denotes both growth and completion in a cycle. When drawn on a circular graph, the torus is the infinity sign, implying perpetual motion.

If you look down through the torus, you see the upper originating and lower returning parts of the spiral. If you ignore the depth and look at just the pattern, you see two curves, one right and the other left, coming together in a large heart shape and within that another, but inverted and smaller. While the spirals of this shape appear to go in different directions, if you take a wire and bend it in the torus shape with three and a half turns and the beginning and end meeting, then look down on it and you will see the heart within a heart. You will also notice that the initial counterclockwise movement creates both the depth and the illusion that the second part of the spiral has changed directions and is the opposite of the first. Yet this is a continuous process. *As above, so below,* is another way of saying that.

Physics, the Torus and the Schumann Resonance

The Einstein-Eddington formula for the universe is called the *hypersphere.* Arthur M. Young noted this formula matches that of a torus, not of an open doughnut but of the apple form with an infinitely small core, which reconciles the differing shapes predicted by Relativity and Quantum theories. The Twister Theory is vying for the top spot in physicists' search for that which unites everything; it has toroidal shape. The other dominant view is Super String Theory, a multi dimensional structure of reality. Drawings of strings look like elongated rather than squashed torus shapes. Computer generated models of the *hypersphere* (or fourth dimension) suggest these theories will be reconciled with the toroidal shape. Similar is the spiraling movement into a black hole, or out of an exploding star.

The planets in our solar system are arranged in the Phi Ratio, one to another. The pulsing or the cycle of the Earth is called the Schumann Resonance. It had been 7.3-7.8 cycles per second (cps), but now appears to be speeding up, having reached 8.6 by 1993. It is predicted to be on its way to 13 cps, the next in a Fibonacci sequence. With the *Earth's heartbeat increasing*, it is expected that our cells will also speed up, trying to match this resonant frequency. (Have you noticed life is "faster" these days?) The Earth's magnetic fields appear to be moving toward a threshold where there may be another polar shift and stabilization at a new resonant frequency of 13 cps. (ref 20).

Biology finds the toroidal shape at the cellular level when reproduction of cells up to the 16th cell division creates a hollow torus, called the morula. All life forms go through these phases. Then again at 512 cells this shape reappears until ultimately the entire body makes up a complex torus. The seven layers of the muscles of the heart are also wound in this shape. The heart works more like a spiraling squeezer than a pump. The heart's electrical signal proceeds around this organ in a toroidal pattern. The electrical field around the heart and brain (or any other electrical generator) is toroidal. When a person's heart rate variability is in a harmonic with abdominal breathing (at about six breaths per minute), biofeedback equipment demonstrates a resonant frequency. This entrained activity can synchronize with brainwave patterns producing an increase of immune system response.

> *For what the centre brings must obviously be*
> *That which remains to the end*
> *And was there from eternity.*
> —*Goethein Westoestlicher Diwan*

Web of Work

The dynamic integration of human nature creates a web of Golden Mean interactions in seven principal learning/growth areas, facilitated by training processes:

1. *Biology,* the brain producing frequencies in golden proportion, coordinated with heart and lung rhythms (utilizing brainwave

biofeedback); muscles and bones aligned in efficient postures—and self-regulation of the physiology.

2. *Emotions,* awareness of feelings, healthy self-esteem, development of courage and compassion, and letting go of (with an oriental perspective of the Elements): anger (wood), greed (earth), possessiveness (metal), sexual frustration (fire), fear (water), and creating new biochemical pathways while balancing neurotransmitters.

3. *Immune system,* using thermal feedback, electro-dermal response, visualization, metaphors, special movements and sounds, and exercises to boost vitality and healthy function.

4. *Chemistry,* optimal nutrition, desensitization and changes in life habits; acupuncture modalities, biofeedback training, and breathing exercises to enhance sustenance to the brain.

5. *Mind,* for clarity of thought, mindful-awareness and empty mind, inner silence and tools, analogies to understand life as a paradoxical reality beyond the monkey mind, and development of discernment.

6. *Energies,* balancing Chi, developing High Will and self-regulation of the bridges of synesthesic expression, increasing and improving the quality, accumulation and circulation of energies, power and forces in all realms.

7. *Higher dimensions,* primordial origin of the life force throughout all of one's bodies. Respect and Wisdom of using the Force of Intention to synthesize the freedom of interdependence among our realms.

With this coherent "web of work"—development of highest potential in daily life and in dreams with the power to enhance the rate of evolution—a quantum jump to freedom occurs. In all of the ancient traditions, the committed student develops, with consistent discipline, the specific energy which allows that individual to do things once thought impossible.

The human has an energetic field in the shape of a torus. It is comprised of different qualities of interactions. Fundamental to one's clear awareness of this form is the inner perception of *the personal Axis*. From that biologic, functional and dynamic structure, we develop the Phi Ratio relationship among brainwaves in the four cranial meridian points called the four horns. Exercises and biofeedback training coordinate the synesthesic abilities, helping the individual to become grounded in a spatial perception of four legs.

When the "centaur aspect" (four legs and horns) is integrated with a disciplined monkey mind, and the heart and breath rate is in harmonic resonance, then the assembler point-bridges between the realms will reverse direction in preparation for the return journey home. Life is transformed into photons that fly in freedom.

Torus is a pattern of wholeness and unity with a spiral sequence expressed through a Golden Mean relationship between segments and the movement that links them to the core of *the axis*. This torus kernel-nature-essence is in each person, and this universal pattern (meta-paradigm) awakens that reality of the bodies-forces-realms nested within. They form a torus pattern when a person has transformed into the most evolved state of Being.

Every Being can use a dynamic process to interconnect the bodies of matter, energies, movements and dimensions through biological self-regulation, functional flowing of energetic and electromagnetic fields, and the development of **inner keys** that allow bridging among dimensions into a Web of Wisdom. This concept is complex and transcends linear thinking. The axes (spinal cord-axis of time; resonance between the heart and second skin-axis of space; and the rainbow-cocoon axis) dialogue in the same language (Inner Song) to make an infinitely free movement with the pulse of Awareness traveling in a spiral toroidal shape.

The torus has the zero point in the core (the central axis), where one cycle has been completed and the next is in the formative state. It is the calm at the center of chaos (the safe place). This movement is completed when two circularities are formed, perpendicular to each other, in an evolutionary Phi Ratio spiral that is recursive and reflexive. When we pay attention to the coordination of the breath, then the heart rate and the Phi Ratio of the frontal-orbital brain areas move in rhythmic harmony with Ki circulation in the Extraordinary Meridians, and the cycle of inhalation-exhalation takes the torus form. "Being the breath" is an attitude in which the wild monkey mind surrenders and becomes quiet, creating an inner silence. This is the vertical axis of the two circularities.

Self-regulation of the physiology causes electrochemical and energetic change which allows synesthesic *fractal expression* to illuminate the second skin from the sacred point in the heart of the human body (the zero point). This is where all of the primordial seeds of our realms have their presence. This radiating field from the heart is the second axis-circularity of the movement of the torus. When the brain has undergone extensive biofeedback training, it develops a special state of harmony called the *dance of the horns*. These electrical brain frequencies in high power (in Golden Mean relationship to each other) allow the manifestation of a state of Awareness, a vibration sound—an Inner Song. This symphony can be seen on brainwave maps as mandalas. This unification of the realms causes the force needed to quantum jump from the real zero point.

> *What I call alone*
> *Is to forget both alone and not-alone,*
> *And again to forget the one who forgets:*
> *This is truly to be alone.*
> —*Sengai Master*

Healthy Physiology and Change Management

Information, by itself, cannot modify our personal energy if we do not sustain discipline, high intention and a flexible attitude to do the conscious movements. An impeccable style of life (a warrior concept) facilitates healthy physiology in all our dimensions of being. This harmonic physiology is the result of internal discipline, with a clear intention that the monkey mind stops its interference and petty distractions. *Unconditional commitment* to the totality of life is a requirement; achievement is not possible with "if, but, or might." Such prerequisites are not easy tasks, but most important to regulate is the physiology.

Due to habits, childhood experiences and trauma, and an array of stressors on and in the body for years, the mind has worked regularly with suboptimal neurochemistry, brainwaves without harmonic resonance, and explosions of hormones. The neuromodulators of our emotions are triggers for reflexive behavioral and mental responses during social and emotional pressures. Changing all of these acquired patterns takes years of persistence to achieve. Modern technology can help to reduce that time.

Old Conditioned Responses

As previously discussed, our thoughts are linked to emotional chemistry (neurotransmitters). What we *think* creates modifications in the neuro-physiological paths, brainwave frequencies, chemical modulators and transmitters, as well as in the actual spatial position of the neuronal fibers. Personal *reactions* can result from associations with experiences from childhood. Those repetitive reactions will quickly become automatic, conditioned rigid responses. However, we can modify those patterns if we change the quality of our thoughts with *intention*, use techniques to manage the emotions, practice movements for *flexibility* and use precise, scientific (biofeedback) information, which reduces the time of discipline needed for building the path of awareness of the pure self.

The physical body is attached to *habits* (old automatic mistakes) and has an instinctive *fear of change*. Only a healthy physiology, capable of self-regulation, without rigid, inflexible structures of self-concept can give us the possibility to reach our intended goals. In life, there may be no such thing as a free lunch, but to be alive in awareness is only for the strongest seekers of freedom.

Sovereignty

Life in human form is an opportunity to execute sovereignty (to make one's own decisions). That birthright was denied to many people, and especially to women during millennia of male-dominated societies. Religions (accusing Eve of sin), cultures (enslaving women and children for sexual pleasure), and some societies today disallow women's choices, just as they discriminate based on inherent sexual orientation. In all time periods, there are also special people who take a risk to be "different," regardless of their gender and socio-sexual situation. They execute sovereignty. These can be named as: 1) Pre-cursors, 2) Pioneers, and 3) Inventor-Discoverors.

Pre-cursor people understand principles beyond those accepted by the culture and environment in their time. On many occasions they have paid with their lives to be different. They have an idea or concept, other knowledge or value, but they only "prepared the land (told others near them) to sustain the seeds" for the next generation who develop the conditions for those seeds to germinate. Few modern people can name *them* because the story only gets told for those who win a battle, show the product, or make the money. Leonardo da Vinci was a pre-cursor creator of the submarine, the helicopter, and many other out-of-the-box ideas for his time. Jean De Arc, a young warrior, had a mission for France that transcended her life, the betrayal of the king and the fire of the Inquisition of that epoch.

Pioneers are capable of reading the unconscious collective for the upcoming steps of the evolution of humanity, or learning from pre-cursors. They use the *right timing* in exposing their ideas and concepts to larger numbers of those representing "fertile land to grow the seeds." Human history records secrets schools, brotherhoods and alchemy fraternities. Many of them were killed—either for religions reasons (Giovanni Bruno by the Inquisition), or poisoned by government (Socrates), or tortured by military dictators (many places in South America and Africa). Some are ostracised by politics like General Patton after WWII.

Science has ignored Inventor-Discoverors. Rosalind Franklin, who worked with Maurice Wilkins at Randall's laboratory at London, showed to him the X-ray photographs of DNA and crystallographic portraits. However, her meaningful role in learning the structure of DNA was not honored by the three men—Watson, Crick and Wilkins—receivers of the 1962 Nobel prize for discovering the genetic material. Environmentalist Dian Fossey lived almost 18 years among gorillas, studied their behaviors and relationships to humans. She was killed at night in her cabin at Karisoke Research Center, Rwanda, Africa because of her intention to protect mountain gorillas from hunters and poachers.

However, progress is an inherent force that can be slowed like the water behind a dam, but never stopped. And in a right moment someone discovers, invents or proves, then a new paradigm arrives. Einstein is a great example, completely changing physics in the last century. We are in a wonderful time during a new state of chaos for modern life. The common attractor points are Quantum Physics, Modern Art, Music with meaning and vibrational effects, paradoxical thinking, brain plasticity, and the claim for empowerment as: "Unity—realizing the connectedness of us all, promoting teamwork in peace and harmony."

Every paradigm change takes place in society over about 20 to 50 years, and we are perhaps in the beginning of one of those cycles. When ideas and concepts become common sense and accepted as knowledge by the average person (as well as the media culture), that time is only a first step. At that time, other pre-cursors will start pushing their ideas, and humanity will maintain, thanks to them, the process of evolution.

The Future of the Mind and brainwave biofeedback

Tom Collura PhD suggests that we are now in a *consciousness revolution,* and that it is accelerating. The information revolution has progressed to the point that room-sized computers of before are now the size of our handheld personal computers and cellphones. In time, these handheld items will all merge into a single wearable or implantable device which will play directly into the ears and eyes. It will allow us communication and entertainment with an interface that is responsive to brainwaves. This can represent progress or limit our freedom, depending on safeguards of this interface system. Progress to higher level of awareness requires freedom, and technology needs to be applied with the discernment to not limit free will.

In the last century, it became acceptable to look into the mental realm using a variety of techniques and agents; it was routine to try new religions, belief systems, and other mental pursuits. There is a new interest in meditation, spirituality, mental development, and empowerment programs, training seminars, and group and personal enhancement experiences. "The inner self" is finally becoming more important than "the outer self."

The future of individual and collective consciousness may be affected by brainwave biofeedback. It is a means to precisely *navigate your inner space.* The compass and GPS changed navigation and exploration of the outer world, and brainwave biofeedback can do that for the inner world.

Expect to explore and discover inner realms and dimensions that are now only fleetingly glimpsed by a select few. The rare insight or *mental breakthrough*—will be callable on demand, and this will transform individual and collective consciousness.

What we now take for granted would have been inconceivable 80 years ago (a lifetime ago). We walked on the moon and routinely travel across the world in a day. The human heart is replaceable by a mechanical pump, and you can call worldwide on a satellite cellphone. Look forward 100 years (during the lives of your grandchildren), and imagine the study of consciousness as part of physics, and there is a *hard* science built around the phenomena of Mind. Equations like Einstein's field equations incorporate consciousness as a part of the Quantum Field. This includes other dimensions, and physics now explains the "other-world/other-side." We consider *intention* a force, like the other physical forces. The physical components of consciousness are known, and artificial consciousness—sentient machines are created.

During your lifetime, there was a time nobody heard of computers. Children are now "computer wizards." Your indigo grandchildren will be the "brain wizards" of the future. There will some day be a scientific understanding of direct mind-to-mind communication. Clairvoyance will be taught in school, and some will learn psychokinesis. One will develop the mind with the same commitment and precision that we now use developing the body. Determination and knowledge will be applied to the development of the brain and mind in a "Mind Spa"—for new millennium brain-builders. Mind development will become as important as physical exercise.

A cellphone may eventually be unnecessary as direct mental communication is learned by some. Rather than buying a cell phone, you may see a brainwave biofeedback trainer or join a "Mind Spa" that specializes in training this skill. The training will also develop other abilities that today lie latent in all of us. Put on an EEG "cap," and the system will read your brainwaves, analyze, and determine the best learning program. The training will be configured based upon analysis of your brain, and automatically train a sequence to help you accomplish your goals. Ongoing progress evaluation will allow the training to automatically adapt. Feedback may include virtual reality, abstract metaphors, and even real-time scans.

Without psychoactive drugs, you will self-regulate your own mental health and function, handling depression, anxiety, attention disorders and other mind issues. A mental/sensory immersion system will allow exploration of virtual reality using sound, sights, physical sensations, and smell. One could learn to do out-of-body experiences and remote viewing. Shared experiences with direct mind-to-mind communication (similar to current couples/group brainwave biofeedback) will create new ways of being with others, transforming relationships and entire social structures. With many brains continually connected, a new form of consciousness may emerge. The next major revolution, called "*hyperconsciousness*" by Collura, is where we explore other dimensions through the power of the mind in awareness, with direct travel via consciousness. Through advanced development of the *physiology of awareness*, we may find ourselves living in different realms, more than our 3-dimensional life now. With these new capacities, we can create peace.

"Mindmasters" will develop mental powers by way of work on the brain and mind in a "Mind Spa" with advanced intensive training. When brainwave biofeedback reaches its full potential, the state of the human mind will create a *leap in human evolution*. With brain mastery and consciousness exploration, we will use much more of the "unused 70%" of our brain physiology. Global hyperconsciousness is a first step toward a true supercivilization. In a great leap, we will reach into other dimensions, and beyond.

Life in awareness and inner freedom

Life in awareness and inner freedom is not a recipe, but we can cook better with a clean kitchen, plenty of modern tools, fresh food, and a healthy, harmonic fire. Any cooking process is a unique personal challenge, never repeating in the exact same manner, and . . . yet never ending.

We are on the path to our final freedom, the realization of our purpose, the light and power that lies within and beyond. Being in unity with all while living within the light (and beyond) would provide the potential of being anywhere, at any time, in any form, thus serving the ultimate purpose of creating, learning, and finding the way home to our true and eternal nature. We are, after all, in part the fallout of stardust, the slowest frequency and densest part of light, breathed out from the great Oneness (? Big Bang). And just as it is the nature of light to travel distances in wholeness, and to be holographic, so is this fractal pattern embedded within our every breath and heartbeat. This demystifies the knowledge and skills that have been kept secret for ages waiting for the right circumstances for their proper use in realizing our greater potentials. It is the moment to use our inner keys to open the doors to the safe, wise use of our powers. Three universal goals for mankind are to be healthy, to be efficient, and to be happy.

Michael Schneider in his Beginner's Guide to Constructing the Universe comments, "The recognition of the Phi relationship structuring nature's forms gives us a passkey to our inner selves." Science, technology and ancient wisdom together will help us develop our powers and highest-level function for ourselves, humanity, the planet, the cosmos, and beyond. Life is a journey. With wisdom, courage, and energetic balance, we must make our choices, because where we decide to go is our birthright.

Thank you.

Liana Mattulich
David Paperny

Glossary

Ascension—term used by religions to express out-of-body experiences, and after-death awareness with immersion in the Quantum Field

Awareness—the individual state of inner power with pristine wisdom, where, in addition to our physical existence, is another dimension; Awareness is a pristine identity as essence of you

Axis—an electro-chemical path, where neurons carry information throughout the body to the central nervous system; a "flowing circuit of light," an image analogy of our essence

Being Presence—neurological coherence occurring after achieving an increased thermal state; one of the stages and states of awareness

Being—refers to the whole reality of a person, the physical aspect with energetic realms and electromagnetic fields superimposed

Boundless Awareness—signals of the non-local state, fed by High Intention; the resulting condition of Being is called by some: the Mind of God or the Zero Point

Creative plasticity—the flexible ability of brain activity that results in a high quality of work and art

Dantien—the primal force of life energy center in the lower abdomen (aka Tanden)

Empowerment—self-work creating a life of health, efficiency, and happiness

Energy spectrum—different frequencies of energy in the universe, represent and correlate to different planes of consciousness

Enlightenment—state in which everything everywhere is One

Fibonacci sequence—Fibonacci spiral is the pattern in nature by which all things grow, by adding what went before to what exists now. It progresses as 0 1 1 2 3 5 8 13 21 34 55, etc. It is Nature's way of modifying this ideal Golden Ratio with an individual starting point. *The body* grows in Fibonacci patterns, as do all living forms in some way (e.g. the nautilus shell which shows the pattern most visibly).

Five horns—areas of the brain as keys for Awareness and higher states of Being; points/doors where biology interacts with the internal energy paths

Flexibility—the brain's plasticity, an inherent functionality of natural learning of the most efficient pathways and ease of modification

Fractal mathematics—geometric designs that portray the universal relationship of fractal forms as duplicate copies of original mathematic variations

Glia cells—The cerebellum (the smaller, lower back part of the brain) has more glia cells than both of the two upper hemispheres and it is paramount in perceiving the gravitational field. Glias record and recover memories, help with spatial and time orientation, are involved in paranormal abilities, and are one of the first electrical signals in many brain nerve pathways; glia cells are bridges to the highest human potentials.

High gamma—brainwave frequencies above 40 Hertz, found in people in enlightened states; can be as high as 126 Hertz (or more) with harmonic brainwaves resonant between them at different locations on the scalp

High Intention—This energy shapes our life's course, giving us new meaning and goals. Similarly, a galaxy sends out bursts of star formations, which are new products in the universe, new life forms; it is High Will akin to the light and energy of a quasar.

High Will—Intense discipline and exercises are needed to extract this strong force, a special quality and level of power and awareness that changes and opens up one's perceptions.

Higher consciousness—equivalent to Awareness (in some schools)

Inner Keys—Inner work unlocks and opens doors of wisdom, using *inner keys*. We achieve states of higher awareness through these *personal cues* that can be recalled at will. For example, we define our axis in order to create a unique, personal Inner Key, to be used at will. Everyone can learn to interconnect the bodies of matter, energies, movements and dimensions through biological self-regulation, functional flowing of energetic fields, and the development of psycho-physiological **inner keys** that allow bridging among dimensions.

Intention—Our thoughts are raw material (like dough) which need the fire of intention (energy) to transform that dough into bread. *Intention* is Energy. Energy flows where attention goes. If you identify your Intention daily, and keep it in mind all day, you will automatically act to fulfill that intention.

Life Force—one of the three primordial forces of this multidimensional universe

Light—the energy of Awareness; the Light Body based in photons; the primordial Light Force of the process of dimensional creation from the pristine dark cosmos; the origin from matter-antimatter universes

Meridian—An acupuncture meridian is a preferred path where energy moves. Chi travels through (the acupuncture) meridians and is distributed through the body by these channels. The twelve principle meridians are named after the organs. This unique form of energy is capable of integrating and providing vital nourishment, leading us into another dimension of Awareness. Besides physical anatomy, the spine is also the location of the central energetic meridians. This central ocean of energy contains Chi that is sent out to the various meridian pathways. Acupuncture points lie on these channels or rivers of energy.

Monkey mind—the wild, noisy and disruptive mind with mundane thoughts. The superficial thinking mind, lacks control, and is occupied with insubstantial topics, habits and entangled feelings. The wild animal mind engages in impulsive, undisciplined mental responses. Compulsive and addictive behaviors originate here.

Neuroplasticity—the brain's ability to change and be flexible and responsive to new learning, thoughts, will and intention (see Flexibility)

Optimal Performance—a balanced, efficient state of healthy quality of life and a joyful personal life of success accomplished by self-work

Original smile—expression in Buddhism' practices about the pristine state of transcendent; our *essence,* where we originated beyond matter-form in a realm of infinite possibilities; the starting point of universal life

Phi ratio /Golden Mean /Golden Proportion—a universal mathematical relationship; can be viewed as an essential energy with multiple levels of expression

Pristine field—(original, pure) program /movement/ Inner Song; our essence in the highest expression

Psychophysiology—the physical body function as it is influenced by mind, emotion, and immune system

Quantum Field continuity / Universal Mind / Quantum Mind / Mind of God / Zero Point Field—the original and only universal energy field of pure infinite potentials; the absolute

Quantum Observer—The "observer effect" in physics is that: seeing actually creates matter. Seeing is creating. "The *Observer* of an experiment can alter what happens in the experiment because of the Observer's influence of the Quantum field" in physics.

Raw spectrum of EEG—histogram display of all the individual frequencies of the EEG signal showing the rhythmic increases and decreases in height (power/amplitude)

Soul—the energetic record (accessible by some) that reconnects us to our past experiences, wisdom, and ultimately back to Universal Mind

Spirit—the light energy in photons (particle-waves) as presence of the absolute inside of us

Synesthesia—the ability to perceive multiple sensory information; the senses of hearing, smell, vision, kinesthesia, and taste being received at the same time. A capacity for multi-sensory experiences beyond usual psychological reference; allows second attention to open the electro-magnetic field to increase personal perceptions and facilitate new physiologic pathways

Three-leg position—The Axis energetically extends from the head down the back to the sacrum, which extends through the two physical legs. An additional energetic path is the tail extending into/to the ground, called the third leg.

Torus—a geometric shape; the logarithmic spiral in Phi Ratio, also known as the Fibonacci spiral. Humans have an energetic field in the shape of a torus: a pattern of unity in a spiral sequence that links to the core of the axis. This torus kernel-nature-essence is in each person as the reality of the bodies-forces-realms nested within. They form a torus pattern when a person has transformed into the most evolved state of Awareness/Being.

Transformation—the upward spiral of evolution beginning at the simplest level, to the joy experienced in psycho-physiological self-regulation, and to transcendent states of being

Universal Wisdom—the collective a-temporal wisdom from all the souls of all life forms in the universe and Beyond

Appendix

RESPONSIBLE OPEN SELF-EXPRESSION PROCESS

Once you have decided to replace negative feelings in a situation with a willingness to communicate, you can begin to *search* for your hurt, anger, fear, guilt and sadness. First ask yourself: "**What does this situation *remind me of?***" Then you may actually recall a past negative experience. This can help you understand why you are reacting with hurt, anger, fear, guilt or sadness now. Here are the three processes you can use in *any* situation:

1) **SEARCH PROCESS**: When you are upset in a situation, you first ask yourself:

> *What does this remind me of ?*

   * Then explore your hurt by asking:

> *What was done to me?*
> *What seems unfair ?*
> *How much hurt and resentment am I feeling ?*

   * Then explore your anger by asking:

> *What do I want or expect ?*
> *What am I not getting ?*
> *How much anger and blame am I feeling ?*

   * Then explore your fear by asking:

> *What will harm me ?*
> *What will I lose ?*
> *How scared and worried am I ?*

* Then explore your guilt by asking:

> *What am I ashamed of ?*
>
> *What seems to be my fault ?*
>
> *How guilty and unworthy am I feeling ?*

* Then explore your sadness by asking:

> *What have I permanently lost ?*

* Then ask:

> *Which of the 5 am I **Mostly** feeling ?*
>
> *What is the **Opposite** of that feeling ?*
>
> *What **Else** am I really feeling ?*
>
> *What would I really **like** to happen ?*
>
> *What would I **also like** ?*
>
> *What would I **prefer** ?*

2) **WILLINGNESS PROCESS**:

Next ask yourself:
Am I willing and able to communicate responsibly and openly at this time ?

If not, excuse yourself, take a break, and repeat to yourself:

. . . "*I can decrease* (the Mostly) *with my* (the Opposite)." Think about the situation's truth.

3) **SELF-EXPRESSION PROCESS**:

Responsibly, openly, and honestly say:

"I am / I feel (the Mostly) . . .
"I also am/feel (the Else) . . .
. . . since / because / when (I/we) . . . *[avoid "you"]*
"I need/want to (the Opposite) . . . you.
"I would really like . . . .
"I would also like . . . .
"I would prefer . . . .
"I (the Opposite) . . .

> *The ROSE situation pneumonic:*
> REMIND me of
> done to me / unfair / HURT
> expect / not getting / ANGER
> harm / lose / FEAR
> ashamed / fault / GUILT
> lost / SADNESS

Mostly / Opposite / Else
Like / Also like / Prefer

---

willing/able?
I decrease—[Mostly] with—[Opposite]
The truth.

I am/feel [Mostly]
also feel [Else]
want [Opposite]
would [Like]
would [Also like]
would [Prefer]
I—[Opposite]

Test your understanding (answers at end of Appendix):

QUIZ #1: Match the feeling to definition.
1. Hurt, 2. Anger, 3. Fear, 4. Guilt, 5. Depression

The negative feeling about what you think someone has done to you.
Suspecting that you will lose something important to you.
Frustration because you want or expect something.
Blaming yourself for bad results.
The result of unmet expectations.
Concern or dread of harm.
A sense of being unworthy and ashamed.
Disappointment and frustration because you believe what happened to you was unfair.
Caused by being sedentary.

QUIZ #2: Match the reaction to definition.
1. Resistance, 2. Rejection, 3. Repression, 4. Revenge

Putting up an emotional barrier.
Total destruction of trust.
Emotional numbness and apathy.
Emotional or physical disconnection.
When feelings are put away to simply make peace.
Not really listening to understand.
Fatal for communication.
Pushing away to relieve resentment.

QUIZ #3: Match the feeling:
> 1-Resentment, 2-Blame, 3-Worry, 4-Self-Criticism

> The feeling that goes along with hurt is.
> The feeling that goes along with fear is.
> The feeling that goes along with guilt is.
> The feeling that goes along with anger is.

QUIZ #4: Match the feeling to definition.
> 1. Love, 2. Forgiveness, 3. Trust, 4. Confidence, 5. Happiness/Joy

> What you must have for yourself before you can give it to others.
> Needed for you to give love, gratitude and praise.
> An important step in resolving negative feelings.
> The willingness to depend and rely on someone.
> Accepting your faults and going beyond self-criticism and fear of failure.
> Not possible in the presence of fear.
> The one attitude that allows you to get past your hurt and resentment.
> Needed for you to express yourself fully, and to stop hiding who you really are.
> The most powerful emotion.

QUIZ #5: Opposite Quiz:
> 1-Love, 2-Forgiveness, 3-Trust, 4-Confidence

> The feeling that is opposite to hurt is_.
> The feeling that is opposite to fear is_.
> The feeling that is opposite to guilt is_.
> The feeling that is opposite to anger is_.

Now let's handle 8 situations . . .

> 1. You: "I washed your car.
> Response: "It still looks dirty to me.
> Mostly: hurt.

> 2. You: "When are you going to stop smoking?
> Response: "I don't even want to talk about it.
> Mostly: anger.

3. You: "Let's go see a counselor together.
Response: "I've had it with you. I don't need this any more.
Mostly: fear.

4. You: "Hello.
Response: "You haven't paid me back the money you promised.
Mostly: guilt.

5. You are a teenager.
Stated to you: "I found cigarettes in your bedroom.
Mostly: anger, Also: guilt, fear, hurt.

6. You had planned to meet.
Stated to you: "You're late again.
Mostly: guilt, Also: hurt, fear, anger.

7. You are an employee.
Stated to you: "This is the fourth time your cash register has
    come up short.
Mostly: fear, Also: guilt, hurt, anger.

8. You are washing the dishes.
Stated to you: "Be careful with the dishes.
Mostly: hurt, Also: anger, guilt, fear.

Situation Processes:

For each situation, we will do the Search, Willingness, & ROSE processes:

Situation 1-Mostly: hurt. You: "I washed your car.
Response: "It still looks dirty to me.

(Search process): * Ask yourself:
What does this remind me of ?
—My dad was never satisfied with me.
What was done to me?
—All my work and effort was put down.
What seems unfair ?
—No appreciation of my efforts.
How much hurt/resentment am I feeling ?
—Much.
What do I want or expect ? &

What am I not getting ?
—Acknowledgement.
How much anger and blame am I feeling ?
—Some.
What will harm me? 0
What will I lose ? 0
How scared and worried am I ? 0
What am I ashamed of ?
—My work.
What seems to be my fault ?
—Possibly a poorly done job.
How guilty and unworthy am I feeling ?
—Some.
Which of the 4 am I mostly feeling ?
—Hurt.
What is the opposite of that feeling ?
—Love & caring.
What else am I really feeling ?
—Anger & Guilt.
What would I really like to happen ?
—To have my work appreciated.
What would I also like ?
—To be complimented for my efforts.
What would I prefer ?
—Acknowledgement before criticism.

(Willingness process): If not willing and able to communicate responsibly and openly at this time, excuse yourself, take a break, and repeat to yourself: "I can decrease hurt with my Love & caring." The truth is that I washed the car.

(ROSE process): Openly & honestly say:

> "I feel hurt when my work and effort is not appreciated.
> "I also feel angry when I'm not acknowledged, and guilty that possibly I did a bad job.
> "I need to Love & care about you.
> "I would really like to have my work appreciated.
> "I would also like to be complimented for my efforts.
> "I would prefer acknowledgement before criticism.
> "I love & care about you.

Situation 2-Mostly: anger. You: "When are you going to stop smoking? Response: "I don't even want to talk about it.

(Search process): * Ask yourself:
What does this remind me of?
—My first partner would shut me up.
What was done to me?
—My conversation was cut off cold.
What seems unfair?
—I asked with good intentions.
How much hurt/resentment am I feeling?
—Some.
What do I want or expect?
—I expect a willingness to discuss it.
What am I not getting?
—Serious respect and attention.
How much anger and blame am I feeling?
—Much.
What will harm me? 0
What will I lose? 0
How scared and worried am I? 0
What am I ashamed of? 0
What seems to be my fault?
—The way I asked my question.
How guilty and unworthy am I feeling?
—Some.
Which of the 4 am I mostly feeling?
—Anger.
What is the opposite of that feeling?
—Forgiveness & understanding.
What else am I really feeling?
—Hurt & Guilt.
What would I really like to happen?
—I would like to have a discussion.
What would I also like?
—Respect and attention to my concern.
What would I prefer?
—Not to have discussion cut off cold.

(Willingness process): If not willing and able to communicate responsibly and openly at this time, excuse yourself, take a break, and repeat to yourself:

"I can decrease anger with my Forgiveness & understanding." The truth is that the smoking is occurring.

(ROSE process): Openly & honestly say:

> "I am angry because of your unwillingness to discuss it.
> "I also feel hurt when conversation is cut off, and guilty about the way I asked the question.
> "I want to Forgive & understand you.
> "I would really like to discuss it.
> "I would also like respect and attention to my concerns.
> "I would prefer not to have discussion cut off cold.
> "I forgive you.

Situation 3-Mostly: fear. You: "Let's go see a counselor together. Response: "I've had it with you. I don't need this any more.

> (Search process): * Ask yourself:
> What does this remind me of ?
> —Being dumped by my first partner.
> What was done to me?
> —My suggestion was ignored.
> What seems unfair ? 0
> How much hurt/resentment am I feeling ?
> —Some.
> What do I want or expect ? 0
> What am I not getting ? 0
> How much anger & blame am I feeling ? 0
> What will harm me ?
> —I may be dumped and alone again.
> What will I lose ?
> —I may lose my partner.
> How scared and worried am I ?
> —Much.
> What am I ashamed of ? 0
> What seems to be my fault ?
> —A failure to communicate well.
> How guilty and unworthy am I feeling ?
> —Some.
> Which of the 4 am I mostly feeling ?
> —Fear.
> What is the opposite of that feeling ?

—Trust & acceptance.
What else am I really feeling ?
—Hurt & Guilt.
What would I really like to happen ?
—To try to solve the problem.
What would I also like ?
—To be assured I won't be dumped.
What would I prefer ?
—To talk it out.

(Willingness process): If not willing and able to communicate responsibly and openly at this time, excuse yourself, take a break, and repeat to yourself: "I can decrease fear with my Trust & acceptance." The truth is that we are not communicating well.

(ROSE process): Openly & honestly say:

"I am scared that you will leave me.
"I also feel hurt that my suggestion was ignored, and guilty since
    I may be failing to communicate well.
"I need to Trust & accept you.
"I would really like to try to solve the problem.
"I would also like assurance that you are not going to leave me.
"I would prefer to talk it out.
"I trust and accept you.

Situation 4-Mostly: guilt. You: "Hello.
Response: "You haven't paid me back the money you promised.

(Search process): * Ask yourself:
What does this remind me of ?
—Ruining a childhood friendship.
What was done to me? 0
What seems unfair ? 0
How much hurt/resentment am I feeling?0
What do I want or expect ? 0
What am I not getting ? 0
How much anger & blame am I feeling? 0
What will harm me ? 0
What will I lose ?
—This relationship.
How scared and worried am I ?

—Some.

What am I ashamed of ?

—Breaking a promise.

What seems to be my fault ?

—That I failed to pay money back.

How guilty and unworthy am I feeling ?

—Much.

Which of the 4 am I mostly feeling ?

—Guilt.

What is the opposite of that feeling ?

—Confidence & self-worth.

What else am I really feeling ?

—Fear.

What would I really like to happen ?

—To be able to keep my promise.

What would I also like ?

—To preserve this relationship.

What would I prefer ?

—To pay back a little at a time.

(Willingness process): If not willing and able to communicate responsibly and openly at this time, excuse yourself, take a break, and repeat to yourself: "I can decrease guilt with my Confidence & Self-worth." The truth is that I promised to pay.

(ROSE process): Openly & honestly say:

"I feel guilty that I haven't kept my promise.

"I am also worried about our relationship.

"I want to be Confident that I can pay you back.

"I would really like to be able to keep my promise.

"I would also like to preserve this relationship.

"I would prefer to pay a little at a time.

"I am confident we can work this out.

Situation 5-Mostly: anger, Also: guilt, fear, hurt.

You are a teenager. Stated to you: "I found cigarettes in your bedroom.

(Search process): * Ask yourself:

What does this remind me of ?

—The snooping in my things last year.

What was done to me?
—Accused.
What seems unfair ?
—My parents smoke.
How much hurt/resentment am I feeling ?
—Some.
What do I want or expect ?
—Bedroom privacy.
What am I not getting ?
—Trust.
How much anger and blame am I feeling ?
—Very much.
What will harm me ?
—Punishment.
What will I lose ?
—Privileges.
How scared and worried am I ?
—Pretty much.
What am I ashamed of ?
—My desire to smoke.
What seems to be my fault ?
—That I smoke.
How guilty and unworthy am I feeling ?
—Pretty much.
Which of the 4 am I mostly feeling ?
—Anger.
What is the opposite of that feeling ?
—Forgiveness & understanding.
What else am I really feeling ?
—Guilt & Fear.
What would I really like to happen ?
—To be trusted.
What would I also like ?
—More privacy.
What would I prefer ?
—Not to be punished, but helped.

(Willingness process): If not willing and able to communicate responsibly and openly at this time, excuse yourself, take a break, and repeat to yourself: "I can decrease anger with my Forgiveness & understanding." The truth is that I smoke.

(ROSE process): Openly & honestly say:

> "I am angry because I want trust and privacy.
> "I am also ashamed of smoking and scared of being punished.
> "I want to Forgive & understand you.
> "I would really like to be trusted.
> "I would also like more privacy.
> "I would prefer not to be punished, but helped.
> "I forgive & understand what happened.

Situation 6-Mostly: guilt, Also: hurt, fear, anger.
You had planned to meet. Stated to you: "You're late again.

> (Search process): * Ask yourself:
> What does this remind me of ?
> —Unfair punishment in front of class.
> What was done to me?
> —I was accused.
> What seems unfair ?
> —There is a good reason I was late.
> How much hurt/resentment am I feeling ?
> —Pretty much.
> What do I want or expect ?
> —A chance to explain.
> What am I not getting ? 0
> How much anger and blame am I feeling ?
> —Some.
> What will harm me ?
> —A bad reputation.
> What will I lose ?
> —A friend.
> How scared and worried am I ?
> —Pretty much.
> What am I ashamed of ?
> —I said I would be on time.
> What seems to be my fault ?
> —I am usually late.
> How guilty and unworthy am I feeling ?
> —Very much.
> Which of the 4 am I mostly feeling ?
> —Guilt.

What is the opposite of that feeling ?
—Confidence & self-worth.
What else am I really feeling ?
—Hurt & Fear.
What would I really like to happen ?
—To usually be on time.
What would I also like ?
—A chance to explain.
What would I prefer ?
—A better reputation.

(Willingness process): If not willing and able to communicate responsibly and openly at this time, excuse yourself, take a break, and repeat to yourself: "I can decrease guilt with my Confidence & self-worth." The truth is that I am often late.

(ROSE process): Openly & honestly say:

>"I feel guilty when I am late.
>"I also feel hurt because I was accused, and I'm scared about our friendship.
>"I want to be Confident about being on time for you.
>"I would really like to usually be on time.
>"I would also like a chance to explain.
>"I would prefer a better reputation.
>"I am confident I can improve.

Situation 7-Mostly: fear, Also: guilt, hurt, anger.
You are an employee. Stated to you:
"This is the fourth time your cash register has come up short.

>(Search process): * Ask yourself:
>What does this remind me of ?
>—Being blamed for a broken toy.
>What was done to me ?
>—I was blamed.
>What seems unfair ?
>—It may not be my fault.
>How much hurt/resentment am I feeling ?
>—Pretty much.
>What do I want or expect ?

—Benefit of the doubt.
What am I not getting ? 0
How much anger and blame am I feeling ?
—Some.
What will harm me ?
—A bad reputation.
What will I lose ?
—My job.
How scared and worried am I ?
—Very much.
What am I ashamed of ?
—Not doing my job right.
What seems to be my fault ?
—That money may be missing.
How guilty and unworthy am I feeling ?
—Pretty much.
Which of the 4 am I mostly feeling ?
—Fear.
What is the opposite of that feeling ?
—Trust & acceptance.
What else am I really feeling ?
—Guilt & Hurt.
What would I really like to happen ?
—To keep my job.
What would I also like ?
—To be able to account for the money.
What would I prefer ?
—To not be blamed if it may not be my fault.

(Willingness process): If not willing and able to communicate responsibly and openly at this time, excuse yourself, take a break, and repeat to yourself: "I can decrease fear with my Trust & acceptance." The truth is that the register appears to be short.

(ROSE process): Openly & honestly say:

"I feel scared of losing my job.
"I also feel guilty about maybe not doing my job right, and hurt because it may not be my fault.
"I want to trust that you'll help me.
"I would really like to keep my job.
"I would also like to be able to account for the money.

"I would prefer to not be blamed if it may not be my fault.
"I trust that we can work this out.

Situation 8-Mostly: hurt, Also: anger, guilt, fear.
You are washing the dishes. Stated to you: "Be careful with the dishes.

(Search process): * Ask yourself:
What does this remind me of ?
—My mother nagging me as a child.
What was done to me ?
—I was called careless.
What seems unfair ?
—I always have to do the dishes.
How much hurt/resentment am I feeling ?
—Very much.
What do I want or expect ?
—To share the chores.
What am I not getting ?
—Appreciation for my work.
How much anger and blame am I feeling ?
—Pretty much.
What will harm me ? 0
What will I lose ?
—This happy relationship.
How scared and worried am I ?
—Some.
What am I ashamed of ?
—Breaking some dishes before.
What seems to be my fault ?
—Some missing dishes.
How guilty and unworthy am I feeling ?
—Pretty much.
Which of the 4 am I mostly feeling ?
—Hurt.
What is the opposite of that feeling ?
—Love & caring.
What else am I really feeling ?
—Anger & Guilt.
What would I really like to happen ?
—To share this chore.
What would I also like ?
—Appreciation for my work.

What would I prefer ?
—Assistance rather than criticism.

(Willingness process): If not willing and able to communicate responsibly and openly at this time, excuse yourself, take a break, and repeat to yourself: "I can decrease hurt with my Love & caring." The truth is that I am washing the dishes.

(ROSE process): Openly & honestly say:

"I feel hurt because I am always doing the dishes.
"I also feel angry when I get no appreciation for it, and guilty because of other broken dishes.
"I need Love & caring from you.
"I would really like to share this chore.
"I would also like appreciation for my work.
"I would prefer assistance rather than criticism.
"I love and care about you.

Answers:

QUIZ #1: 1 3 2 4 2 3 4 1 5
QUIZ #2: 1 4 3 2 3 1 4 2
QUIZ #3: 1 3 4 2
QUIZ #4: 1 4 2 3 4 5 2 3 1
QUIZ #5: 1 3 4 2

With practice, you will become very adept at the ROSE process.
Now consider what approaches really do and do not work in life . . .

What Works in Your Life

WHAT *WILL* WORK FOR YOU	WHAT *WILL NOT* WORK FOR YOU
SELECTIVE LISTENING, QUIETLY	PREJUDGING
COMING FROM YOUR ESSENCE	SMOKESCREEN, MASK, NICE & PHONY
DIGESTING AN IDEA, TO KNOW	SWALLOWING AN IDEA, TO KNOW ABOUT
TAKING A RISK	PLAYING IT SAFE
SOLUTION ORIENTED	PROBLEM ORIENTED
PARTICIPATION	SIDELINES
GIVING, SHARING, CARING	TAKING
US	ME & THEM
BEING CREATIVE	COMPLAINING
KEEPING AGREEMENTS	BREAKING AGREEMENTS
CONSTRUCTIVE THINKING	DESTRUCTIVE THINKING
SELF-HONESTY	UNREALISTIC EXPECTATIONS
NOTICING OPPORTUNITIES	MEDIOCRITY
DUMPING ON THE FLOOR	DUMPING ON OTHERS
MAKING MISTAKES, FAILURES	FEAR OF FAILURE
URGENCY	"SOMEDAY"
INTEGRITY	JUSTIFICATION
CHANGE OF ATTITUDE OR VIEWPOINT	SKEPTICISM AND RESISTANCE
POSITIVE EMOTIONAL INVOLVEMENT	DWELLING ON RESENTMENT
BALANCE	TENSION
CHANGE	AVOIDANCE
CONTROL OBSTACLES	ATTACK
ENTHUSIASM	COMPLACENCY
CLEAR INTENTION, VISUALIZE RESULTS	BRINGING UP PAST NEGATIVE
INNOVATION	DECEPTION
THE FACTS	YES, BUT. .
100% COMMITMENT	INTELLECTUALIZING
PERSISTENCE	RATIONALIZATION
"I AM . . ."	"YOU ARE . . ."
"I FEEL . . . ."	"IT'S THEIR FAULT."
"I CAN . . ."	"I CAN'T"
POSITIVE GOSSIP	VULGARITIES, NAME CALLING
OPEN COMMUNICATIONS	SHOULDS, OUGHTS, MUSTS
SPONTANEITY	INVALIDATING
BE OF SERVICE	BEND THE RULES
PRACTICE	GUILT
THE TRUTH	BEING A VICTIM
GROWTH	DECAY
GETTING EXCITED	FEAR & ANGER
WIN-WIN	REVENGE
IMAGINATION	ULTIMATUM
UNCONDITIONAL LOVING	STRINGS ATTACHED

Constructive:	Destructive:
TOLERANCE	CRITICISM
PATIENCE	CONDEMNING
ENCOURAGEMENT	HOSTILITY
CONFIDENCE	SHYNESS
PRAISE	RIDICULE
APPRECIATION	SHAME
FAIRNESS	FIGHTING
JUSTICE	GUILT
&	
SECURITY	
ACCEPTANCE	
FRIENDSHIP	
LOVE	
FORGIVENESS	

References-Bibliography

Books:

Alberti, Michael L. Stand Up, Speak Out. Publisher: Pocket books: 1990 & Stand Up, Speak Out, Talk Back! by Robert E. & Emmons, (Paperback—1975)

Bennett, J. G. Enneagram Studies. Publisher: Red Wheel/Weiser: 1983

Benson, H. The Relaxation Response. 1975 Wm.Morrow &Co Publishers, New York, NY

Besant, A. Man and His Bodies. London: The Theosophical Publishing House. (1975).

Blavatsky, H. Isis Unveiled, Vols. 1 & 2. Pasadena, California: Theosophical University Press. (1976).

Bohm, David. Wholeness and the implicate order. 1980, Routledge/TJ International Ltd, London.

Bowman, Carol. Children's past lives. New York: Bantam, 1998.

Callahan, R.J. Five minute phobia cure. Wilmington: Enterprise. (1985).

Callahan, R.JCallahan Techniques: Thought Field Therapy: Basic Diagnostic Training, Step A & B. (1998). La Quinta, CA (www.TFTrx.com)

Callaway, E. Brain electric potentials and individual psychological differences. Grune & Stratton, New York. (1975). ISBN-10: 0808908820

Capra, Fritjof. The Tao of Physics: an Exploration of the Parallels Between Modern Physics And Eastern Mysticism, Publisher: Bantam Books (1977) ISBN-10: 0553240137

Castaneda, Carlos. The Art of Dreaming. 1993 Harper Collins Publishers ISBN 0-06-017051-4

Castaneda, Carlos. Magical Passes. Harper Perennial (1998) ISBN-10: 0060928824

Chopra, Deepak. Life After Death-The burden of proof. Harmony Books, NY 2006

Chopra, Deepak. Ageless Body, Timeless Mind: The Quantum Alternative to Growing Old. Harmony Books (November 16, 1993) ISBN-10: 0517598183

Collin, Rodney. The Theory of Celestial Influence. Samuel Weiser (1971) ISBN-10: 0722400195

Cook, Theodore Andrea. The Curves of Life / The Curves of Life (Dover Books Explaining Science), 1979, unabridged 1978 republication of the London 1914 edition ISBN 0-486-23701 (Divine Proportion)

Dalai Lama, the. Sleeping, Dreaming, and Dying. Somerville, MA: Wisdom Publications, 1997.

DeAnglelis, Barbara. How to Make Love All the Time, Dell Publishing, New York, NY 1987

Dewey, G.D. Fractals in Molecular Biophysics, Oxford University Press, Inc, New York (1997) pp. 120-166

Dunlap, Jay C., Loros, J., and DeCoursey, P. Chronobiology: Biological Timekeeping. 2004 Sinauer Associates; 1 edition (May 8, 2003) ISBN-10: 087893149X ISBN-13: 978-0878931491

Evans, Wentz, trans. The Tibetan Book of the Dead. London: Oxford University Press, 1960

Goleman, Daniel. Emotional Intelligence. 1995 Bantam Books NY, NY

Green, Elmer & Alice—of the Meninger Fdn. Beyond Biofeedback. 1989 Publisher: Knoll 1989

Hageseth, Christian. A Laughing Place: The Art and Psychology of Positive Humor in Love and Adversity. Publisher: Berwick Pub Co (1988) ISBN-10: 0962063908

Hill, Napoleon. Think and Grow Rich. 1972 Hawthorn Books, New York, NY

Hutchison, Michael. Mega-brain: new tools and techniques for brain growth and mind scientific exploration. & Mega Brain Power: Transform Your Life With Mind Machines and Brain Nutrients. Hyperion Books, 1994

Jung, C. Psychology and the East. (1978), Princeton, New Jersey: Princeton University Press.

Jung, C. G. Sincronicidad. Pub: Editorial Sirio, S.A.; 2nd edition (1990) ISBN-10: 8486221277

Kabat-Zinn, Jon. Wherever You Go, There You Are. Hyperion (1994) ISBN-10: 0786880708

Keyes, Ken, Jr. The Hundredth Monkey. Mass Market Paperback—1985

Leadbeater, C. A Textbook of Theosophy. (1995). Wheaton, Illinois: The Theosophical Publishing House

Masunaga, Shizuto & Ohashi, Wataru. Shiatsu Zen. Publisher: Ediciones Paidos Iberica (1994) ISBN-10: 8449300061

McArthur, David & Bruce. The Intelligent Heart: Transform Your Life With the Laws of Love. 1997: A.R.E. Press 1997 1st.Edition

Moody, Raymond A. Life After Life. New York: Bantam, 1975

Naimy, Mikhail. The Book of Mirdad: The Strange Story of a Monastery Which Was Once Called the Ark. Paperback by: Watkins Publishing Ltd; New Ed edition (July 2002) ISBN-10: 1842930389, ISBN-13: 978-1842930380

Orlick, T. In Pursuit of Excellence. 1980 Human Kinetics, Champaign, IL

Ostrander, S. & L. Schroeder. Superlearning 2000: New Triple Fast Ways You Can Learn, Earn, and Succeed in the 21st Century. Dell Publishing, New York, NY 1994

Paddison, Sara. The Hidden Power of the Heart: Discovering an Unlimited Source of Intelligence. 1998, Planetary—Boulder Creek, CA 95006 ISBN 187905243-1

Pert, Candice. Molecules Of Emotion: The Science Behind Mind-Body Medicine. (Paperback—Feb 17, 1999) Touchstone, New York, NY 1997-9 & 1997, Scribner, 1230 Avenue of the Americas, New York. NY 10020

Pribram, Karl. Brain and perception. June 1, 1992 in Brain and Perception: Holonomy and Structure in Figural Processing (John M Maceachran Memorial Lecture Series) by Karl H. Pribram (Hardcover—Jun 1, 1991)

Robbins, Jim. A Symphony in the Brain. Grove Press, New York, 2000.

Leibenluft E, Rosenthal N, et al. Light therapy in patients with rapid cycling bipolar disorder: preliminary results. *Psychopharmacol Bull.* 1995;31(4):705-10.

Roshi, Philip Kapleau. The Three Pillars of Zen: Teaching, Practice, and Enlightenment. Anchor Books 1989

Rossi, Ernest L. Ph.D, David B. Cheek. MD. Mind-Body Therapy. 1988, W.W. Norton & Co. Inc. 500 5th Avenue., New York. NY. 10110

Satinover, J. The quantum brain, the search for freedom and the next generation of man. 2001 John Wiley & Sons, New York, NY

Schneider, Carol & Edgar S. Wilson. Foundation of Biofeedback Practice. Biofeedback Society of America (1985). ASIN: B00070UCWY

Schwartz, Gary E. The Afterlife Experiments: Breakthrough Scientific Evidence of Life After Death. William Simon, 2002 PocketBooks, New York, NY

Seki, Hideo, PhD. The Science of Higher Dimensions: Qi and cosmic consciousness. Sawayaka Publishing Co., Ltd., Hong Kong, 1995, published by: Win Honest Planning Ltd.

Silverman, M, Mallett, R. A galactic super-fluid? In Quantum Superposition: Counterintuitive Consequences of Coherence, Entanglement, and Interference (The Frontiers Collection) (Hardcover) by Mark P. Silverman, Frontiers Collection; Springer-Verlag, Berlin 2008

Simonton, Carl O. Getting Well Again. Bantam Books (1984) ASIN: B000K0OLVE

Smith, Manuel. When I say no, I feel guilty. 1975 Bantam Books

Steiner, R. (1999). Introducing Anthroposophical Medicine. New York: Anthroposophic Press.

Steiner, R. (1990). Freud, Jung, and Spiritual Psychology. Great Barrington, MA: The Anthroposophic Press.

Stevenson, Ian. Children who remember previous lives. Charlottesville, Virginia: University Press of Virginia, 1987.

Stevenson, Ian. Twenty cases suggestive of reincarnation. Charlottesville, Virginia: University Press of Virginia, 1974.

Stevenson, Ian. Where reincarnation and biology intersect. Westport, Connecticut: Praeger, 1997.

Stevenson, Ian. Reincarnation and Biology: A Contribution to the Etiology of Birthmarks and Birth Defects. Westport, Connecticut: Praeger, 1997.

Stroebel, C. QR the Quieting Reflex. 1982 Putnam Pub Group

Tart, C. T. Altered States of Consciousness. 1969 John Wiley & Sons

Walker, E.H. The Physics of Consciousness. Perseus Press: Boston, MA. (2000).

Walker, E. H. The Natural Philosophy and Physics of Consciousness, in The Physical Nature of Consciousness, edited by Philip Van Loocke and John Benjamins, Amsterdam/Philadelphia pp. 63-82. (2001).

Wambach, Helen. Life Before Life. New York: Bantam, 1979.

Wambach, Helen. Reliving Past Lives: The Evidence Under Hypnosis. New York: Bantam, 1978.

Winfree, Arthur T. When Time Breaks Down: The Three-Dimensional Dynamics of Electrochemical Waves and Cardiac Arrhythmias. Princeton University Press 1987

Young, Arthur. The Reflexive Universe: Evolution of Consciousness. (Paperback—Aug 1984), Delecorte Press trade PB, 1976.

Zajone, Arthur. Catching the Light, the Entwined History of Light and Mind. Oxford University Press, USA; New Ed edition (April, 1995) ISBN-10: 0195095758

Papers:

Achterberg J, Cooke K, Richards T, Standish LJ, Kozak L, Lake J. Evidence for correlations between distant intentionality and brain function in recipients: a functional magnetic resonance imaging analysis. J Altern Complement Med. 2005 Dec; 11(6):965-71.

Albert, A, Andrasik, F, Moore, L, Dunn, B. Theta/beta training for attention, concentration and memory improvement in the geriatric population. Applied Psychophysiology & Biofeedback, 23(2), 109. Abstract. (1998).

Beloff, J. (1990). "Could There Be a Physical Explanation for Psi?" Available: http://moebius.psy.ed.ac.uk/~ dualism /papers/physical. html . Based on Beloff's paper at the Third International Conference of the S.P.R., Edinburgh in April, 1979; see also: Could There Be a Physical Explanation for Psi?, The Relentless Question: Reflections on the Paranormal (pp. 123-132). Jefferson: McFarland & Company, Inc.

Bettermann H, von Bonin D, Fruhwirth M, Cysarz D, & Moser M. Effects of speech therapy with poetry on heart rate rhythmicity and cardiorespiratory coordination. International Journal of Cardiology, Jul., 84(1), 77-88. (2002)

Boynton, T. Applied research using alpha/theta training for enhancing creativity and well-being. Journal of Neurotherapy, 5(1-2), 5-18. (2001).

Brock, M. "Chronobiology and Aging." Journal of American Geriatric Society. 1991; pages 74-91

Brown, J. H., Enquist, B. J., West, G. B. The fourth dimension of life: Fractal geometry and allometric scaling of organisms. Science, 284:1677-1678. (1999).

Brown, S.W. and Blodgett J. "EEG Kappa Rhythm During Transcendental Meditation and Possible Perceptual Threshold Changes Following." in The Psychobiology of Transcendental Meditation: A Literature Review, ed. D. Kanellakos. Menlos Park, CA: W A Benjamin, 1974.

Cobb, D.E., Evans, J.R. The use of biofeedback techniques with school-aged children exhibiting behavioral and/or learning problems. Journal of Abnormal Child Psychology, 9, 251-281. (1981)

Collura, Thomas F. "Brain, Mind, and Neurofeedback: The Next 100 years." NeuroConnections-A joint newsletter from the ISNR and the AAPB Neurofeedback Division, October 2007. Pp.9-12.

Cowan, Jonathan, The projection and reception of electroholomorphic fields by the brain: a proposed mechanism. ISSSEEM, 1991

Crawford & Vasilescu. Differential EEG pattern activity of low and high sustained attention adults during decision-making tasks. Annual Scientific Meeting of the Society for Psychological Research. Toronto, Canada 1993

Egner, T., Gruzelier, J. H. Ecological validity of neurofeedback: Modulation of slow wave EEG enhances musical performance. NeuroReport, 14(1), (2003).

Emoto M. Healing with Water. J Altern Complement Med. 2004 Feb;10(1):19-21. I.H.M. Research Institute, Tokyo, Japan. info@hado.net

Gasser, T., Verleger, R., Bacher, Lubar, J.F., Gross, D.M., Shively, M.S., & Mann, C.A. Differences between normal, learning disabled and gifted children based upon an auditory evoked potential task. Journal of Psychophysiology, 4, 470-481. (1990)

Godshall, Gary S. "Transformational Effect of Inner Feedback," Pres. Address, Biofeedback Society of CA, 22nd annual convention, San Francisco, 1996, Quarterly Newsletter Winter 1997, V 13, No.1.

Hardt, J. V. Alpha EEG feedback: closer parallel with Zen than Yoga. Biocybernaut Institute, 1993

Hardt, J. V. Creativity increases in scientists through Alpha EEG feedback training. Biocybernaut Institute, 1993

Humphreys, Reginald and Eagan-Deprez, Kathleen. Anthroposophical Hypnosis: Integrating Hypnosis and Anthroposophical Medicine. 2008, Independent publication: Reginald Humphreys, PhD, Dallas TX (booklet).

Jibu M, Hagan S, Hameroff SR, Pribram KH. Quantum optical coherence in cytoskeletal microtubules: implications for brain function. *Biosystems*. 1994;32(3):195-209.

Kornhauser, S.H. Alpha conditioning therapy. American Journal of Electromedicine, 116-119. (1989)

Lee, Ching-tse, Lee, Bernard, Cea, J, Lin T. Brain wave pattern: effects of auditory stimulation based on the five element theory. ISSSEEM, 1991

Lubar, J.F. Discourse on the development of EEG diagnostics and biofeedback for attention-deficit/hyperactivity disorders. Biofeedback and Self-Regulation. 16, 201-225. (1991)

Lubar, J. F. Neocortical dynamics: Implications for understanding the role of neurofeedback and related techniques for the enhancement of attention. Applied Psychophysiology & Biofeedback, 22(2), 111-126. (1997).

Lutz A, Greischar LL, Rawlings NB, Richard M, Davidson RJ. Long-term meditators self-induce high-amplitude gamma synchrony during mental practice. *Proc Natl Acad Sci U S A*. 2004 Nov 16;101(46):16369-73.

McCraty, R, Tiller W, Atkinson, M. Head-Heart Entrainment. ISSSEEM, Fifth Annual Conference, 1995

Paperny, D., Sakai, C., Callahan, R.J. Therapeutic dissociations of negative affect from cognitive precipitants of affective disorders using thought field therapy. Paper presented at the Scientific Meeting of the American Society of Clinical Hypnosis, Baltimore, Maryland. (February 2000)

Radin D, Hayssen G, Emoto M, Kizu T. Double-blind test of the effects of distant intention on water crystal formation. Explore (NY). Institute of Noetic Sciences, Petaluma, CA 94952. 2006 Sep-Oct; 2(5):408-11

Rakovic, Dejan. Neural networks, brain waves, and ionic structures: Biophysical basis of consciousness. ISSSEEM, 1991

Sakai C, Paperny D, Mathews M, Tanida G, Boyd G, Simons A, Yamamoto C, Mau C, Nutter L. "Thought Field Therapy clinical applications: utilization in an HMO in behavioral medicine and behavioral health services." J Clin Psychol. 2001 Oct; 57(10):1215-27 .

Sime W, Ravizza K. A four-year experience in mental toughness training. Sport Psychology Conference, San Antonio, 1980

Sime, W. E. Raymer K. Helping students cope with the challenges of today's and tomorrow's world. Dept. of Education Eleventh Annual Conference, Nebraska, 1991

Tansey, M.A. Wechsler (WISC-R) changes following treatment of learning disabilities via EEG biofeedback training in a private practice setting. Australian Journal of Psychology, 43, 3, 147. (1991)

Underwood, Anne. Real Rhapsody in Blue: A quirky phenomenon that scientists once dismissed could help explain the creativity of the human brain. Newsweek Dec 1, 2003, p.67

Walker, E. H. The Nature of Consciousness. Mathematical BioSciences 7, 131-178. (1970).

Walker, E. H. Information Measures in Quantum Mechanics. Physica B 151, 332-338, 1988. (1988).

Publications related to Brainwave Biofeedback:

Adrain, E. D., Yamagiwa, K. The Origin of the Berger Rhythm. Brain, 58, 232-351. (1935).

Buchsbaum, M. S., et al. "Simultaneous cerebral glucography with positron emission tomography and topographic electroencephalography" in Pfurtscheller, G. et al, (Ed.), Brain Ischemia: Quantitative EEG and Imaging Techniques, Process in Brain Research. Amsterdam: Elsevier, 1984.

Buchsbaum, M. S., Capelletti, J., Coppola, R., Regal, F., King, A. C., van Kammen, D.P. New methods to determine the CNS effects of antigeriatric compounds: EEG topography and glucose use. Drug Devel. Res., 2, 489-496. (1982).

Colby, C. L. The neuroanatomy and neurophysiology of attention. Journal of Child Neurology, 6, (Suppl.), S88-S116. (1991).

Cooper, R., Crow, H. J., Walter, W. G., Winter, A. L. Regional control of cerebral vascular reactivity and oxygen supply in man. Brain Res, 3, 174-191. (1966).

Darrow, C. W., Graf, C. G. Relation of electroencephalogram to photometrically observed vasomotor changes in the brain. Journal of Neurophysiology, 8, 449-461. (1945).

Davis, H., Wallace, W. Factors affecting the electroencephalographic changes induced by hyperventilation. American Journal of Physiology, 133, 258. (1941).

Duffy, F., Iyer,V., Surwillo, W. Clinical Electroencephalography and Topographic Brain Mapping: Technology and Practice, Springer-Verlap. (1989).

Duffy, F. H., Denckla, M. B., Bartels, P. H., Sandini, G. Dyslexia: Regional differences in brain electrical activity by topographic mapping. Annals of Neurology, 7, 412-420. (1980).

Fried, R. The Psychology and Physiology of Breathing in Behavioral Medicine. Clinical Psychology and Psychiatry. New York, Plenum. (1993).

Fried, R. What is Theta? Biofeedback and Self-Regulation: Vol. 18, No. 1, Plenum Publishing Corp., 53-58. (1993).

Fuller, P. W. Computer estimated alpha attenuation during problem solving in Children with learning disabilities. EEG and Clinical Neurophysiology, 38, 149-156 (1977)

Haier, R. J. Cerebral Glucose Metabolism and Intelligence, Dept. of Psychiatry and Human Behavior College of Medicine University of CA, Irvine; in Vernon, P. A., (Ed.), Biological Approaches to the Study of Human Intelligence, Ablex Pub. Corp., Norwood, New Jersey. 316-332.

Hughes, J. R., Myklebust, H. R. The EEG in a controlled study of minimal brain dysfunction. Electroencephalography and Clinical Neurophysiology, 31, 292. (1971).

Huttenlocher, P. R. Synaptic density in human frontal cortex: Developmental changes and effects of aging. Brain Research, 163, 195-205. (1979).

Ingvar, D. H., Soderberg, U. Cortical blood flow related to EEG patterns evoked by stimulation of the brain stem. Acta. Physiol. Scand., 42, 130-143. (1958).

Ingvar, D. H., Slug, I. A. Regional cerebral blood flow and EEG frequency content in man. Scand. Jour. Clin. Lab. Invest., 23, Suppl., 47-66. (1969).

Ingvar, D. H., Sjolund, B., Arbo, A. Correlation between dominant EEG frequency, cerebral oxygen uptake and blood flow. Electroencephalography Clin. Neurophysiol., 41, 268-276. (1976).

Jensen, A. R., Cohn, S. J., Cohn, C. M. G. Speed of information processing in academically gifted youths and their siblings. Personality and Individual Differences, 10 (1), 29-33. (1989).

Lindsley, D. B. Electrical potentials of the brain in children and adults. Jour. Gen. Psychology, 19, 285-306. (1938).

Lubar, J, Deering, W. Behavioral approaches to neurology. Academic Press. (1981).

Lubar, J. O., Lubar, J. F. Electroencephalographic biofeedback of SMR and beta for treatment of attention deficit disorders in a clinical setting. Biofeedback and Self-Regulation, 9, 1-23. (1984).

Lubar, J. F. Changing EEG activity through biofeedback applications for the diagnosis and treatment of learning disabled children; in Theory and Practice. Ohio State University, 24, 106-111. (1985).

Lubar, J. F., Bianchini, K. J., Calhoun, W. H., Lambert, E. W., Brody, Z. H., Shabsin, H. Spectral analysis of EEG differences between children with and without learning disabilities. Journal of Learning Disabilities, 18, 403-408. (1985).

Lubar, J. F., Mann, C. A., Gross, D. M., Shively, M. Differences in semantic event related potentials in learning disabled, normal, and gifted children. Biofeedback and Self-Regulation, 17, 41-57. (1992).

Lubar, J. F., Swartwood, M. O., Swartwood, J. N., O'Donnell, P. Evaluation of the effectiveness of EEG neurofeedback training for ADHD in a clinical setting as measured by changes in T. O. V. A. scores, behavioral ratings, and WISC-R performance. Biofeedback and Self-Regulation, 20, 83-99. (1995).

Lubar, J. F., Swartwood, M. O., Swartwood, J. N., Timmermann, D. Quantitative EEG and auditory event-related potentials in the evaluation of Attention-Deficit/Hyperactivity disorder: Effects of methylphenidate and implications for neurofeedback training. Journal of Psychoeducational Assessment (Monograph Series Advances in Psychoeducationl Assessment) Assessment of Attention-Deficit/Hyperactivity Disorders, 143-204. (1995).

Mann, C. A., Lubar, J. F., Zimmerman, A. W., Miller, B. A., Muenchen, R. Quantitative analysis of EEG in boys with attention deficit/hyperactivity disorder (ADHD): a controlled study with clinical implications. Pediatric Neurology, 8, 30-36. (1992)

Maximilian, V. A., Prohovnik, I., Risberg, J., et al. Regional blood flow changes in the left cerebral hemisphere during word pair learning and recall. Brain Lang., 6, 22. (1978).

Mody, C. K., et al. Computerized EEG frequency analysis and topographic brain mapping in Alzheimer's disease. In Zappulla, R. A., et al (Eds.), Windows on the brain. Vol. 620. New York, NY, Academy of Sciences, 45-56. (1991).

Mountcastle, V. B., Plum, F., Geiger, S. The Nervous System, Neurophysiology, in section 1: Handbook of Physiology: A critical, comprehensive presentation of physiological knowledge and concepts. American Physiological Society, Bethesda, Maryland, 643-674. (1987).

Obrist, W. D. The electroencephalogram of healthy aged males. in Birren, J. E., Butler, R. N., Greenhouse, S. W., Sokoloff, L., Yarrow, M. R., (Eds.) Human Aging: A biological and behavioral study (Public Health Service Publication 986), Washington, D. C., Government Printing Office, 77-93. (1963).

Obrist, W. D., Sokoloff, L., Lassen, N. A., Lane, M. H., Butler, R. N., Feinberg, I. Relation of EEG to cerebral blood flow and metabolism in old age. Electroenceph. Clin. Neurophysiol., 15, 610-619. (1963).

Rasey, H. W., Lubar, J.F., McIntyre, A., Zoffuto, A. C., Abbot, P.L. EEG Biofeedback for the enhancement of attentional processing in normal college students. Journal of Neurotherapy, 1, 15-31. (1996).

Risburg, J, Maximilian, A, & Prohovnik. Changes of cortical activity patterns during habituation to a reasoning test. Neuropsychological, 15, 793. (1977).

Roy, S. & Sherrington, C. J. The regulation of the blood supply of the brain. Journal of Physiology, (London), 11, 85-108. (1890).

Schafer, E. W. P. Neural adaptability: a biological determinant of behavioral intelligence. International Journal of Neuroscience, 17, 133-191. (1982).

Seifert, A. R., Lubar, J. F. Reduction of epileptic seizures through EEG Biofeedback training. Biological Psychology, 3, 157-184. (1975).

Senf, G. M. Neurometric brainmapping in the diagnosis and rehabilitation of cognitive dysfunction. Cognitive Rehabilitation, Nov./Dec., 2037. (1988).

Slug, I. A. Quantitative EEG as a measure of brain dysfunction. In Pfrutscheller, G. (Ed.), Ibid. 65-94. (1984).

Spiel, G. (1987). Is there a possibility of differentiating between children with minimal cerebral dysfunction by means of computer-assisted automatic EEG analysis? Advances in Biological Psychiatry, 16, 171-177.

Tansey, M. A. EEG sensorimotor rhythm biofeedback training: Some effects on the neurologic precursors of learning disabilities. International Journal of Psychophysiology, 1, 163-177. (1984).

Tansey, M. A. Righting the rhythms of reason: EEG biofeedback training as a Therapeutic modality in a clinical office setting. Medical Psychotherapy, 3, 57-68. (1990).

Tansey, M. A. Wechsler (WISC-R) changes following treatment of learning disabilities via EEG biofeedback training in a private practice setting. Australian Journal of Psychology, 43, 147-153 (1991a).

References for Chapter 3—Western and Oriental Medicine, Two Halves of the Whole Picture

Cho, Z.H., Ph. D. New Findings of the Correlation between Acupoints and Corresponding Brain Cortices Using Functional MRI. Proceedings of the National Academy of Science, excerpt from Acupuncture Alliance Forum, Spring 1999. p16. Dept of Radiological Sciences, University of CA 92697

Eisenberg, D, Davis R, Ettner S, Appel S, Wilkey, S, Rompay M, Kessler R. Trends in alternative medicine use in the United States 1990-1997. JAMA 1998; 280(18):1569-1575.

Gallo, Fred, Energy Psychology. 1999: CRC Press LLC, 2000 Corporate Blvd N.W., Boca Raton, FLA 33431

Helms, Joseph M. Acupuncture Energetics: a clinical approach for physicians. Medical Acupuncture Publishers, Berkeley, CA 1995.

Jarrett, Lonney. Nourishing Destiny. Spirit Path Press, Stockbridge MA, 1998, pp.57, 300-312.

Kenyon, Julian. Modern Techniques of Acupuncture. HarperCollins (November 1984) ISBN-10: 0722507518

Maciocia, Giovanni. The foundations of Chinese Medicine. Churchill Livingston, London England, 1989, pp. 67-105.

Seem, Mark, Ph.D. Acupuncture Energetics. Healing Arts Press, Rochester VT, 1991, pp. 17-28.

Teeguarden, Iona Marsaa. The Joy of Feeling: Body mind Acupressure. Japan Publications, Inc., Tokyo and New York 1978, p. 55.

Worsley, J.R. Traditional Chinese Acupuncture, Vol. 1, Meridians and Points. Element Books Ltd., Whiltshire UK. 1982.

Suggested Reading

Abrams, Michael. "Can You See With Your Tongue?" Discover, June 2003.

Budzynski, T.H. Brain brightening: Can neurofeedback improve cognitive process? Biofeedback, 24(2), 14-17. (1996).

Fields, R. Douglas. "The Other Half of the Brain." Scientific American, 2004. *www.journals.cambridge.org/jid*

Green, Elmer and Alyce. Beyond Biofeedback. Knoll Publishing, Ft. Wayne, IN. 1977.

Grossenbacher, Peter G. and Christopher T. Lovelace. "Mechanisms of Synesthesia: Cognitive and Physiological Constraints." Trends in Cognitive Sciences, Vol. 5, No. 1, January 2001.

Gurdjieff, G. I. Beelzebub's Tales to His Grandson: All And Everything: 1st Series (All and Everything Series 1). Paperback by: Penguin (Non-Classics); New Ed edition (August 1, 1999) ISBN-10: 0140194738, ISBN-13: 978-0140194739

Gurdjieff, G. I. The Inner Journey: Views from the Gurdjieff Work (PARABOLA Anthology Series). Paperback by: Morning Light Press; Pap/Dvdr edition (March 28, 2008) ISBN-10: 1596750219, ISBN-13: 978-1596750210

Ho, M. W. The Rainbow and the Worm: The Physics of Organisms. World Scientific Publishing Co., London, England 1998, reprinted 2006. [Work on coherent energy, liquid crystalline and acupuncture]

Lutz, Antoine, Lawrence L. Greischar, Nancy B. Rawlings, Matthieu Ricard and Richard J. Davidson, "Long-term Meditators Self-Induce High-Amplitude Gamma Synchrony During Mental Practice," University of Wisconsin and Princeton University, Proc. National Acad Sci.November 16, 2004; v101;no.46. (see: www.pnas.org/cgi/doi/10.1073/pnas.0407401101)

Othmer S., Othmer S.F. EEG biofeedback training for hyperactivity: Attention Deficit Disorder, specific learning disabilities, and other disorders. EEG Spectrum, Inc., Encino, CA 91316.

Ramachandran, Vilayanur S. and Edward M. Hubbard. "Hearing Colors, Tasting Shapes," Scientific American, May 2003.

Turner, Michael S. "Absurd Universe" in Origin and fate of the universe: special cosmology issue of Astronomy, 2004.

Shah, Idries. The Exploits of the Incomparable Mulla Nasrudin / The Subtleties of the Inimitable Mulla Nasrudin. Paperback by Octagon Press, Limited; New Ed edition (June 1989) ISBN-10: 0863040403, ISBN-13: 978-0863040405

Shah, Idries. The Sufis. Paperback by: Anchor (January 5, 1971) ISBN-10: 0385079664, ISBN-13: 978-0385079662

Shapiro, F. Eye Movement Desensitization and Reprocessing: Basic Principles, Protocols and Procedures (2nd ed.)., New York: Guilford Press. (2001). (www.EMDR.com)

Wilson, Edgar S, MD, "The Transits of Consciousness," Subtle Energies, Vol. 4, Number 2, 1991, pp.178-186.

Specific References

1—Graham, D. Experimental Data Demonstrating Augmentations of Ambient Gravitational and Geomagnetic Fields. *Space Technology and Applications International Forum* CP813, 2006 American Institute of Physics, p1256-1263.

2—Particle Physics And Cosmology: The Quest For Physics Beyond The Standard Model(s): Tasi 2002 Boulder, Colorado, USA, June 2002 (Hardcover) by Howard E. Haber (Editor), Ann E. Nelson (Editor), World Scientific Publishing Company (September 30, 2004) ISBN-10: 9812388923

3—Cherkin DC, Sherman KJ, Hogeboom CJ, Erro JH, Barlow WE, Deyo RA, Avins AL. Efficacy of acupuncture for chronic low back pain: protocol for a randomized controlled trial. *Trials*. 2008 Feb 28;9(1):10.
&
Chou R, Qaseem A, Snow V, Casey D, Cross JT Jr, Shekelle P, Owens DK. Diagnosis and treatment of low back pain: a joint clinical practice guideline from the American College of Physicians and the American Pain Society. Clinical Efficacy Assessment Subcommittee of the American College of Physicians; American College of Physicians; American Pain Society Low Back Pain Guidelines Panel, Oregon Health & Science University, Portland, Oregon, USA. Ann Intern Med. 2007 Oct 2; 147(7):478-91. Summary for patients in: Ann Intern Med. 2007 Oct 2; 147(7):I45.

4—Pacioli, Lucas. Divine Proportion. Abaris Books (June 1, 2008) ISBN-10: 0898350654
&
Young, Arthur. The Geometry of Meaning. Anodos Foundation (December 1976) ISBN-10: 0440049873
&
Ghyka, Matila. The Geometry of Art and Life. Dover Publications; 2 edition (June 1, 1977), ISBN-10: 0486235424
&

Huntley, H. E. The Divine Proportion. Dover Publications (June 1, 1970) ISBN-10: 0486222543

5—Sul JY, Orosz G, Givens RS, Haydon PG. Astrocytic Connectivity in the Hippocampus. *Neuron Glia Biol.* 2004 Feb;1(1):3-11.

6—Sataric, M.V, Zakula, R.B, and Tuszynski, J.A. A model of the energy transfer mechanism in microtubules involving a single soliton. Nanobiology 1, 445-456 (1992).
&
Hameroff, S, Nip A, et al. Conduction Pathways In Microtubules, biological quantum computation and consciousness. *Biosystems* 2002, 64(1-3):149-168
&
Walker, Evan. Dualism, Causal Loops in Time, and the Quantum Observer Theory of Paraphysical Phenomena. Walker Cancer Research Institute, Inc., at http://www.newdualism.org/papers/E.H.Walker/Dualism.html

7—Stuart Hameroff's website "Quantum Consciousness." *http://www. quantumconsciousness.org/publications.html*
&
Davia, Christopher. Life, Catalysis and Excitable Media: A Dynamic Systems Approach to Metabolism and Cognition, p255-292 in The Emerging Physics of Consciousness. The Frontiers Collection: ISSN 1612-3018; Springer Berlin Heidelberg 2006; ISBN 978-3-540-23890-4 (Print) 978-3-540-36723-9 (Online) http://www.springerlink.com/content/g78444834162p322/

8—Smith, Jr., Frank D. (Tony). Penrose-Hameroff Quantum Tubulin Electrons, Chiao Gravity Antennas, and Mead Resonance. Cartersville— August 2002 [January 2003] (contributed to Quantum Mind 2003— Consciousness, Quantum Physics and the Brain, March 15-19, 2003, University of Arizona, Tucson, AZ

9—Thirteen/WNET New York and David Grubin Productions. Secret Life of the Brain. PBS video, 2001 Educational Broadcasting.

10—Silk JS, Dahl RE, Ryan ND, Forbes EE, Axelson DA, Birmaher B, Siegle GJ. Pupillary reactivity to emotional information in child and adolescent depression: links to clinical and ecological measures. *Am J Psychiatry.* 2007 Dec; 164(12):1873-80.
&.
Forbes EE, Christopher May J, Siegle GJ, Ladouceur CD, Ryan ND, Carter CS, Birmaher B, Axelson DA, Dahl RE. Reward-related decision-

making in pediatric major depressive disorder: an fMRI study. *J Child Psychol Psychiatry.* 2006 Oct;47(10):1031-40.

11—Kraft, U. Train Your Brain: Mental exercises with neurofeedback may ease symptoms of attention-deficit disorder, epilepsy and depression—and even boost cognition in healthy brains. *Scientific American MIND.* February 1, 2006 http://www.sciam.com/article.cfm?id=train-your-brain

12—Leutwyler, K. Glia Cells Help Neurons Build Synapses. *Scientific American,* January 29, 2001 http://www.sciam.com/article.cfm?id=glia-cells-help-neurons-b

13—Ramtha. Consciousness & Energy® technique in: Beginner's Guide to Creating Reality: 3rd Ed., JZK Publishing, Yelm, WA 2004

14—Marcer, P.J., Schempp, W. Model of the Neuron Working by Quantum Holography. Informatica 21:519–534 (1997)

15—Radin, Dean. The Conscious Universe. Harper, San Francisco (1997)

16—Mitchell, E. Nature's Mind: The Quantum hologram. National Institute for Discovery Science website *www.nidsci.org/articles/mitchell_hologram. php* Abstract is on Institute of Noetic Sciences website *www.ions.org* & In *IONS magazine* (March 2008): Edgar Mitchell, Sc.D., Institute of Noetic Sciences, Sausalito, CA.

17—Van Flandern, T. What the Global Positioning System tells us about Relativity, in: Open Questions in Relativistic Physics, ed. by F. Selleri, Apeiton, Montreal (1998).

18—Lehrer PM, Vaschillo E, et al. Biofeedback treatment for asthma. *Chest.* 2004 Aug;126(2):352-61.

19—Cousins, Norman. Anatomy of an Illness as Perceived by the Patient. 1979 WW Norton & Co, New York, NY

20—Glatzmaier G, Olson, Peter. Probing the Geodynamo. *Scientific American* April 2005, p.51-7